TECHNOLOGY, HEALTH, AND LAW IN LIFE AND DEATH

This book brings together leading global scholars to examine the legal, ethical and social implications of biotechnological innovations in healthcare throughout the lifecycle – from the potential of life being formed outside the womb to the possibility of life after death.

Biotechnological innovations in healthcare have extended the life span of human beings in the 21st century. Emerging health technologies have resulted in human beings living longer, and improving the quality of their lives and their deaths. What were once considered matters of science fiction have now become a reality in a burgeoning field of boundary-pushing advancements. However, emerging health technologies require careful regulation and ethical scrutiny. There must be a balance between what can be done and what should be done in technology, health and law.

This book uniquely takes the reader on a journey of the life cycle – from before the cradle to beyond the grave – of biotechnological innovations to better understand what healthcare of the present and future might hold. It examines how emerging health technologies are profoundly disrupting legal knowledge of life and death in the developed world.

The book makes a significant and original contribution to the field of health law and bioethics by adopting a socio-legal perspective in examining the legal, ethical and social implications of technologies that create, sustain and foster life and death.

Technology, Health, and Law in Life and Death

Before the Cradle to Beyond the Grave

Edited by
Neera Bhatia

•HART•
OXFORD • LONDON • NEW YORK • NEW DELHI • SYDNEY

HART PUBLISHING

Bloomsbury Publishing Plc

Kemp House, Chawley Park, Cumnor Hill, Oxford, OX2 9PH, UK

1385 Broadway, New York, NY 10018, USA

Bloomsbury Publishing Ireland Limited, 29 Earlsfort Terrace, Dublin 2, D02 AY28, Ireland

HART PUBLISHING, the Hart/Stag logo, BLOOMSBURY and the Diana logo are trademarks of Bloomsbury Publishing Plc

First published in Great Britain 2025

A catalogue record for this book is available from the British Library.

A catalogue record for this book is available from the Library of Congress.

Library of Congress Control Number: 2025945742

ISBN: HB: 978-1-50997-881-6
ePDF: 978-1-50997-883-0
ePub: 978-1-50997-882-3

Typeset by Compuscript Ltd, Shannon

For product safety related questions contact productsafety@bloomsbury.com

To find out more about our authors and books visit www.hartpublishing.co.uk. Here you will find extracts, author information, details of forthcoming events and the option to sign up for our newsletters.

For Luke and Chiara

FOREWORD

Studying health law brings such unique and meaningful satisfaction because it engages with some of the most fundamental aspects of being human. It operates at the intersections of birth, life and death, shaping the legal responses to our most intimate experiences. As science advances in unpredictable ways, health law compels us to confront complex questions about autonomy, dignity, accountability and fairness. This book demonstrates why the field is both fascinating and significant, because the questions it addresses are so crucial.

In an age of rapid technological advancement, health law stands as both a safeguard and a guide. It attempts to navigate the delicate balance between technological progress and ethical responsibility, between personal freedoms and shared obligations. This collection provides essential insights on how emerging technologies are reshaping the legal landscape. Each chapter engages deeply with the ethical, social and legal questions that arise from technological innovations, offering critical insights that both illuminate and interrogate contemporary legal norms.

Part I, *Birth*, ventures into the foundational stage of the life cycle, exploring the implications of reproductive technologies that influence and shape human bodies. The separate examinations of stem cell-based embryo models and ectogestation open up intriguing possibilities about how the two might one day be integrated. Part II, *Life*, turns to technologies that enhance life and human capabilities, examining their legal and ethical implications. Part III, *Death*, demonstrates that our relationship with death is undergoing radical transformation. It discusses emerging technologies that could blur the boundaries between life and death, matter and data, compelling a rethinking of legal, ethical, and philosophical understandings of what it means to die, and perhaps, not to.

Technology is transforming healthcare at a pace few could have imagined. These advances bring extraordinary potential, but they also raise deeply complex legal and ethical questions. It is not enough to wait and respond to innovation, we must anticipate its impact and develop frameworks that can guide it responsibly.

Reactive regulation can deepen existing inequalities and have unforeseen consequences. When the law lags behind technological advancements, it struggles to provide effective safeguards or protect rights amid change. By taking steps to address these issues proactively, we open the door for informed discussions, inclusive policy development and legal frameworks that evolve alongside innovation.

This book offers a critical and timely intervention in that process. It brings together voices that understand the urgency of looking forward, of asking not just what can be done, but what ought to be done. By addressing the legal implications of emerging health technologies before they are fully embedded in practice, we are better equipped to shape a future that is not only technologically advanced, but also legally coherent and ethical.

This volume is not just an important academic exploration but a call to action urging policymakers, scholars, and scientists to engage with the evolving challenges of regulating technologies that redefine the boundaries of birth, life and death. The question uniting each part is clear: how should our legal institutions evolve to meet the demands of a world where biotechnological innovations continue to stretch the limits of the possible?

It is with great enthusiasm and respect for the contributors' work that I commend this book to all those seeking to understand and shape the future of health law and technology.

Emma Cave
Professor of Healthcare Law
Durham University, United Kingdom

ACKNOWLEDGEMENTS

I would like to thank each of the contributors for sharing their intellectual scholarship and ideas, as well as their shared enthusiasm in bringing this edited collection to life. I am grateful to the team at Hart (Bloomsbury) for assisting me throughout the process – from concept to completion. In particular, Sinead Moloney for our initial discussion and ongoing support from Verity Stuart and Roberta Bassi. You have been a dream team to work with. An edited collection is by no means an easy feat, it takes many months to manage, write and complete, and this would not have been possible without the collective effort of everyone involved. Finally, I thank my family for their support.

CONTENTS

Foreword vii
Emma Cave

Acknowledgements ix
List of Contributors xiii

Introduction 1
Neera Bhatia

PART I
BIRTH

1. *Ectogestation and Reproductive Justice* 9
Zoe L Tongue

2. *The Sexual and Reproductive Health Revolution of FemTech will not be Sufficiently Regulated: The Current Regulatory Gaps in the Protection of FemTech Users* 27
Manna Mostaghim

3. *When is a Stem Cell-Based Embryo Model Equivalent to a Natural Human Embryo?* 41
Julian Koplin and Neera Bhatia

PART II
LIFE

4. *An NHS Medical Devices Information System: Reconciling Patient Safety and Patient Choice?* 65
Jean McHale

5. *Parents, Children and Open-source Artificial Pancreas: Morality in the Era of Healthcare Financialisation* 83
Giles Birchley

6. *Neuroethics, Governance, and the Brain* 105
Nathan Higgins, Stephanie K Slack, John Gardner and Adrian Carter

PART III
DEATH

7. *Life After Death? The Ethical, Legal and Social Implications of Cryonics* 131
Emma Kowal and Neera Bhatia

8. *New Funerary Methods: Technological Innovation, Sustainability, and the Role of Law* 147
Heather Conway and Gerard Kelly

9. *The Digital Afterlife: Grieving Digitally After Death* 165
Matthew Groves and Prue Vines

Index 181

LIST OF CONTRIBUTORS

Neera Bhatia, Associate Professor and Director of the Law, Health and Society Research Unit, School of Law, Deakin University, Australia

Giles Birchley, Lecturer in Healthcare Law and Ethics, University of Bristol, United Kingdom

Adrian Carter, Associate Professor, School of Philosophical, Historical, and International Studies, Monash University, Australia

Heather Conway, Professor of Property Law and Death Studies, Queen's University Belfast, Northern Ireland

John Gardner, Senior Lecturer at the School of Social Sciences and Director of the Monash Bioethics Centre, Monash University, Australia

Matthew Groves, Distinguished Professor of Law, Deakin University, Australia

Nathan Higgins, PhD candidate, Monash University, Australia

Gerard Kelly, Senior Lecturer, Queen's University, Belfast, Northern Ireland

Julian Koplin, Lecturer in Bioethics, Monash University, Australia

Emma Kowal, Distinguished Professor of Anthropology and Co-Convenor of the Science and Society Network, Deakin University, Australia

Jean McHale, Professor of Healthcare Law and Director of the Centre for Health Law Science and Policy, University of Birmingham, United Kingdom

Manna Mostaghim, PhD Candidate, London School of Economics, United Kingdom

Stephanie K Slack, PhD, Monash University, Australia. She is currently a Policy Manager in the Health Sector

Zoe L Tongue, Lecturer in Law, University of Leeds, United Kingdom

Prue Vines, Professor of Private & Commercial Law, University of New South Wales, Australia

Introduction

NEERA BHATIA

Biotechnological innovations in healthcare have extended the lifespan of human beings in the twenty-first century. Emerging health technologies have not only resulted in human beings living longer, but also improved the quality of their lives and their deaths – reshaping the ultimate human experience. Matters that were once considered within the realm of science fiction have now become a reality in the burgeoning field of medical and scientific advancement. While biotechnological innovations hold great promise, they require well-considered regulation and ethical scrutiny. There must be a balance between what *can be* done in healthcare and what *should be* done. This edited collection brings together leading scholars[1] to critically explore and examine the legal, ethical, and social implications of biotechnological innovations in healthcare throughout the lifecycle – from the potential of life being formed outside the womb to the possibility of life after death as we understand it today.

These robust contributions highlight how emerging health technologies are profoundly disrupting legal knowledge and ethical understanding of life and death in the developed world. In adopting a socio-legal perspective, contributors to this collection examine healthcare and related technologies, considering the role of regulation, policymakers and various associated challenges. This is especially important to consider in cases where there is scientific uncertainty, ambiguity or ethical controversy. By addressing these questions, this collection situates contemporary biotechnological developments within broader social, cultural, and ethical contexts. This collection uniquely takes the reader on a journey of the life cycle, from before the *cradle* to beyond the *grave*, of biotechnological innovations to better understand what healthcare of the present and future might hold. This edited collection is divided into three parts that respond to different aspects of the relationship between technology, health and the law throughout the life cycle.

The first part of this collection explores the ethical, legal and social implications of health and technology relevant to issues before birth to create, influence, shape and sustain human life.

[1] I wish to thank Associate Professor Marc Trabsky, Monash Law School, for his involvement and discussions in the early stages of drafting and preparing this edited collection.

Part I – Birth

The first of these contributions examines some of the current debate, legal and ethical issues that surround the future potential for growing babies outside of the womb. This chapter explores the contentious issue of ectogestation and reproductive justice. It explores how ectogestation might expand or constrain reproductive decision-making, enabling (biological) reproduction for people experiencing infertility, those who do not want to gestate, and LGBTQ+ couples who cannot become pregnant. At the same time, gendered norms around reproduction and the regulation of ectogestation technologies have the potential to undermine such decision-making. Additionally, this chapter considers how ectogestation has the potential to improve health outcomes for pregnancy-related risks and reduce maternal and infant mortality. However, it also has the potential to heighten existing regional, national, and international inequalities in access to healthcare and reproductive technologies, particularly considering restrictive legal regulation and unequal global distribution.

The second contribution in this edited collection considers data privacy and legal protection for users of wearable 'FemTech' monitoring devices, focusing on the United Kingdom. These types of 'FemTech' products have been marketed as digital tools to empower women to take control of their health and well-being. Despite this, industry practices for 'FemTech' products have increasingly faced scrutiny due to insufficient legal protections afforded to users regarding privacy policies for sensitive information that is recorded.

The final chapter in this part of the collection investigates the various ways that embryo models are being used, and the legal and ethical ambiguities that they raise. It considers how the ethical issues highlighted by these embryo-like entities can be best addressed by lawmakers, policymakers, and regulators. This contribution argues that current debates over how to regulate stem cell-based embryo models are stuck in the wrong question: whether these entities legally or biologically count as 'embryos'. Instead, it argues that we should ask whether they share the morally relevant features of human embryos – such as sentience or developmental potential that justified embryo research restrictions in the first place. This stance should lead us to reject double standards for research with 'natural' and 'synthetic' embryos, and to consider whether current restrictions on embryo research should be revised altogether, such that research limits are tied to the actual features that make an entity worthy of moral consideration.

Part II – Life

The second part of this collection includes three chapters that examine different technologies used to improve or enhance life, while also pushing against the limits of legal norms.

The first of these contributions explores the evolution of information technology concerning medical devices, enabling a much broader range of access to information concerning an individual medical device and how a patient reacts to that device. This chapter examines the legal, ethical and regulatory challenges that might be posed by the development of a National Health Service (NHS) medical devices information system from the perspectives of patient safety, clinical decision making and patient information and clinical research. Additionally, this chapter discusses the original consideration of these issues in England leading up to the passage of the Medicines and Medical Devices Act 2021 and the role of Medical Devices Registries and more recent developments. It analyses the legal and ethical issues raised by the development of a Medical Device Information system and existing mechanisms for regulatory oversight and scrutiny, and whether there is a case for a new regulatory approach in this area for the future.

The second contribution in this collection discusses the use of 'artificial pancreas' technology that consists of 'closed loop' devices that automate the process of blood glucose monitoring and insulin delivery. This technology was developed by grassroots users using open-source technologies to convert off-the-shelf insulin pumps and continuous glucose monitoring into closed-loop devices capable of acting as artificial pancreases and has promised to revolutionise the burden of treatment for type 1 diabetes. Commercial versions of the technology have followed, and some universal healthcare systems, for example, the National Health Service (NHS) in the United Kingdom (UK), have committed to making the commercial technology available to children with type 1 diabetes. Many parents, globally and in the UK, nevertheless use open-source technology, either because of its more user-centred model or because they are unwilling to wait for commercial devices. This chapter considers the law, ethics and morality of parental decisions to use open-source technologies to deliver their child's treatment, through the frame of the economic and commercial evolution of healthcare delivery.

The final chapter in this part of the collection investigates the area of neuroethics. The research and development of medical and commercial neurotechnologies raises ethical, social, and legal issues. This might include, for example, trials of implantable neurotechnologies that carry significant surgical risks and stringent eligibility criteria that may undermine informed consent if treatment-refractory participants view their involvement in the trial as a 'last-resort'. Novel neurotechnologies also raise justice issues, including whether these expensive neurotherapies will only be accessible to the wealthy few and whether research participants will be able to afford the continuation of care after the trial ends. Novel neurotechnologies may have the potential to alter a person's decision-making, motivation or preferences in ways that bypass their autonomous control. As these technologies become more ubiquitous, there are growing concerns that specific kinds of data collected by neurotechnologies raise unique and unprecedented threats to privacy, confidentiality, and freedom of thought. This chapter reviews the current state of neurotechnology research and identifies three critical challenges faced by efforts to design global neurotechnology governance. In so doing, this contribution argues that proponents of neurorights tend to promote rights inflationism and are tainted by neuroexceptionalism and neuroessentialism. The chapter offers some recommendations for the governance of research and development of novel neurotechnologies through a variety of mechanisms that advocate for value pluralism, interdisciplinary stakeholder involvement, and design justice while supporting innovation.

Part III – Death

The final part of this collection includes three chapters that focus on technology, health and the law as it relates to death. These contributions question our fundamental understanding of death in its conventional form, and the rituals and practices that surround death and the afterlife.

The first contribution in this part of the collection considers the ethical, legal, and social implications that surround cryonics (alternatively called cryogenics), a belief in life beyond biological death using advanced biomedicine and technology. Cryonics provides technological optimism, replacing metaphysical forces as the path to immortality. Some supporters of cryonics contend that future scientific breakthroughs in areas such as nanotechnology or regenerative medicine might allow for the reanimation and restoration of cryopreserved individuals, granting a form of life extension. Cryonics is often associated with 'transhumanist' philosophies that seek to surpass biological limitations through technological enhancement. This chapter explores the likelihood of a cryopreserved body or brain being restored to life in the future and examines a range of questions about the innovative use of technology related to cryonics and how such technology *could* or *should* be regulated. Further, this chapter asks how we should understand this new approach to immortality, focusing on developments and discourse in Australia and the United Kingdom.

The second contribution in this part of the collection evaluates how alternative methods for disposing of a corpse, such as alkaline hydrolysis, are disrupting funerary laws and procedures.

Whilst advances in healthcare technology have increased life spans, biological death remains inescapable. One consequence of this is the reality of physical human remains. Burial and cremation have dominated the funerary landscape, but new technologies such as alkaline hydrolysis (AH) and natural organic reduction (NOR) have now emerged as alternative funerary methods. The legal and environmental aspects of these technological innovations are the focus of this chapter. By exploring jurisdictions' differing approaches to legalising AH and NOR, this chapter interrogates the role and limits of law. The chapter locates the evaluation of these new funerary methods within the context of the climate emergency and assesses the contested nature of sustainability as it relates to funerary methods.

While law acts as a legitimising and regulatory tool in the emerging phase of new funerary methods, this remains a policy sphere where there is de minimis state intervention. The chapter concludes by examining the law's limitations in this evolving funerary landscape.

The final chapter in this collection examines the legal and ethical implications of the digital afterlife. The law of death has long focused on the disposal of the human body and the assets of the deceased. The body and assets are dissipated after death according to rules of succession. However, new technologies have created new parts of our lives, which are not property in the strict sense. This chapter examines the digital aspects of a person's life that continue after death. In particular, the digital presence of people can be preserved, even expanded, after death through digital remembrance. It can even be expanded through AI (artificial intelligence) based avatars. The new digital afterlife creates the one thing succession law never counted on – immortality.

In a time when individuals are increasingly questioning their relationship with life and death, there is also a global interrogation of legal institutions that regulate different aspects of healthcare and technology. The question that unites each part of this tripartite collection is how emerging health technologies challenge the law and how such technologies should *or* could be regulated. It is hoped that this edited collection is a valuable resource for scholars, students and practitioners in law, health and the social sciences.

PART I

Birth

1

Ectogestation and Reproductive Justice

ZOE L TONGUE

I. Introduction

In Tloto Tsamaase's novel *Womb City*, artificial womb technology exists in a futuristic Botswana and allows the protagonist to conceive a child, despite her infertility.[1] In one passage, the protagonist ruminates on how she feels about gestating her child this way, stating 'I am relieved I don't have to carry my children.'[2] Yet the control that the government and the corporation owning the 'Wombcubator' has is quite sinister; the protagonist is warned that the device could be switched off, or the foetus requisitioned for someone else, if they did not keep up their monthly payments.[3] In our present, artificial womb technology is being prototyped for human use by scientists in the Netherlands.[4] As Tsamaase's novel explores, ectogestation could have various potential benefits for people capable of becoming pregnant.[5] However, it also has the potential to be used oppressively, thus raising numerous regulatory questions.

In this chapter, I address some of the legal and ethical issues surrounding ectogestation before I go on to explore the impacts of artificial womb technology through the lens of the reproductive justice framework. This framework centres on the experiences of people from marginalised groups and has been used to critique the structural gendered, racialised, and class-based biases that exist in reproductive healthcare. I apply this framework to the idea of reproductive choice in relation to ectogestation, highlighting the inaccessibility of existing fertility technologies for many people and the prevalent denial of choice in maternity care settings. I then consider the adoption of ectogestation globally and its potential impact on communities in the Global South.[6] In the current political and economic climate, ectogestation has the potential

[1] T Tsamaase, *Womb City* (Erewhon Books, 2024).

[2] ibid.

[3] ibid.

[4] Perinatal Life Support, 'Progress', see perinatallifesupport.eu/progress/.

[5] In this chapter, I will use the terms 'pregnant people' and 'people capable of becoming pregnant' to be inclusive of trans, non-binary, and gender-expansive individuals.

[6] The term 'Global South' is not a geographical descriptor but is used to refer to underdeveloped states in Central and South America, Asia, and Africa which have had limited geopolitical

to exacerbate existing reproductive inequalities and could be used in coercive and dehumanising ways. Thus, I conclude by considering how a rights-based approach to regulating ectogestation might facilitate reproductive justice.

II. The Artificial Womb

The term 'ectogenesis' was coined by British scientist JBS Haldane in 1924 to refer to the growth of an organism in an artificial environment as opposed to the body.[7] Ectogenesis has long been a feature of science fiction, beginning with Aldous Huxley's 1932 novel *Brave New World* (which was published in response to Haldane's speculations), a novel featuring embryos fertilised in test tubes and gestated in 'hatcheries'.[8] In 1978, the first baby was born using in-vitro fertilisation (IVF) – referred to in the media as the first 'test tube baby'[9] – and scientists have been attempting to develop artificial womb technology for at least three decades.[10] In 1992, a Japanese scientist reported the successful partial gestation of a foetal goat in an artificial womb made of rubber, though the experiment was ultimately unsuccessful due to technical failures.[11] However, in 2017, researchers in Philadelphia published that they were able to gestate multiple foetal lambs for up to four weeks at the end of their gestational period in an artificial womb system called the 'Bio Bag'.[12] Far from the high-tech incubators that feature in much science fiction, the Bio Bag is effectively a plastic bag filled with artificial amniotic fluid, with a mechanical placenta doing much of the work.[13]

The purpose of developing the Bio Bag was not, however, to create an alternative to embodied gestation but to develop an extracorporeal gestational system to support extremely premature infants, preventing respiratory failure in these neonates.[14] In response to the claim that this technology was *not* ectogenesis (as the foetus was only supported by the technology after a period of ordinary gestation) but a form of neonatal incubation, Elselijn Kingma and Suki Finn advanced

influence. The term 'Global North' is used to refer to wealthier states in North America, Europe, and parts of Oceania. See J Letzing, 'What's in a name? For the 'Global South,' it depends on who you ask' (*World Economic Forum*, 31 July 2023) www.weforum.org/stories/2023/07/what-s-in-a-name-for-the-global-south-it-depends-on-who-you-ask/.

[7] JBS Haldane, *Daeladus, or Science and the Future* (Dutton, 1924) 63.

[8] A Huxley, *Brave New World* (Chatto & Windus, 1932); DN James, 'Ectogenesis: A Reply to Singer and Wells' (1987) 1(1) *Bioethics* 80, 81.

[9] C Nugent, 'What It Was Like to Grow Up as the World's First "Test-Tube Baby"' (*Time*, 25 July 2018) time.com/5344145/louise-brown-test-tube-baby/.

[10] P Klass, 'The Artificial Womb is Born' (*The Guardian*, 29 September 1996) www.nytimes.com/1996/09/29/magazine/the-artificial-womb-is-born.html.

[11] ibid.

[12] EA Partridge et al, 'An extra-uterine system to physiologically support the extreme premature lamb' (2017) 25(5) *Nat. Comm.* 15112.

[13] ibid 2–4; ZL Tongue, 'Ectogestation as Emancipation: A Feminist Science Fiction' in A Green, M Travis and K Tranter (eds), *Cultural Legal Studies of Science Fiction* (Routledge, 2024) 306–307.

[14] Partridge et al (n 12) 2.

the definition of ecto*gestation* for partial ectogenesis – 'development after being "born-by-location-change" but before being "born-by-physiology-change": i.e. development outside the maternal body that prevents the physiological transformation from fetus to neonate.'[15] This definition built on Elizabeth Chloe Romanis' definition of the subject of ectogestation – a 'gestateling' rather than a foetus or neonate.[16] However, while Kingma and Finn do not include full ectogenesis, which they refer to as 'the "babies in bottles" vision often espoused in science-fiction',[17] I adopt the terminology of ectogestation for both partial and full gestation in an artificial womb, in keeping with several other scholars,[18] for two reasons: first, for linguistic simplicity; and second, to emphasis the gestational labour involved in both pregnancy and artificial wombs, and to distinguish it from science fictional forms of ectogenesis which would not require the normal gestational time period of humans (such as cloning). I will instead use the labels 'partial' and 'full' to distinguish between the two forms of ectogestation where necessary.

The development of ectogestation is currently limited to its partial form as an improved alternative to current neonatal care. While this technology has not yet been tested on human foetuses, researchers in the Netherlands are currently developing the proof-of-concept for their 'perinatal life support system' which they expect to be ready within five years.[19] Full ectogestation remains far from a reality, but longer periods of ectogestation have been possible in the non-human realm; scientists in Japan have created an artificial womb to support mid-term lanternshark embryos – this being a species of shark that gestates foetuses for 18-months rather than laying eggs.[20] It should be noted here that this technology was only successful due to the fact that these shark embryos have external yolk sacs carrying necessary nutrients.[21] However, this nonetheless illustrates the future possibilities for artificial womb technology. As partial ectogestation is developed and improves over time, it may become possible to artificially gestate for longer periods of time, eventually leading to full ectogestation. This comes with a wealth of ethical and regulatory issues that ought to be considered in anticipation of this technology – and as Donna Drucker has noted, the law rarely anticipates scientific advancements but merely responds

[15] E Kingma and S Finn, 'Neonatal incubator or artificial womb? Distinguishing ectogestation and ectogenesis using the metaphysics of pregnancy' (2020) 34(4) *Bioethics* 323, 360.

[16] EC Romanis, 'Artificial womb technology and the frontiers of human reproduction: conceptual differences and potential implications' (2018) 44 *J. Med. Ethics* 751, 751.

[17] Kingma and Finn (n 15) 356.

[18] See eg A Bidoli, 'More than an idea: why ectogestation should become a concrete option' (2024) *J. Med. Ethics* [online ahead of print]; J-Y Lee, E Di Nucci and A Bidoli, 'Does ectogestation have oppressive potential?' (2023) *J. Soc. Phil.* [online ahead of print].

[19] Perinatal Life Support (n 4).

[20] T Tomita et al, 'One-year extra-uterine life support for viviparous shark embryos: first technological application to mid-term embryos' (2024) 2 *Front. Fish Sci.* 1.

[21] ibid.

to them once they have happened, leaving numerous regulatory gaps and problems.[22]

III. Legal, Ethical, and Feminist Perspectives

There is, however, a growing body of academic literature on the ethics and future regulation of ectogestation. In terms of the development of this technology, concerns have been raised over the legal and ethical implications of experimenting with partial ectogestation using human embryos or foetuses. Seppe Segers notes that most countries allowing embryo research adopt a legal limit of 14 days for the in vitro growth of an embryo after fertilisation, while the testing of artificial womb technology on foetuses about to be born extremely prematurely would carry with it a host of moral problems.[23] Balancing these issues against the benefits of potentially life-saving treatment for premature neonates, Segers argues in favour of the development of this technology provided that a threshold of acceptable risk is established for human trials.[24] Segers and Romanis have expanded on the importance of 'value sensitive design' in the development of partial ectogestation, which must be conscious of the impact on testing artificial womb technology on the (former) pregnant person as well as the foetus/gestateling.[25]

Other scholars have speculated on circumstances in which partial ectogestation could be useful, beyond supporting premature gestatelings. One such claim relates to the potential for ectogestation to be used as an 'alternative' or 'solution' to abortion, in that the foetus could be removed from the pregnant person's body and transferred to an artificial womb to continue gestating.[26] Catherine Overall, for example, distinguishes between evacuation of the uterus and the death of the foetus, and argues that while the former is essential for bodily autonomy, there is no right to the latter.[27] For Overall, the development of partial ectogestation would therefore come with a moral obligation to continue the gestation of a foetus that could survive uterine evacuation.[28] However, feminist scholars have sought to defend abortion rights against these claims.[29] Claire Horn highlights

[22] DJ Drucker, *Fertility Technology* (Fertility Technology, 2023) 103.

[23] S Segers, 'The path toward ectogenesis: looking beyond the technical challenges' (2021) 22(59) *BMC Med. Eth.* 1, 10.

[24] ibid 12.

[25] S Segers and EC Romanis, 'Ethical, Translational, and Legal Issues Surrounding the Novel Adoption of Ectogestative Technologies' (2022) 15 *Risk Manag. Healthc. Policy* 2207, 2210.

[26] See eg W Simkulet, 'Abortion and Ectogenesis: Moral Compromise' (2020) 46 *J. Med. Eth.* 93; J Räsänen, 'Ectogenesis, abortion and right to the death of the fetus' (2017) 31(9) *Bioethics* 697; P Singer and D Wells, *The Reproduction Revolution: New Ways of Making Babies* (Oxford University Press, 1984) 116–34.

[27] C Overall, 'Rethinking Abortion, Ectogenesis, and Fetal Death' (2015) 46(1) *J. Soc. Philos.* 126, 129.

[28] ibid 130.

[29] See eg EC Romanis and C Horn, 'Artificial Wombs and the Ectogenesis Conversation: A Misplaced Focus? Technology, Abortion, and Reproductive Freedom' (2020) 13(2) *Int. J. Fem. Approaches Bioeth.*

that access to abortion is about autonomy more broadly, rather than just *bodily* autonomy – autonomy in this broader sense 'can only be enacted if it is enabled by a relational framework of positive resources that would allow a person to end or carry on with a pregnancy, and to be provided with resources for support in either instance.'[30] Ectogestation will nonetheless impact upon the abortion debate and legislation in practice, particularly that which rests on 'viability' as a moral threshold, and Horn therefore argues that abortion must be fully decriminalised ahead of this technology.[31]

Unsurprisingly, broader issues around reproductive autonomy feature prominently in the feminist literature on ectogestation. Feminist scholars have highlighted the importance of re-centering people capable of becoming pregnant instead of a narrow focus on foetuses – particularly in relation to developing the technology and speculation on abortion.[32] To centre the perspectives of pregnant people also requires considering the uses, benefits, and risks of partial and full ectogestation beyond supporting premature neonates. This includes the recognition of pregnancy loss in the context of partial ectogestation and the need for psychological support where a pregnancy ends prematurely, and the choice to use partial ectogestation as a mode of childbirth.[33] Anna Nelson highlights that the latter must also come with the choice *not* to opt for partial ectogestation; while some may argue that ectogestation would have a social benefit in the context of alcohol or drug use, to forcibly require a pregnant person to end their pregnancy early in favour of an artificial womb would have a significant impact on their autonomy and human rights.[34]

Finally, in speculating on the development of full ectogestation, feminist scholars have debated the emancipatory potential of removing gestation from the human body. The radical feminist Shulamith Firestone advocated in the 1970s for ectogestation as a site of gender equality as part of a broader socialist revolution.[35] Contemporary scholars have taken up the claim that ectogestation could liberate women from the biological inequalities surrounding pregnancy, challenge gender roles around childrearing, therefore promoting

174; E Kendal, 'Pregnant people, inseminators and tissues of human origin: how ectogenesis challenges the concept of abortion' (2020) 38 *Monash Bioeth. Rev.* 197; S Langford, 'An end to abortion? A feminist critique of the "ectogenetic solution" to abortion' (2008) 31(4) *Women Stud. Int. Forum* 263.

[30] C Horn, 'Ectogenesis is for Feminists: Reclaiming Artificial Wombs from Antiabortion Discourse' (2020) 6(1) *Catalyst* 1, 6.

[31] C Horn, 'Abortion Rights after Artificial Wombs: Why Decriminalisation is Needed Ahead of Ectogenesis' (2021) 29(1) *Med. Law Rev.* 80.

[32] See eg Romanis and Horn (n 29); N Roesner, 'Beyond a Medicalized View of Reproduction: Recentering Pregnant People in the Ethics of Ectogenesis' (2023) 23(5) *Am. J. Bioethics* 102; L Cannold, 'Women, Ectogenesis and Ethical Theory' (1995) 12(1) *J. Appl. Philos.* 55.

[33] EC Romani and V Adkins, 'Artificial placentas, pregnancy loss and loss-sensitive care' (2024) 50 *J. Med. Eth.* 299; A Nelson, 'Should Delivery by Partial Ectogenesis Be Available on Request of the Pregnant Person?' (2022) 15(1) *Int. J. Fem. Approaches Bioeth.* 1.

[34] Nelson (n 33) 17.

[35] S Firestone, *The Dialectic of Sex*, first pub. 1970 (Verso, 2015) ch 1.

further workplace inequalities, and expand reproductive choice.[36] However, on the other side of the debate, some scholars are sceptical of the emancipatory potential of this technology and instead highlight its potential use in furthering reproductive oppression and removing many people's reproductive autonomy.[37] Indeed, Firestone herself acknowledged that without the prior elimination of the economic class system and sex distinction, ectogestation 'does not guarantee once the biological basis of their oppression has been swept away that women and children will be freed.'[38] Firestone thus warns that this new technology 'may be used against them to reinforce the entrenched system of exploitation'[39] and I have explored this elsewhere in the context of current reproductive rights issues in the US.[40] The assumption in much of the literature that ectogestation will improve reproductive outcomes has often been blind to Global South perspectives and the scale of global inequalities in access to reproductive healthcare and fertility technologies.

IV. Intersectionality and Reproductive Justice

An intersectional lens therefore must be adopted in considering the impact of ectogestation on people capable of becoming pregnant. Kimberlé Crenshaw coined the term intersectionality to demonstrate how discrimination on the grounds of gender and race combine, and is experienced differently to sexism or racism alone.[41] This theory has been developed to capture the lived experiences of people situated along the intersecting lines of gender, race, sexuality, disability, nationality, religion, and other characteristics. Intersectionality was central the development of the reproductive justice framework, advanced by women of colour in the 1990s. Sister Song, a reproductive justice collective based in the US, defines reproductive justice as 'the human right to maintain personal bodily autonomy, have children, not have children, and parent the children we have in safe and sustainable communities.'[42] The framework identifies reproductive oppressions along intersectional lines and how the broader socio-economic context, including culture and environmental factors, affect one's reproductive decision-making.[43]

[36] For an overview of these arguments, see Tongue (n 13) 293–96.
[37] ibid 297–99.
[38] Firestone (n 35) 11.
[39] ibid.
[40] Tongue (n 13) 300.
[41] K Crenshaw, 'Demarginalizing the Intersection of Race and Sex: A Black Feminist Critique of Antidiscrimination Doctrine, Feminist Theory, and Antiracist Politics' (1989) 1 *U. Chi. Legal. F.* 139.
[42] Sister Song, 'Reproductive Justice', www.sistersong.net/reproductive-justice.
[43] LJ Ross and R Solinger, *Reproductive Justice: An Introduction* (University of California Press, 2017) 69.

A central focus of the reproductive justice movement is how marginalised communities have historically been denied the choice to have children.[44] As Angela Davis noted in the 1980s, while 'women of color are urged, at every turn, to become permanently infertile, white women enjoying prosperous economic conditions are urged, by the same forces, to reproduce themselves.'[45] Early feminist movements for birth control, for example, were steeped in racialised and gendered ideas of motherhood; notable birth control advocates Marie Stopes and Margaret Sanger did so on the basis that it would allow for white racial progress.[46] In settler colonial countries such as the US, Black and Indigenous women were subjected to forced sterilisation alongside the growth of the birth control movement.[47] In the US, the experiments which shaped modern gynaecology were conducted on enslaved Black women without their consent and usually without anaesthesia.[48] Coercive sterilisation has also been experiences in other contexts; in India Gyan Prakesh has explored how the language of family planning was used to mask population control policies during The Emergency (1975–1977), a political period in which lower caste and Muslim men were subjected to forced or coerced sterilisation and poor women were offered financial incentives to undergo sterilisation or use long-acting reversible contraceptives.[49] Coercive contraceptive practices continue within the global family planning context, particularly in the Global South, in order to meet development goals.[50]

This framework and context provokes an analysis of exactly who may benefit or be harmed by the development of artificial womb technology. Horn and Romanis highlight that the 'biological realities of such a process are that the only way in which such technology can be developed is by experimenting on the bodies of pregnant persons, and on preterm neonates.'[51] They go on to highlight that the development of partial ectogestation is likely to entrench inequalities in reproductive healthcare; pregnant people who are already marginalised within the healthcare system, predominantly Black women and those who are socio-economically disadvantaged in countries such as the US and the UK, are 'more likely to be those who give birth prematurely and therefore to be those

[44] ZT Luna '"The Phrase of The Day": Examining Contexts and Co-Optation of Reproductive Justice Activism in the Women's Movement' (2011) 32 *Res. Soc. Mov. Confl. Change* 219, 224.

[45] A Davis, *Women, Race, and Class* (Vintage Books, 1983) 221.

[46] J Carey, 'The Racial Imperatives of Sex: birth control and eugenics in Britain, the United States and Australia in the interwar years' (2012) 21(5) *Women Hist. Rev.* 733, 738–41.

[47] Y Suarez-Balcazar et al, 'Reproductive justice for Black, Indigenous, Women of Color: Uprooting race and colonialism' (2023) 73(1–2) *Am. J. Comm. Psych.* 159, 161–62.

[48] D Cooper Owens, *Medical Bondage: Race, Gender, and the Origins of American Gynecology* (University of Georgia Press, 2017) 1–3.

[49] G Prakesh, *Emergency Chronicles* (Princeton University Press, 2019) 258–68.

[50] L Senderowicz, '"I was obligated to accept": A qualitative exploration of contraceptive coercion' (2019) 239 *Soc. Sci. Med.* 112531.

[51] C Horn and EC Romanis, 'Establishing Boundaries for Speculation About Artificial Wombs, Ectogenesis, Gender, and the Gestating Body' in C Dietz, M Travis and M Thomson, *A Jurisprudence of the Body* (Palgrave Macmillan, 2020) 235.

persons encouraged to submit their preterm neonate to clinical trials of these technologies.'[52] This is of particular concern from a reproductive justice perspective, given the history and continuing legacies of marginalised people being denied reproductive autonomy.

There has so far been a somewhat limited engagement with the reproductive justice framework in the context of ectogestation. Horn has applied reproductive justice to the issue in the context of existing healthcare inequalities and the criminalisation of conduct during pregnancy in the UK, the US, and Canada, which again disproportionately impacts Black and poor pregnant people.[53] I have similarly discussed the likelihood of ectogestation to exacerbate reproductive injustice in light of racialised and socio-economic inequalities in access healthcare, the potential for corporate control over artificial womb technology, and the rollbacks we have seen on reproductive and LGBTQ+ rights in the Global North.[54] However, much of the feminist literature on ectogestation adopts a focus on reproductive choice which, as will be explored in the following section, is limited in scope. Moreover, this literature tends to adopt a perspective focusing on the Global North, but the development of reproductive and fertility technologies has global implications. This chapter therefore seeks to contribute an undertheorised perspective to the literature on ectogestation by addressing the reproductive justice implications surrounding the 'choice' to use artificial womb technology, and how this technology may deepen inequalities on a global scale.

V. Ectogestation and Reproductive 'Choice'

Mainstream reproductive rights movements in the Global North have typically adopted a liberal conception of reproductive choice, focusing on the legalisation and provision of reproductive healthcare in order to enable autonomous individual decision-making. However, reproductive justice scholars and activists have been critical of this approach. Joan Chrisler, for example, argues that the language of choice reflects individualist thinking, suggesting that there is a 'marketplace' of appealing options open to all consumers, ignoring the social, economic, and political conditions that frame the choices available to different people.[55] Individual choice is dependent upon 'a series of enabling conditions' as women are unable to exercise their autonomy 'whenever their livelihood is endangered, public health and education systems are inadequate, and cultural diversity is not respected.'[56]

[52] ibid 247.
[53] C Horn, 'Ectogenesis, inequality, and coercion: a reproductive justice-informed analysis of the impact of artificial wombs' (2023) 18 *BioSocieties* 523.
[54] Tongue (n 13) 300.
[55] JC Chrisler, *Reproductive Justice: A Global Concern* (Praeger, 2012) 3.
[56] S Corrêa, *Population and Reproductive Rights* (Zed Books, 2002) 85.

Choice thus assumes that all people can decide for themselves whether or not to have children; it assumes that all people have the resources to pay for sexual and reproductive healthcare; and it assumes that all people own and control their bodies, their health, and their relationships.[57] For many, this is not the case. As such, the framework of reproductive justice is based on broader understanding of reproductive autonomy which is situated in 'structural, institutional, and relational contexts that shape the nature of this care and the extent to which choice can be exercised'.[58]

In the context of reproductive technologies, Greta Gaard argues that 'feminists have lost discursive control over the word "choice": instead, the term has been commodified and sold back to women as consumers'.[59] The global surrogacy industry has been widely critiqued for its potentially exploitative practices, whereby couples from the Global North pay a surrogate (often from the Global South) to carry their pregnancy to term.[60] However, exploitative capitalist practices also exist more widely in the global fertility market, which includes many for-profit companies such as international egg donation agencies, and finance corporations offering loans specifically for fertility treatment, which can cost tens of thousands of dollars in some countries.[61] Private companies offering in-vitro fertilisation (IVF) often charge more for 'add-ons' including medication, hysteroscopy, assisted 'hatching' to help the embryo break out of the protein layer coating the egg, and time-lapse imaging.[62] Many of these add-ons have unclear results in terms of improving the outcomes of IVF, or may be actively harmful.[63] Donna Drucker also highlights that IVF has also been accompanied by 'elective' egg freezing where women wish to postpone having children, which she describes as 'a decision to enter into a long-term relationship with a company that will inevitably shift over time'.[64] It is the company here, and not the prospective parent, in control of the future of those eggs.

While 'choice' over reproduction has increased for the minority of people who can afford it, the industry is led by profitability rather than the reproductive rights of its consumers. Thus, the global economy of fertility technology has been described as an

> unevenly developed, highly gendered, multi-actor networks of globalized reproduction in which the reproductive capacities, skills, bodies, biologies, and labors of oocyte vendors, surrogate carriers, and tissue providers are increasingly deployed and

[57] Chrisler (n 55) 1.

[58] Horn (n 53) 526.

[59] G Gaard, 'Reproductive Technology, or Reproductive Justice? An Ecofeminist, Environmental Justice Perspective on the Rhetoric of Choice' (2010) 15(2) *Ethics Environ.* 103, 105.

[60] See eg R Limki, 'On the coloniality of work: Commercial surrogacy in India' (2017) 25(4) *Gend. Work Organ.* 327; A Pande, 'Global reproductive inequalities, neo-eugenics and commercial surrogacy in India' (2015) 64(2) *Current Soc.* 244; N Fixmer-Oraiz, 'Speaking of Solidarity: Transnational Gestational Surrogacy and the Rhetorics of Reproductive (In)Justice' (2013) 34(3) *Frontier* 126.

[61] Drucker (n 22) 87; 148.

[62] ibid 171–72.

[63] ibid 171.

[64] ibid 94–95.

> marketized to fulfil the reproductive needs of intended parents and the capital accumulative needs of the fertility industry.[65]

Who is a consumer of fertility technologies is therefore often contingent on one's financial resources, and on the financial resources of their country of residence. The availability of fertility technology is also political, serving broader reproductive and population goals – whether that is to encourage the reproduction of certain citizens, or restrict it. For example, China has controlled the number of children its citizens are permitted to have since 1980, starting with a one-child policy aimed at reducing population growth.[66] In this context, access to IVF was carefully regulated, including prohibitions on its use for single women.[67] However, in 2016, the one-child policy was replaced with a two-child policy and in 2021, a three-child policy due to concerns over the ageing population.[68] China has now relaxed some of its restrictions on IVF, offering free assisted reproductive technologies and encouraging egg freezing in order to promote a higher birth rate.[69] Access to IVF in China has not been a matter of choice, as its availability (at least legally, as there has been illegal use of fertility technologies in the country)[70] has been dependent on governmental population policy, and continues to be denied to single and queer prospective parents.[71] Rachelle Chadwick argues, in relation to consumer choice framings in the birthing context, that those in the Global North are 'ostensibly free to make individual "choices" (…) while the overdetermination and ontological politics of these choices is often overlooked.'[72] This can also be seen in relation to fertility technologies, as the ability of a person to exercise 'choice' over their use is shaped by the political climate and one's individual resources.

At the same time, the medicalisation of reproduction, pregnancy, and childbirth undermines and restricts the choices that are available to many people capable of becoming pregnant. In the Global North, structural racism within healthcare results in significantly higher maternal mortality rates for Black pregnant people

[65] S Vertommen, B Parry and M Nahman, 'Global Fertility Chains and the Colonial Present of Assisted Reproductive Technologies' (2022) 8(1) *Catalyst* 1, 4.

[66] G Baochang, W Feng, G Zhigang and Z Erli, 'China's Local and National Fertility Policies at the End of the Twentieth Century' (2007) 33(1) *Pop. Develop. Rev.* 129.

[67] L Zhu, 'Procreative rights denied? Access to assisted reproduction technologies by single women in China' (2021) 8(1) *J. Law Biosci.* 1.

[68] W Feng, B Gu and Y Cai, 'The End of China's One-Child Policy' (2016) 47(1) *Stud. Fam. Plann.* 83; D Stanway and T Munroe, 'Three-child policy: China lifts cap on births in major policy shift' (*Reuters*, 1 June 2021) www.reuters.com/world/china/china-says-each-couple-can-have-three-children-change-policy-2021-05-31/.

[69] K Magramo, 'China to offer free fertility treatment in bid to boost record low birth rate' (*CNN World*, 8 February 2023) edition.cnn.com/2023/02/08/china/china-ivf-fertility-treatment-national-healthcare-intl-hnk/index.html.

[70] *Reuters*, 'China launches campaign to crack down on illegal fertility treatments' (11 July 2023) www.reuters.com/world/china/china-launches-campaign-crack-down-illegal-fertility-treatments-2023-07-11/.

[71] H Tao, 'A desirable future or unaffordable hope? Queer people becoming parents through assisted reproductive technology (ART) in Guangdong, China' (2022) 25(4) *Cult. Health Sex.* 413.

[72] R Chadwick, *Bodies That Birth: Vitalizing Birth Politics* (Routledge, 2018) 3.

than their white counterparts.[73] In this context, the hospital is 'the site of antiBlack misogynistic violence, the space that seeks to curtail Black women's reproductive freedom.'[74] Obstetric violence, a terminology emerging from feminist activists in Latin America as a way of describing the structural mistreatment of birthing people across the world, has been recognised on a global level.[75] This phenomenon is gendered, but also occurs across intersectional lines – Davis uses the term 'obstetric racism' to capture the racialised iterations of obstetric violence.[76] Obstetric violence includes, among other forms of abuse, refusals of treatment or the provision of medical treatment (such as a caesarean section) without informed consent. There are countless example of coerced or forced reproductive healthcare, from the pressure that was put on pregnant people across Latin America to opt for caesarean sections during COVID-19 lockdowns,[77] to the women with intellectual disabilities who experienced forced abortions in a Moldovan neuropsychiatric asylum.[78] Obstetric violence has been recognised as a form of gender-based violence by the UN Special Rapporteur on Violence Against Women.[79] In 2007, Venezuela criminalised some forms of obstetric violence, including non-consensual or coerced medical treatment.[80] However, obstetric violence remains prevalent and has not been addressed by most countries, so even those experiencing high-risk pregnancies may be reluctant to engage with formal maternity care.[81]

For Maureen Sander-Staudt, ectogestation promises 'a wider spectrum of reproductive choice for women'.[82] However, given the current inequalities in access to fertility technology, this choice is likely to be heavily dependent on one's country of residence and socio-economic status. Further, ectogestation could exacerbate obstetric violence, particularly in relation to non-consensual treatment – the debates that have been had over ectogestation as an alternative to abortion or where the pregnant person is using drugs or alcohol would certainly point to the

[73] E Dayo, K Christy and R Habte, 'Health in colour: black women, racism, and maternal health' (2023) 17 *Lancet Reg. Health* 100408.

[74] JC Nash, *Birthing Black Mothers* (Duke University Press, 2021) 93.

[75] P Quattrocchi, 'Obstetric Violence Observatory: Contributions of Argentina to the International Debate' (2019) 38(8) *Med. Anth.* 762.

[76] D-A Davis, 'Obstetric Racism: The Racial Politics of Pregnancy, Labor, and Birthing' (2019) 38(7) *Med. Anth.* 560.

[77] D Rea, L Carrión and D Cariboni, 'Women across Latin America "under pressure" to have C-sections during COVID-19' (*OpenDemocracy*, 16 July 2020) www.opendemocracy.net/en/5050/women-latin-america-pressure-c-sections-covid/.

[78] See *G.M. and Others v The Republic of Moldova* App. No. 44394/15 (ECtHR, 22 November 2022).

[79] UN General Assembly, 'A human rights-based approach to mistreatment and violence against women in reproductive health services with a focus on childbirth and obstetric violence' (11 July 2019) UN Doc. A/74/137.

[80] R Pérez D'Gregorio, 'Obstetric violence: a new legal term introduced in Venezuela' (2010) 111 *Int. J. Obstet. Gynecol.* 201.

[81] R van der Waal, 'Undercommoning Anthrogenesis: Abolitionist Care for Reproductive Justice' (2024) 42(2) *Soc. Text* 159, 1.

[82] M Sander-Staudt, 'Of Machine Born? A Feminist Assessment of Ectogenesis and Artificial Wombs' in S Gelfand and JR Shook (eds), *Ectogenesis: Artificial Womb Technology and the Future of Human Reproduction* (Rodopi, 2006) 112.

potential for ectogestation to become mandated in some instances. Horn argues that while ectogestation might not be forced in this way, there is the possibility that 'practices of offering ectogenesis without provision of actual informed consent or under coercive circumstances' could occur, given the prevalence of coercive treatment in contemporary reproductive medicine.[83] In the obstetric violence literature, scholars have noted that the healthcare providers are willing to ignore, dismiss, or override the pregnant person's requests where their behaviour or decision-making is deemed to pose a threat to the foetus, or is contrary to their medical advice.[84] Without addressing these issues, ectogestation is likely to curtail – rather than expand – the reproductive choices of many pregnant people.

VI. Ectogestation in Global Context

Maternal and infant mortality rates vary significantly across the world. In 2020, there were approximately 287,000 maternal deaths, and 95 per cent of these occurred in low- and middle-income countries.[85] In 2022, there were approximately 2.3 million newborn deaths, with the highest neonatal mortality rates in sub-Saharan Africa and southern and central Asia.[86] The Sustainable Development Goals for 2030 therefore include targets aimed at a significant reduction in preventable maternal and infant mortality.[87] This global disparity relates to the socio-economic resources of each country and their budgetary allocation for healthcare, access to sexual and reproductive healthcare more broadly, including education and family planning, and demographic inequalities, including access for those living rurally and those from already marginalised groups.[88] Many causes of maternal and infant mortality are preventable with access to treatment – these issues often relate to 'inadequate healthcare infrastructure, limited access to prenatal care, and cultural barriers inhibiting women's autonomy in reproductive decision-making'.[89] Ectogestation could potentially make a significant difference in reducing maternal and infant mortality rates *if* its use is also supported by improved healthcare infrastructure, maternity services, and reproductive rights protection.

[83] Horn (n 53) 592.

[84] See eg Chadwick (n 72) 27–28; S Cohen Shabot, '"You are Not Qualified" – Leave it to us": Obstetric Violence as Testimonial Injustice' (2021) 44 *Hum. Stud.* 635.

[85] L Say et al, 'Global causes of maternal death: a WHO systematic analysis' (2014) 2(6) *Lancet Glob. Health* 323.

[86] World Health Organization, 'Newborn mortality', see www.who.int/news-room/fact-sheets/detail/newborn-mortality.

[87] World Health Organization, 'SDG Target 3.1 Maternal mortality', see www.who.int/data/gho/data/themes/topics/sdg-target-3-1-maternal-mortality; World Health Organization, 'SDG Target 3.2 Newborn and child mortality', see www.who.int/data/gho/data/themes/topics/indicator-groups/indicator-group-details/GHO/sdg-target-3.2-newborn-and-child-mortality.

[88] Say and others (n 85) 327–28.

[89] F Oluwafunmilayo Omolola, EO Oduwole and A Adebayo, 'Ectogenesis and the Challenges of African Motherhood in Contemporary Society' (2023) 8(2) *Nasara J. Philos.* 1, 3.

However, it is important that technologies developed in the Global North are not expanded globally without consideration of the 'ongoing colonial relations between capital accumulation, extraction, and [assistive reproductive technologies]'.[90] Echoing the reproductive justice movement's focus on the denial of reproductive choice, Sigrid Vertommen, Bronwyn Parry, and Michal Nahman highlight the 'shared reproductive hardships and struggles of formerly colonized and enslaved peoples against exploitation, dispossession, elimination, and dehumanization'[91] that continue to be felt within global fertility chains and family planning initiatives. Thus, as Fabiyi Oluwafunmilayo Omolola, Ebunololuwa Oduwole, and Aina Adebayo argue, it is necessary to examine ectogestation from a decolonial and reproductive justice perspective, particularly in thinking beyond the Global North.[92] This requires an examination of how the use of ectogestation could further entrench exploitative, coercive, and dehumanising practices, particularly where there is a high risk of maternal or infant mortality and the pregnant person wants to refuse the use of an artificial womb. As already mentioned above, current family planning efforts operating in the Global South are often coercive in nature.[93] Rishita Nandagiri has highlighted how the 'voluntariness' of such family planning programmes is interpreted in service of development goals, in particular those aimed at reducing fertility levels, improving health outcomes, and serving overall economic development.[94] In this context, the reproductive rights and autonomy of the women in targeted countries are secondary to these broader goals.[95] Thus, the use of ectogestation as a solution to maternal and infant mortality thus risks 'explicitly locating a normal pregnancy as a source of danger and providing justification for medical intervention'[96] in service of the same goals.

The potential for coercion also comes from the fact that it cannot be assumed that ectogestation will be embraced in all contexts – while many feminist scholars in the Global North have largely embraced the potential of ectogestation, perspectives from the Global South are more varied, with concerns raised about its impact in some communities. For example, Babajide Olugbenga Dasaolu, Emmanuel Ofuasia, and Ibiyemi Sheriff Olasunkanmi highlight that there 'is little emphasis on the cultural implications of such technologies for the values of African society' and point to the hesitance to embrace ectogestation in African feminisms.[97] They

[90] Vertommen, Parry and Nahman (n 65) 6.

[91] ibid 9.

[92] Omolola, Oduwole, and Adebayo (n 89) 14.

[93] See Senderowicz (n 50); V Boydell, RD Smith and Global LARC Collaborative (GLC), 'Hidden in plain sight: A systematic review of coercion and Long-Acting Reversible Contraceptive methods (LARC)' (2023) 3(8) *PLOS Glob. Pub. Health* e0002131.

[94] R Nandagiri, 'What's so troubling about "voluntary" family planning anyway? A feminist perspective' (2021) 75(S1) *Pop. Stud.* 221, 226.

[95] ibid.

[96] EC Romanis, D Begović, MR Brazier and AK Mullock, 'Reviewing the womb' (2021) 47 *J. Med. Eth.* 820, 825.

[97] B Olugbenga Dasaolu, E Ofuasia and IS Olasunkanmi, 'Perceptions of Ectogenesis among Prominent African and Western Feminists' (2022) 17(2) *Int. J. African Renaiss. Stud.* 84, 94–96.

argue that ectogestation could face resistance as many 'African societies view the act of giving birth as a very important event in a woman's life'.[98] Religious beliefs are also likely to shape receptiveness to new reproductive technologies; Haniwarda Yaakob argues that, in the Malaysian context, socio-cultural and Islamic beliefs place great emphasis on pregnancy and motherhood, and religious authorities are likely to be influential in the legal regulation of new technologies such as the artificial womb.[99] Omolola, Oduwole, and Adebayo are slightly less hesitant in embracing the potential of this technology, arguing that ectogestation offers a 'promising solution to the multifaceted challenges' surrounding African maternal mortality rates.[100] However, they do also raise concerns over 'the monetization of reproductive and the possible erosion of cultural values, even as it promises safer pregnancies and healthier results'.[101] In contrast with feminists from the Global North who view ectogestation as having emancipatory potential, Omolola, Oduwole, and Adebayo raise issues relating to the reproductive autonomy available to women in may socio-cultural settings.[102] They do, however, highlight the usefulness of ectogestation in making motherhood possible for those that currently cannot sustain a pregnancy.[103]

Reproductive justice in the context of ectogestation requires equitable access to this technology across the globe, including those in the Global South, which in turn requires that artificial womb technology is not prohibitively expensive. The cost of ectogestation could exacerbate reproductive inequalities for all socio-economically disadvantaged people,[104] but this gap in access would be heightened for those living in lower-income countries. However, while expanding access to ectogestation to all those wishing to use it is important, this could also be a double-edged sword; artificial womb technology could also be a source of reproductive injustice if used coercively or imposed upon communities without cultural sensitivity. Given the current lack of regulation for the global fertility market and current coercive reproductive practices, reproductive justice in this context seems unlikely without careful boundaries around its use.

VII. Ectogestative Justice – A Rights-Based Approach

Many of the issues with the global fertility market relate to the lack of legal regulation and the proliferation of for-profit companies offering services that are

[98] ibid 93.

[99] H Yaakob, 'Setting the Boundaries of Individual Reproductive Autonomy: The Case of Artificial Womb' (2022) 13(2) *UUM Journal of Legal Studies* 1, 11, 19.

[100] Omolola, Oduwole and Adebayo (n 89) 3.

[101] ibid 5.

[102] ibid 4.

[103] ibid 4.

[104] Horn and Romanis (n 51) 248.

inaccessible to many. To limit the potential injustices surrounding ectogestation, international regulation will be necessary – but this must be underpinned by a human rights agenda, incorporating intersectional and diverse perspectives on its use. The right to health, which includes sexual and reproductive healthcare, requires that healthcare facilities are available, accessible, acceptable, and of a high quality.[105] The Committee on Economic, Social, and Cultural Rights (CESCR) has also commented on the right to access up-to-date scientific technologies, including in the sphere of sexual and reproductive healthcare.[106] This must include the incorporation of a gender-sensitive approach from the first stage of technological development, and the impact of scientific advancements on women and girls should be evaluated throughout.[107] The CESCR also placed emphasis on 'the protection of women's free, prior and informed consent in treatments or scientific research'.[108] When artificial womb technology moves to the human trials stage, this gender-sensitive human rights approach will provide important boundaries for its development and eventual use. Cultural sensitivity and consultation with women and pregnant people from different countries and demographics will also be an important step to ensuring the appropriateness of this technology.

The reproductive justice lens also highlights the importance of reproductive autonomy. In the context of family planning programmes, Leigh Senderowicz has proposed the incorporation of 'contraceptive autonomy' as an indicator for family planning goals in order to promote a reproductive rights-based model and reduce instances of coercion.[109] Senderowicz highlights that this would frame autonomous *non-use* of contraception as a positive outcome.[110] The incorporation of reproductive autonomy principles in the regulation and promotion of ectogestation would similarly prioritise autonomous reproductive decision-making, recognising and respecting the reasons why some people may decide not to use an artificial womb, even where it would have therapeutic benefits. As already highlighted above, international human rights bodies place great emphasis on free and informed consent to reproductive healthcare.

There are, of course, limitations to the rights-based approach to ectogestation. International human rights treaties place the responsibility for rights protection on individual states, which is harder to guarantee when concerned with a global industry and companies operating across borders. Placing requirements on the states that allow for ectogestation to protect human rights would at least mitigate against some potential harms, requiring due diligence in relation to non-governmental

[105] CESCR, 'General Comment No. 22 on the Right to Sexual and Reproductive Health (Article 12 of the ICESCR)' (2 May 2016) UN Doc. E/C.12/GC/22, paras 12–21.

[106] CESCR, 'General Comment No. 25 on Science and Economic, Social and Cultural Rights' (30 April 2020) UN Doc. E/C.12/GC/25.

[107] ibid paras 29–33.

[108] ibid para 33.

[109] L Senderowicz, 'Contraceptive Autonomy: Conceptions and Measurement of a Novel Family Planning Indicator' (2020) 51(2) *Stud. Fam. Plann.* 161.

[110] ibid 161.

organisations. However, there is no requirement that states assist other states in meeting their human rights obligations, meaning that there is no obligation on higher-income states to assist lower-income states in fulfilling the right to health. In fact, higher-income states may actively hinder this; in 2020, it was reported that richer countries were hoarding COVID-19 vaccines whilst many people in lower-income countries could not access treatment.[111] People in lower-income countries may lack voluntary access to ectogestation once it is developed because of existing structural inequalities, and the global disparities in access to healthcare is difficult to address through the human rights frame, as it only places responsibilities on individual states for their own citizens.

Moreover, as the UN Special Rapporteur on Violence Against Women has identified, gender-based violence and intersectional discrimination is pervasive in the reproductive healthcare context.[112] This, too, must be addressed if the development of reproductive technologies is to avoid exacerbating these existing gendered harms. The Special Rapporteur makes numerous recommendations in relation to the right to 'receive dignified and respectful reproductive health-care services and obstetric care' including addressing underlying structural inequalities, the creation of a national strategy on maternity care, the effective application of informed consent standards, the review of all laws and practices which perpetuate discrimination (including intersectional discrimination), and accountability mechanisms for victims of obstetric violence.[113] Obstetric violence, harmful gender stereotypes around pregnancy and motherhood, and other reproductive rights violations must be addressed before ectogestation could have the liberatory potential that some scholars argue it has. This technology *could* facilitate reproductive justice, but only if states are committed to realising reproductive rights and reproductive autonomy for all.

VIII. Conclusion

Ectogestation has the potential to significantly improve health outcomes for extremely premature infants and people experiencing high risk pregnancies. The development of full ectogestation, whilst currently speculative, could also open up more reproductive choices for people currently unable to become pregnant, and for those who do not want to become pregnant. However, the development of this technology also poses numerous ethical and legal challenges, and could undermine rather than facilitate reproductive justice. Those developing and regulating future reproductive technologies ought to pay attention to the ways in which people

[111] BBC News, 'Rich countries hoarding Covid vaccines, says People's Vaccine Alliance' (9 December 2020) www.bbc.co.uk/news/health-55229894.
[112] UN General Assembly (n 79) para 15.
[113] ibid paras 75–82.

from marginalised groups have experienced oppressive, coercive, and exploitative practices in the past and the present. Ectogestation could exacerbate current inequalities surrounding reproductive choice, which relate to socio-economic status and political contexts and are felt along intersectional lines. Moreover, while global access to artificial womb technologies will be important to avoid perpetuating these injustices, it is important to consider how ectogestation could be used coercively to meet certain development goals – particularly as some communities may be hesitant to embrace this new technology due to cultural norms and values. I have therefore argued that in order to limit this potential for harm, the development and application of ectogestative technologies must be guided by respect for human rights principles. However, without tackling the gendered stereotypes and violence that pervades global reproductive healthcare settings, reproductive justice in the context of ectogestation will not be possible.

2

The Sexual and Reproductive Health Revolution of FemTech will not be Sufficiently Regulated: The Current Regulatory Gaps in the Protection of FemTech Users

MANNA MOSTAGHIM

I. Introduction

FemTech, a portmanteau for Female Technology, encapsulates a broad spectrum of products. The products span from non-invasive lifestyle products like jewellery; to non-technological items like 'sanitary towels, tampons, female condoms, or the contraceptive pill'; to sex toys;[1] to digital interfaces that collect sensitive health information on an individual's menstrual cycle, sexual behaviours and medications.[2] However, FemTech digital tools like menstrual cycle trackers, fertility trackers and apps that provide pregnant people with health information are the most associated with the FemTech moniker.[3]

FemTech could facilitate the provision of greater access to healthcare services and better research for women's sexual and reproductive health.[4] According to a 2024 article in the *Financial Times*, 'pretty much everywhere you look in women's health there has been under-investment and under-innovation so there are huge

[1] K Albury, Z Stardust and J Sundén, 'Queer and Feminist Reflections on Sextech' (2023) *Sexual and Reproductive Health Matters* 31.

[2] D Hofman, 'FemTech: Empowering Reproductive Rights or FEM-TRAP for Surveillance? (*Medical Law Review*, 2024), see academic.oup.com/medlaw/advance-article/doi/10.1093/medlaw/fwae035/7810195?login=true.

[3] 'GOV.UK. 'Women's Health Strategy for England'. See www.gov.uk/government/publications/womens-health-strategy-for-england/womens-health-strategy-for-england.

[4] 'FemTech | McKinsey'. See www.mckinsey.com/industries/healthcare/our-insights/the-dawn-of-the-femtech-revolution.

opportunities'.[5] The FemTech industry has subsequently positioned itself as acting in service to closing gaps in under resourced sexual and reproductive health services.[6] Alongside facilitating an easier collection of data from a larger sample of women in under researched areas of women's health.[7]

The domestic legislation of the United Kingdom (UK) has not kept pace with the developments in emerging technologies like FemTech and the vulnerabilities that they may pose to user's privacy.[8] There are no codified and specific privacy protections for FemTech users in the UK and there is a lack of clarity on a FemTech user's rights to privacy protections within other forms of pre-existing legislation.[9] Nor have legal jurisdictions made legislation to compel the FemTech industry to institute better practices in protecting data privacy or better providing notice to FemTech users. Legal enforcement mechanisms are also unwilling or unable, to prosecute FemTech providers that may not adequately safeguard a user's right to privacy.[10] Rather, legal enforcement agencies are more likely to use FemTech data to prosecute members of the population. A policy agenda must therefore be developed to assist policymakers, the FemTech industry and its users to mitigate threats from the use of FemTech.

The lack of regulation of the FemTech industry and the subsequent threats to FemTech users have been aggregated across numerous studies that pertain to several legal jurisdictions. For example, the use of FemTech data in the prosecution of abortion has been repeatedly identified as a threat (especially in the United States).[11] But there are other current, emerging, and immediate threats to FemTech users from the use of FemTech apps that are underexplored within the literature. Namely, other implications of sharing FemTech data with law enforcement; the commodification of FemTech data sold to third parties; the utilisation of FemTech for intimate partner violence (IPV); employment

[5] S Stacey, 'Privacy Fears Sap Potential of Female Fertility Tech Start-Ups' *Financial Times* (25 June 2024) www.ft.com/content/56585c50-7608-49f3-998d-a7e100e0ddc7.

[6] B Corbin, 'Digital Micro-Aggressions and Discrimination: FemTech and the "Othering" of Women' (*Nova Law Review*, 2020), see ssrn.com/abstract=3630435; RL Healy, 'Zuckerberg, Get out of My Uterus! An Examination of Fertility Apps, Data-Sharing and Remaking the Female Body as a Digitalized Reproductive Subject' (2021) 30(4) *Journal of Gender Studies*, see doi.org/10.1080/09589236.2020.1845628.

[7] 'FemTech Forward 2024: Transforming Women's Health with Tech'. See www.wrh.ox.ac.uk/news/femtech-forward-2024-transforming-women2019s-health-with-tech.

[8] M Mehrnezhad, T Van Der Merwe and M Catt, 'Mind the FemTech Gap: Regulation Failings and Exploitative Systems' (2024) 3 *Frontiers in the Internet of Things*, see doi.org/10.3389/friot.2024.1296599; A Scatterday. 'This Is No Ovary-Action: Femtech Apps Need Stronger Regulations to Protect Data and Advance Public Health Goals' (2022) 23 (636) *North Carolina Journal of Law and Technology.*

[9] C McMillan, 'Monitoring Female Fertility Through "Femtech": The Need for a Whole-System Approach to Regulation' (2022) 30 (3) *Medical Law Review*, see doi.org/10.1093/medlaw/fwac006; Scatterday (n 8).

[10] Mehrnezhad, Van Der Merwe and Catt (n 8).

[11] K Spector-Bagdady and MM Mello. 'Protecting the Privacy of Reproductive Health Information After the Fall of Roe v Wade' (2022) 3(6) JAMA Health Forum, see doi.org/10.1001/jamahealthforum.2022.2656.

protections; and the use of FemTech digital tools in medical settings.[12] This chapter seeks to identify the major threats that require further research, alongside recommendations for a more considered and coordinated approach by policymakers via a policy agenda.

II. The FemTech Revolution

FemTech digital tools often propose solutions to systemic gaps in women's sexual and reproductive healthcare in health systems around the world. In the UK, there are profound gaps in women's sexual and reproductive healthcare services. For example, there are significant wait times for a diagnosis of debilitating reproductive conditions like endometriosis and polycystic ovary syndrome. There have been birth trauma reports in the UK that outline the resource scarcity in maternity care settings, and abortion services are inconsistently provided and subject to waiting lists (despite the time-bound requirements to obtain a legal abortion).[13] The promise of FemTech is that it might provide innovative solutions and services to minimise the impact of the current gaps in sexual and reproductive health services.

The FemTech industry is being posited to provide healthcare solutions, but without being obligated to, or subject to, ethical frameworks in the provision of healthcare information and care standards. FemTech digital tools in the UK are more commonly legally categorised as wellness and lifestyle apps to avoid the more strenuous and exacting conditions placed on medical devices.[14] FemTech providers are 'less regulated and less accountable [to a] range of actors'.[15] Further, due to regulatory gaps, the FemTech industry is permissive to their obligations to FemTech user's privacy. The lack of regulations subsequently minimises the ethical onus and legal obligations for Femtech to safeguard the privacy of their users.[16] It also places the onus of responsibility on the FemTech user to safeguard their privacy, rather than on the FemTech industry.

Medical devices are also required to undergo rigorous research and development to ensure harm is not experienced by the people they are used on. Although FemTech is used – and being proposed to further – supplement gaps in sexual and reproductive health services, it is not subject to the same regulatory processes as medical devices before its release on the market. As a result, FemTech digital

[12] M Mehrnezhad, L Shipp, T Almeida and E Toreini, 'Vision: Too Little Too Late? Do the Risks of FemTech Already Outweigh the Benefits?' (2022) In Proceedings of the 2022 European Symposium on Usable Security, Karlsruhe Germany: ACM. See doi.org/10.1145/3549015.3554204.

[13] FRSH, 'The Sexual and Reproductive Health Workforce Report 2023, (2024), see www.fsrh.org/Common/Uploaded%20files/documents/the-sexual-and-reproductive-health-workforce-report.pdf.

[14] Mehrnezhad, Van Der Merwe and Catt (n 8).

[15] McMillan (n 9).

[16] ibid.

tools have facilitated unwanted pregnancies and the provision of health misinformation.[17] This has resulted in the efficacy and effectiveness of FemTech being uncertain. Nonetheless, the adverse outcomes have not impeded the proliferation of FemTech as a crucial tool to improve women's health and wellbeing – as the industry continues to expand across multiple legal jurisdictions.[18]

Despite the lack of protection for the privacy input into FemTech products, healthcare practitioners (HCPs) are increasingly recommending the use of FemTech products to patients.[19] The utilisation of FemTech products within health systems may falsely impact user perceptions that the ethical standards and obligations of HCPs to safeguard sensitive health information will be replicated within the FemTech products that HCPs endorse. However, there have been no identified guidelines or regulations by HCP industry bodies in the UK that would alert HCPs to potential risks of vulnerabilities to a patient's privacy due to the use of FemTech products. FemTech users who have been recommended FemTech products by HCPs may therefore have further reliance on a false assumption of privacy when inputting their sensitive health information.

III. Problems in Forming a Policy Agenda to Mitigate the Risks of FemTech

The fundamental flaw in the analyses that aggregate the threats of FemTech is fourfold. Firstly, the governance of digital tools often marries the technical illiteracy of policymakers to the gender blindness of digital tool developers.[20] This issue is further compounded by the consistent gender blindness of technical experts in the development of digital tools due to a lack of gender diversity in the industry and a lack of education on gender specific vulnerabilities in technology.[21] To facilitate better dialogue between policymakers and digital tool developers, a policy agenda must be expansive and outline a spectrum of gendered realities for FemTech users.[22]

Second, the technical development of digital tools exists within a different temporal reality to policy bureaucracies. For example, the advances and developments in technology outpace the ability of legislators to make appropriate legislative instruments and regulations. Current, and proposed legal protections

[17] Hofman (n 2).
[18] Healy (n 6).
[19] A Nelson, M Tzanou and T Keren-Paz, 'Recommending Privately-Developed FemTech in Healthcare Part 1: Promises and Pitfalls' (*BMJ Sexual & Reproductive Health blog*, 16 September 2024) blogs.bmj.com/bmjsrh/2024/09/16/femtech-part-1/.
[20] S Frennert, 'Gender Blindness: On Health and Welfare Technology, AI and Gender Equality in Community Care' (2021) 28(4) *Nursing Inquiry*, /doi.org/10.1111/nin.12419.
[21] ibid.
[22] ibid.

for FemTech users need to be expansive to address gaps in technical understanding by policymakers and adaptable for the rapid changes in the industry. Laws that safeguard the privacy of FemTech users should be akin to the General Data Protection Regulation (GDPR) which legislates for data storage rather than on the technical mechanisms. This is because the GDPR recognises that data storage methods may rapidly change, and legal enforcement would need an adaptable legal mechanism to protect users. An analysis on a spectrum of vulnerabilities in tandem – rather than a single issue – may be able to create sufficiently expansive and adaptable set of principles to protect FemTech users.

Third, FemTech poses multiple threats to a user. To portend, or to identify, a single issue with FemTech may then incorrectly minimise or negate other threats to FemTech users. This is especially pertinent due to the expansiveness of the term FemTech; its multiple uses, and therefore multiple avenues for exploitation by third parties. For example, a proposed legislative instrument for menstrual cycle trackers, or fertility trackers, may not adequately consider how sexual and reproductive health data from a sex toy could also subject a FemTech user to vulnerabilities or exploitation by third parties. Subsequent legislation that perceives of the vulnerabilities to FemTech users as single issues, or via an aggregated analysis, will not adequately contend with the multiple threats of FemTech.

A similar study to identify the multiple threats of FemTech for users was conducted by Mehrnezhad et al. via a cybersecurity assessment. The study collated the data collected by the most popular FemTech digital tools and its potential to contribute to harms on FemTech users.[23] The study recognised the necessity for further analyses that identified the ongoing gaps in policymakers to safeguard the privacy of FemTech users.[24] But it had not noted the emerging issues in the utilisation of FemTech by HCPs and medical systems. Nor was there an understanding of the incoherence in the overlapping legal jurisdictions that govern the FemTech industry and safeguards FemTech users.

Fourth, and lastly, the lack of clarity on the privacy protections for FemTech users is also compounded by the diversity of legal regimes wherein which FemTech products are developed and where they are subsequently marketed for use.[25] For example, a FemTech product developed in the US may implement privacy standards of, and be compliant with, legislation from the United States. However, the user of that FemTech product in the UK may assume that their right to privacy is compliant with UK law.[26] Further, there is no significant and consistent clarity as to whether FemTech products developed in one legal jurisdiction but used in another legal jurisdiction 'could still transfer user data

[23] Mehrnezhad, Shipp, Almeida and Toreini (n 12).

[24] ibid.

[25] N Alfawzan, and M Christen. 'The Future of FemTech Ethics & Privacy – a Global Perspective' (2023) 24(1) *BMC Medical Ethics*, see doi.org/10.1186/s12910-023-00976-z.

[26] S Wanni Arachchige Dona, MR Angeles, D Nguyen, P Cooper, L Sweet and A Peeters, 'An Assessment of Ten Popular Pregnancy Applications (Apps) Available for Women in Australia' (2024) 484 *International Journal of Medical Informatics*, see doi.org/10.1016/j.ijmedinf.2024.105354.

to third-party processors … to [other] countries where fewer data protection regulations apply'.[27] A recent study by Pybus and Mir also identified that other subsidiary functions and software within a FemTech app may also be the cause of additional vulnerabilities and be governed by yet another legal jurisdiction.[28] This lack of clarity raises the question about whether the potential benefits of FemTech are sufficient to cancel out systemic issues with the lack of coherence on privacy safeguarding.

IV. A Reflexivity Statement Based on the Principles of Reproductive Justice

Choice in sexual and reproductive health settings is an essential cornerstone of international frameworks on reproductive rights. However, the reproductive justice framework posits that an individual does not 'own, control, or make decisions about their body, health, and relationships'.[29] Choices for sexual and reproductive health are instead dictated by the legal and policy environment that an individual must navigate.[30] For example, if access to sexual and reproductive healthcare is limited and an individual is forced to use FemTech products without strong privacy protections for their data – have they actually consented to sharing their private data?

Meanwhile, the current discussions on FemTech and privacy often examine the interplay between a FemTech user's understanding of their privacy within digital tools and the regulatory gaps. The crux of the analysis is the individual's understanding of whether they are unwittingly sharing information that is not safeguarded for privacy. Within other analyses on the provision of healthcare, the obligation to provide safeguarding is not with the recipient of care, it is with the provider.

A handful of studies confirm that FemTech users would have still downloaded FemTech products even if they knew about the vulnerabilities to their privacy.[31] Or, they would have deleted their FemTech products from their phone, ceasing

[27] L Mekioussa Malki, I Kaleva, D Patel, M Warner and R Abu-Salma, 'Exploring Privacy Practices of Female mHealth Apps in a Post-Roe World'. In *Proceedings of the CHI Conference on Human Factors in Computing Systems*, 1–24. Honolulu HI USA: ACM, 2024, doi.org/10.1145/3613904.3642521.

[28] J Pybus and M Mir, 'Tracking Menopause: An SDK Data Audit for Intimate Infrastructures of Datafication with ChatGPT4o'. (2024) See papers.ssrn.com/sol3/papers.cfm?abstract_id=5054410.

[29] J Chrisler, 'A global approach to reproductive justice: Psychosocial and legal aspects and implications' (2013) 20 *William & Mary Journal of Women and the Law*.

[30] C Onwuachi-Saunders, QP Dang and J Murray, 'Reproductive Rights, Reproductive Justice: Redefining Challenges to Create Optimal Health for All Women' (2019) 9(1) *Journal of Healthcare, Science and the Humanities*.

[31] Wanni Arachchige Dona, Angeles, Nguyen, Cooper, Sweet and Peeters (n 26); D Lupton and S Pedersen, 'An Australian Survey of Women's Use of Pregnancy and Parenting Apps' (2024) 29(4) *Women and Birth* 4.

access to FemTech services. But this poses an interesting question on the immediate issues with FemTech: (1) FemTech users were not aware of the issues with FemTech; (2) FemTech users did not feel like they had a choice in their access and use of FemTech. This is because access to FemTech does not create choices and agency for its users. It instead creates binary choices for a user to either derogate their rights to privacy to access FemTech services or to protect their privacy by not using FemTech.

Ultimately, FemTech users do not believe that they have the choice in their right to privacy with their use of FemTech digital tools. It is the FemTech industry, alongside the legal and policy environment, that will create a shift in safeguarding privacy within digital tools. Commentators believe that investors in FemTech have heeded issues on the increased threat of the use of FemTech data to prosecute abortions after the reversal of *Roe v Wade*.[32] A shift has already occurred with FemTech investors who have begun to impose a pecuniary penalty by not investing in FemTech that 'sell their data to anyone else … That's the bright, red line for us'.[33] Moreover, the market has begun to design FemTech that retains privacy for its users and to remain competitive. Previously established FemTech products have had to adapt their terms of service.[34] But it is still imperative to examine the spectrum of threats that FemTech subjects its users to so that the FemTech industry and policymakers can further evolve to create safer digital tools for users.

The enduring gaps in sexual and reproductive health services for women across the world require innovation. Are FemTech digital tools a suitable solution? Beyond safeguarding the privacy of FemTech users, FemTech has systemic issues within its design and function. This chapter does not adequately examine the disproportionate impact that FemTech has on racially minoritised groups and its entrenchment of gender archetypes. But it is important to note that the impact of FemTech further compounds the difficulty of navigating legal and policy environments for minoritised and marginalised populations.

A lack of enforcement of legal protections or the imposition of more limited choices, is often a feature for minoritised peoples in sexual and reproductive health settings. The poorer treatment for minoritised peoples has been attributed to paternalistic narratives perpetuated in sexual and reproductive health settings. For Mishra and Suresh, FemTech messaging for South Asia persons perpetuates racist archetypes because it portends to be the first providers of education on reproductive health and safe methods of contraception for its users of global majority descent; while it attempts to assist the 'savage' in quelling a '[tendency] to reproduce'.[35] In the UK, there are limited studies to correlate the lack of agency

[32] Stacey (n 5).
[33] ibid.
[34] ibid.
[35] P Mishra and Y Suresh, 'Datafied Body Projects in India: Femtech and the Rise of Reproductive Surveillance in the Digital Era' (2021) www.tandfonline.com/doi/full/10.1080/12259276.2021.2002010.

with adverse outcomes, but persons from racially minoritised backgrounds do experience higher rates of maternal mortality.[36]

The lack of adequate privacy safeguards across digital tools has also made minoritised communities more resistant in their uptake of FemTech. For example, minoritised ethnic communities in the UK that are subject to disproportionate surveillance by the state (ie, persons of African and Caribbean descent) and are more risk averse to using digital tools that require the disclosure of sensitive health information.[37] This is contrary to claims that the accessibility of FemTech tools will provide access and information on currently underrepresented populations within sexual and reproductive health research.[38]

Nelson et al also signal the 'epistemic impact' of Femtech and its devaluation of women's personal testimony on their health.[39] Women's symptoms of 'menstrual and gynecological pain' are often minimised in sexual and reproductive health settings.[40] The Birth Trauma Report in the UK has cited numerous examples of how this devaluation of women's testimony in maternity care settings could be correlated to the adverse outcomes for the physical and mental health of patients. An increased reliance by HCPs on the quantification of symptoms by FemTech may then further devalue women's testimony in sexual and reproductive health settings.[41] Moreover, the ability of FemTech to compound the usurpation of the validity of women's testimony in sexual and reproductive health settings could also prove to be especially detrimental to the wellbeing of people from racially minoritised backgrounds.

Corbin and Healy further claim that FemTech acts as a Trojan horse to reinforce gender stereotypes by misinterpreting health data from FemTech users who have unwittingly provided sensitive health information.[42] Meanwhile, legal commentators and sociologists discuss how a lack of privacy for FemTech user's sensitive health information poses more existential threats to the wellbeing of women and gender minorities.[43] This is because the demand to track menstrual cycles is said to entrench the notion that a woman's contribution to society is via their reproductive capacity and to surveil them as 'monitored subjects' and to make sure that they comply with their roles as mothers and carers.[44] The resulting facilitation

[36] All-Party Parliamentary Group on Birth Trauma. 'Listen to Mums: Ending the Postcode Lottery on Perinatal Care' (13 May 2024, London).

[37] House of Commons, House of Lords – Joint Committee on Human Rights, 'The Right to Privacy (Article 8) and the Digital Revolution: Third Report of Session 2019', 30 October 2019, publications.parliament.uk/pa/jt201919/jtselect/jtrights/122/122.pdf.

[38] GOV.UK (n 3).

[39] Nelson, Tzanou and Keren-Paz (n 19).

[40] ibid.

[41] ibid.

[42] Healy (n 6).

[43] E Hammod and M Burdon, 'Intimate Harms and Menstrual Cycle Tracking Apps' (2024) 55 *Computer Law & Security Review*, doi.org/10.1016/j.clsr.2024.106038.

[44] D Lupton, 'Australian Women's Use of Health and Fitness Apps and Wearable Devices: A Feminist New Materialism Analysis; (2020) 20(7) *Feminist Media Studies* 983 ('Feminist New Materialism Analysis').

of FemTech to endorse the carer archetype for women will allow policymakers to continue to be permissive in employment protections. The current culture of FemTech is therefore not delivering a sexual and reproductive health revolution. It is replicating systemic issues and reinforcing problematic racial and gendered assumptions that deprive women's agency over their health.

V. FemTech: A Threat to Privacy

FemTech products – like menstrual cycle trackers and fertility trackers – collect information about an individual's sexual behaviours, reproductive health and medication intake.[45] FemTech products claim that a user's data will facilitate a women's increased understanding of her health and wellbeing, and/or to self-regulate healthy behaviours.[46] FemTech compels users to input more specific, sensitive health information into its interfaces by claiming that this will create a bespoke experience of the digital tool and better facilitate an improvement to their wellbeing.[47] But cybersecurity experts speculate that vulnerable persons using FemTech apps could have their data used by third parties without their consent or choice.[48] In the UK, there are 'gaps in regulations' that would protect FemTech users' right to privacy for sensitive health information.[49]

A. Sensitive Health Information

The sexual behaviours and reproductive health of a FemTech user are not considered 'sensitive' data by the majority of FemTech digital tools on the market.[50] FemTech users are not aware of the FemTech industry's characterisation of sensitive health data and assume a default standard of privacy on such data.[51] FemTech users report inputting sensitive health information into products like menstrual cycle tracking apps with the assumption that the data collected by the interface will solely be used for their individual purposes.[52] Or, if their data is shared, it will

[45] Mehrnezhad, Shipp, Almeida and Toreini (n 12).

[46] N Alfawzan, M Christen, G Spitale and N Biller-Andorno, 'Privacy, Data Sharing, and Data Security Policies of Women's mHealth Apps: Scoping Review and Content Analysis' (2022) 10(5) *JMIR Mhealth Uhealth*; C Rosas, 'The Future is Femtech: Privacy and Data Security Issues Surrounding Femtech Applications' (2019) 319(15) *Hastings Bus. L.J.*

[47] House of Commons, House of Lords – Joint Committee on Human Rights (n 37); Mekioussa Malki, Kaleva, Patel, Warner and Abu-Salma (n 27).

[48] ibid; Mehrnezhad, Shipp, Almeida and Toreini (n 12).

[49] Mehrnezhad, Van Der Merwe and Catt (n 8).

[50] L Shipp and J Blasco, 'How private is your period?: A systematic analysis of menstrual app privacy policies' (2020) *Proceedings on Privacy Enhancing Technologies* 491–510.

[51] ibid.

[52] J Walker, '84% of Period Tracker Apps Share Data with Third Parties' (*ORCHA*, 21 July 2022) orchahealth.com/period-tracker-apps-share-data/.

contribute to scientific research that could improve women's sexual and reprodutive health across the global population.[53] There is an increasing awareness that there may be a relationship between the use of FemTech products and an increase in targeted advertising, but this has not significantly altered user's behaviours with FemTech.[54]

The assumptions of FemTech users are that an individual has a fundamental right to privacy as it pertains to their sensitive health information[55] and that a FemTech product's safety has been verified by the 'app store' with reference to an individual user's domestic legislation.[56] However, these assumptions are not borne out by the industry practice of FemTech providers.

Users rely on assumptions that the products have a default obligation to provide safeguard measures for their privacy.[57] Terms and conditions are often considered long and full of jargon by FemTech users; and users rely on assumptions that the products have a default obligation to provide safeguard measures for their privacy.[58] Accordingly, two-thirds of the most popular FemTech products do not explicitly state false or misleading notice on a user's right to privacy in their engagement with their product's within the terms and conditions.[59] Instead, the FemTech industry is aware that most user's will not significantly engage with the terms and conditions and privacy policies of digital tools.[60] Or, FemTech products will write incoherent Terms and Conditions with inconsistent provisions on the right to privacy across the FemTech product's Terms and Conditions.[61]

B. Read the Terms and Conditions

Empirical evidence collected on FemTech users' perception and desire for privacy states that they either assume an inherent right to privacy or that their data is protected within FemTech digital tools because of the law.[62] But to read the terms and conditions of the 13 most popular apps in the UK, an individual would

[53] The Information Commissioner's Office, 'Understanding the user experience of fertility and period tracking apps' (October 2023) ico.org.uk/media2/migrated/4029278/understanding-the-user-experience-of-fertility-and-period-tracking-apps.pdf.

[54] M Mehrnezhad and T Almeida. '"My Sex-Related Data Is More Sensitive than My Financial Data and I Want the Same Level of Security and Privacy": User Risk Perceptions and Protective Actions in Female-Oriented Technologies' (2023) arXiv, http://arxiv.org/abs/2306.05956; The Information Commissioner's Office (n 53).

[55] Shipp and Blasco (n 50). Walker (n 52).

[56] Wanni Arachchige Dona, Angeles, Nguyen, Cooper, Sweet and Peeters (n 26).

[57] The Information Commissioner's Office (n 53).

[58] ibid.

[59] House of Commons, House of Lords – Joint Committee on Human Rights (n 37); Mekioussa Malki, Kaleva, Patel, Warner and Abu-Salma (n 27) 1–24.

[60] House of Commons, House of Lords – Joint Committee on Human Rights (n 37).

[61] Pybus and Mir (n 28).

[62] Mekioussa Malki, Kaleva, Patel, Warner and Abu-Salma (n 27); Wanni Arachchige Dona, Angeles, Nguyen, Cooper, Sweet and Peeters (n 26).

require approximately 17 hours.[63] According to a 2019 Report by the UK House of Commons House of Lords Joint Committee on Human Rights, an app user's derogation of a right to privacy is 'bogus'.[64] This is because the derogation to the right to privacy is said to be a result of the terms and conditions being needlessly overcomplicated and individuals being misled to believe that more specific information about their sensitive health information will provide a better user experience of the app. FemTech users are therefore being misled in their use of FemTech tools.

FemTech digital tools provide inconsistent information across their disclaimers. For example, Pybus and Mir identified that across provisions in a single app's terms and conditions, contradictory statements were found to protect a FemTech user's right to privacy.[65] This obfuscates the protections, liabilities and rights that a FemTech user would have whilst engaging with a FemTech interface. Additionally, there has been a recent trend of business enterprises including applicable but broad provisions within terms and conditions.[66] Provisions within the terms and conditions of online services like FemTech can have far reaching consequences.

C. Sharing Data with Third Parties

The commercial viability of FemTech providers is sustained by selling user data to third parties.[67] According to a 2022 report by the Organisation for the Review of Care and Health Apps (ORCHA), 84 per cent of the FemTech products that they assessed 'share the data beyond the developer's system to a third party'.[68] In two-thirds of the 20 most popular FemTech products, notice is given to the product user that their sensitive health information will be shared with third parties.[69] Although any data shared (or sold) to third parties is said to be anonymised, 'an entire sub-industry exists that links these identifiers to peoples' real names and physical addresses'.[70] The potential threat to a FemTech user's privacy from the commercial sale of their sensitive health information is discoverable to FemTech providers and legislators.[71] But FemTech providers are not being required to mitigate this threat via UK legislation.

While 27.5 per cent of FemTech users, surveyed and interviewed within a study by Mehrnezhad and Almeida, reported adverse outcomes from their FemTech

[63] PCMag UK, 'It Would Take 17 Hours to Read the Terms & Conditions of the 13 Most Popular Apps' (4 December 2020) uk.pcmag.com/security/130336/it-would-take-17-hours-to-read-the-terms-conditions-of-the-13-most-popular-apps.

[64] House of Commons, House of Lords – Joint Committee on Human Rights (n 37).

[65] Pybus and Mir (n 28).

[66] ibid.

[67] Mekioussa Malki, Kaleva, Patel, Warner and Rua Abu-Salma (n 27).

[68] Walker (n 52).

[69] Mekioussa Malki, Kaleva, Patel, Warner and Abu-Salma (n 27).

[70] J Cox, 'Data Marketplace Selling Info About Who Uses Period Tracking Apps' (VICE), www.vice.com/en/article/v7d9zd/data-marketplace-selling-clue-period-tracking-data.

[71] Mehrnezhad, Van Der Merwe and Catt (n 8).

data being shared with a third party: 'Eight of them said they have been bothered by personalised ads … and three said they had experienced a password leak'.[72] The identified spectrum of harm to FemTech users may currently seem minimal. However, there is an increased awareness that there has been a creeping scope of the operation of data collection mechanisms in FemTech products and the potentiality of misuse of that data by bad actors.

For example, anti-abortion advocates have used purchased 'anonymised' data to engage in a campaign to target advertisements or redirect Google searches for persons who seek more information on abortions.[73] In a recent study by Malki et al of the 20 most popular FemTech products, '[m]any of the apps in the study were also found to link users' sexual and reproductive data to their Google searches or website visits, posing, as researchers warn, a risk of de-anonymisation for the user and could also lead to assumptions about their fertility status'.[74] Targeted advertisements from bad actors, based on the data collected from users of FemTech products, could therefore redirect FemTech user sites with abortion misinformation[75] or pseudo-medical facilities that actively discourage individuals from having an abortion (ie, a pregnancy crisis centre).[76] The compromised privacy of a FemTech user may therefore place an individual at risk of significant physical harm and mental distress.

D. Law Enforcement

FemTech users in the UK are reported not to be aware that FemTech corporations often reserve the right to share a user's sensitive health information with law enforcement.[77] According to the 2022 ORCHA report, 64 per cent of FemTech apps have shared a user's sensitive health information due to legal obligations. Sensitive health information inputted into FemTech data collection interfaces can, and have been, used as evidence in criminal investigations (e.g. the investigation and prosecution of illegally procured abortions).[78] For example, in the US following

[72] Mehrnezhad and Almeida (n 54).

[73] K Paul, 'Google Earned $10m from Ads Misdirecting Abortion Seekers to "Pregnancy Crisis Centers"' *The Guardian* (15 June 2023), sec. Technology, www.theguardian.com/technology/2023/jun/15/google-misleading-abortion-ads-pregnancy-crisis-centers; V Elliott, 'Antiabortion Disinformation Ads Ran Rampant on Facebook and Instagram' (*Wired*, 27 March 2024) www.wired.com/story/facebook-instagram-anti-abortion-ads-disinformation/.

[74] King's College, 'Female Health Apps Misuse Highly Sensitive Data, Study Finds' (King's College London) www.kcl.ac.uk/news/female-health-apps-misuse-highly-sensitive-data-study-finds.

[75] Elliott (n 73).

[76] Paul (n 73).

[77] Walker (n 52).

[78] J Cao, H Laabadli, CH Mathis, RD Stern and P Emami-Naeini. '"I Deleted It After the Overturn of Roe v. Wade": Understanding Women's Privacy Concerns Toward Period-Tracking Apps in the Post Roe v. Wade Era' in Proceedings of the CHI Conference on Human Factors in Computing Systems, 1–22. Honolulu HI USA: ACM, 2024. doi.org/10.1145/3613904.3642042; P Davis, 'British Police Testing Women for Abortion Drugs (*Tortoise*, 30 October 2023) www.tortoisemedia.com/2023/10/30/british-police-testing-women-for-abortion-drugs/.

the reversal of *Roe v Wade* in 2022,[79] pro-choice activists advised women, and birthing people to delete FemTech products that tracked their menstrual cycles.[80] Activists and commentators signalled that data from menstrual tracking apps would be used as evidence in the prosecution of individuals that have been alleged to illegally procure an abortion in the US.[81] This was based on the previous use of evidence of FemTech data and google searches in the prosecution of abortion cases across the country.[82]

Accordingly, in recent criminal prosecutions across the US and the UK, women who have experienced pregnancy loss have had their Google searches used to verify whether they experienced a miscarriage or had an abortion.[83] However, similar public awareness campaigns have been lacking within other legal jurisdictions where FemTech users are similarly vulnerable to criminal prosecution. Meanwhile, a recent report from the UK notes that FemTech data is being used in the criminal investigation and prosecution of individuals who have allegedly procured an illegal abortion.[84] Criminal investigations have used evidence to prosecute individuals based on conclusions from information in their menstrual cycle tracking app and googling options for pregnancy termination.[85] The use of FemTech data in the prosecution of illegally obtained abortions has become emblematic of the problems with the lack of sufficient privacy protections in the use of digital tools like menstrual tracking apps. But this has not prompted any regulatory or legislative response in the UK.

The facilitation of intimate partner violence (IPV) by FemTech products has yet to be understood. Evidence has largely been attributed to media stories and one-off anecdotal citations in studies.[86] However, there has been increasing recognition that emerging technologies have been increasingly used by abusers to monitor and terrorise their victims.[87] This form of technology-facilitated abuse is difficult to identify by HCPs and other personnel engaged in safeguarding persons from IPV.[88] This lack of knowledge can be attributed to two main factors: a general lack of awareness on FemTech privacy standards, and a lack of training

[79] N Nellore and M Zimmer. 'Femtech Data Privacy Post-Dobbs: A Preliminary Analysis of User Reactions' in Companion Publication of the 2023 Conference on Computer Supported Cooperative Work and Social Computing, (2023) CSCW '23 Companion.

[80] H Moore and J Bhuiyan, 'Should we delete our period tracking apps?' *The Guardian* (5 September 2022), www.theguardian.com/news/audio/2022/sep/05/should-we-delete-our-period-tracking-apps.

[81] McMillan (n 9).

[82] Abortion Rights. 'The Scarlet Google Search: The Use of Digital Data as Evidence in Criminal Conduct for Abortions' (21 June 2023), abortionrights.org.uk/the-scarlet-google-search-the-use-of-digital-data-as-evidence-in-criminal-conduct-for-abortions/.

[83] ibid.

[84] Davis (n 78).

[85] ibid.

[86] S Cook, M Mehrnezhad and E Toreini. 'Bluetooth Security Analysis of General and Intimate Health IoT Devices and Apps: The Case of FemTech' (2024) 23(6) *International Journal of Information Security*, doi.org/10.1007/s10207-024-00883-3.

[87] I Straw and L Tanczer, 'Safeguarding Patients from Technology-Facilitated Abuse in Clinical Settings: A Narrative Review' (2023) 2(1) *PLOS Digital Health*, doi.org/10.1371/journal.pdig.0000089.

[88] ibid.

for HCPs to identify technology-facilitated abuse.[89] Also the facilitation of abuse via FemTech is not included or understood by persons that work in the protection of IPV victims.[90]

VI. Conclusion

FemTech presents a paradox: while it has the potential to address critical gaps in women's healthcare, its lack of regulation poses significant risks to user privacy and safety. A balanced approach is needed – one that acknowledges FemTech's benefits while holding companies accountable for ethical and legal responsibilities. To mitigate the risks posed by FemTech's regulatory gaps, a robust policy framework must be developed.

A lack of privacy is also not the sole threat against FemTech users. New technologies, like FemTech, pose multiple threats to the uncompromised agency and safety of persons vulnerable to IPV.[91] IPV, which is a 'multifaceted phenomenon,' allows abusers to commit violence against individuals via the use of patriarchal social structures.[92] The ability of data from FemTech products to facilitate harassment is increasingly being identified as an emerging threat.[93] However, an acknowledgement of the abuse of these new technologies is sparingly understood in legal regimes that pertain to protecting people from IPV. A future study on legislation for IPV from different legal jurisdictions could therefore propose how to articulate a language to prevent and penalise technology-facilitated abuse via FemTech products. Healthcare providers should also integrate FemTech into care models responsibly (being aware of potential abuses) and ensure it supplements rather than replaces medical guidance.

Further, countries like the UK, which have the infrastructure to enforce the right to privacy, still do not adequately legislate FemTech products. The lack of recognition of FemTech products as medical devices allows the FemTech industry to self-regulate its own standards of privacy. This fundamental lack of privacy protection on the collected data from FemTech interfaces subsequently allows governments to surreptitiously conduct surveillance on FemTech users. The UK, therefore should introduce FemTech-specific regulations modelled after GDPR, requiring explicit consent for data collection and prohibiting the sale of sensitive health information to third parties without user consent.

[89] ibid.

[90] HA Turner, D Finkelhor, K Mitchell and D Colburn, 'Prevalence of Technology-Facilitated Abuse Among Sexual and Gender Minority Youths' (2024) 7(2) *JAMA Network Open*: e2354485. https://doi.org/10.1001/jamanetworkopen.2023.54485; MM Rogers, C Fisher, P Ali, P Allmark and L Fontes, 'Technology-Facilitated Abuse in Intimate Relationships: A Scoping Review' (2023) 24(4) *Trauma, Violence & Abuse*, doi.org/10.1177/15248380221090218.

[91] K MacLure and A Jones, 'Domestic Abuse and Intimate Partner Violence: The Role of Digital by Design' (2021) 23(5) *The Journal of Adult Protection* 282–301.

[92] Straw and Tanczer (n 87).

[93] ibid.

3

When is a Stem Cell-Based Embryo Model Equivalent to a Natural Human Embryo?

JULIAN KOPLIN AND NEERA BHATIA[1]

I. Introduction

In 1946, Jorge Luis Borges published a one-paragraph short story called 'On Exactitude in Science.' In it, Borges describes a fictional empire, and the efforts of the cartographers of that empire to create a perfect map of that empire. The cartographers sought to make these maps increasingly detailed, which required the scale of these maps to increase. Eventually, they produced a map 'whose size was that of the Empire, and which coincided point for point with it.'[2] However, a map of the world built at the same scale as the world turned out to be useless, and the 'map' was abandoned to the animals and beggars that came to inhabit it. Arguably, at this scale, it was no longer a map at all.

Scientists have recently developed models of human embryos that map human embryogenesis to increasingly impressive degrees of exactitude. These embryo models are entities grown from stem cells that resemble 'natural' human embryos. The best such models can recapitulate the development of the human embryo so closely that it no longer seems far-fetched to think that a human embryo model may soon be created that could, if theoretically implanted into the womb, develop to term.

These breakthroughs in modelling human embryogenesis mean that we urgently need to address a thorny question: how should research with stem cell-based models of human embryos be regulated? This is a question on which different jurisdictions and regulatory bodies have taken radically different approaches. It is

[1] The authors thank Tessa Holzman for research assistance related to this chapter.

[2] J Luis Borges, 'On Exactitude in Science' in *Collected Fictions* (Viking Penguin, 1946) 325.

also a question that has serious ethical ramifications, relating to the moral status of these embryo-like structures.

This chapter considers various possible approaches to regulating research with embryo models. We argue that we should not simply rely on existing legal definitions of a 'human embryo', since these were drafted long before the possibility of modelling embryogenesis was even imaginable – and hence were not intended to address the ethical concerns related to embryo model research. We further argue that a double standard for research with 'natural' embryos and embryo models (of the sort proposed, inter alia, by the International Society for Stem Cell Research, or ISSCR) risks introducing arbitrariness into how stringently research with these entities is regulated. In our view, the best approach is to draw up some list of 'morally relevant features' that should trigger research protections, and extend these protections to any entity that possesses these features – regardless of whether they meet legal, biological, or other definitions of a human embryo.

First, however, a note on nomenclature. Much early discussion of embryo models adopted terms like 'synthetic embryos'[3] or 'artificial embryos.'[4] These terms have, however, been criticised, both on the basis that embryo models are made from human biological materials and so are not truly synthetic and on the basis that they differ from 'normal' embryos in certain ways that might make the moniker of 'embryo' misleading.[5] Currently, the term 'stem cell-based embryo models' (SCBEMs) appears to be the most popular, and has been used in several important reports.[6] We adopt it here simply because it is the most common term currently in use. We feel, however, that it is a non-ideal term in at least one respect.

Borges's short story alludes to the problem: a map, made at 1:1 scale with complete accuracy, no longer functions meaningfully as a 'map'; it is, instead, a territory in its own right. An embryo model, if it recapitulates embryonic development closely enough (and, perhaps, were able to be gestated to term) would arguably likewise cease to be a 'model' of an embryo in a meaningful sense. To describe embryo models as *modelling* embryogenesis is potentially misleading; they are, in fact, *undergoing* embryogenesis (or aspects of it). This feature is precisely what generates the distinctive and important moral questions related to embryo model research. It is one which we should not lose sight of.

[3] M Piotrowska, 'Avoiding the Potentiality Trap: Thinking about the Moral Status of Synthetic Embryos' (2020) 38 *Monash Bioethics Review* 166.

[4] JJ Koplin and C Gyngell, 'Emerging Moral Status Issues' (2020) 38 *Monash Bioethics Review* 95.

[5] HL Landecker and AT Clark, 'Human Embryo Models Made from Pluripotent Stem Cells Are Not Synthetic; They Aren't Embryos, Either' (2023) 30 *Cell Stem Cell* 1290.

[6] Cambridge Reproduction, 'Code of Practice for the Generation and Use of Human Stem Cell-Based Embryo Models' (Cambridge Reproduction & Progress Educational Trust 2024) www.repro.cam.ac.uk/scbemcode; Nuffield Council on Bioethics, 'Human Stem Cell-Based Embryo Models: A Review of Ethical and Governance Questions' (2024) www.nuffieldbioethics.org/publication/human-stem-cell-based-embryo-models-a-review-of-ethical-and-governance-questions/.

II. Embryo Models: Current State of the Science

In March 2021, a group of researchers at Monash University, Australia published a groundbreaking article documenting the use of induced human pluripotent stem cells (originally skin cells) to create structures that closely resembled human embryos at the blastocyst stage. The researchers dubbed these models 'iBlastoids.'[7]

iBlastoids were not perfect models; their cellular organisation differs subtly from that of a natural embryo, and it is unclear which aspects of embryonic development are within their capabilities. They also lacked the membrane that normally surrounds the blastocyst, which would be necessary for them to be able to implant in the uterus and develop to full term.[8] Despite these limitations, iBlastoids were an important proof-of-concept for the ability to model human embryogenesis in a dish that paved the way for future advances.

In June 2023, a team of stem cell scientists led by Magdalena Żernicka-Goetz announced the creation of embryo models widely described, in media coverage at the time, as 'synthetic human embryos.'[9] These models, though still imperfect, closely resembled real embryos, exhibiting structures and gene activity similar to those seen in human embryos between 6 and 14 days after fertilisation.[10] However, since they were created using human (embryonic) stem cells rather than a fertilised egg, they fell outside the scope of UK regulation of human embryo research. Indeed, they were apparently allowed to develop *in vitro* to a developmental stage equivalent to just beyond 14 days' *in vitro* development.[11] Notably, this falls slightly beyond the 14-day limit that the UK (alongside many other countries) impose on *in vitro* embryonic development.

Żernicka-Goetz and colleagues' study was quickly eclipsed: mere months later, in September of 2023, a team lead by Jacob H. Hanna announced the creation of 'complete' embryo models featuring not just the types of cells found in the embryo itself but also all the supporting structures needed for development, such as a yolk sac and the beginnings of a placenta. These models behaved much like 'real' embryos, showing early signs of organising themselves into the layers and structures that eventually form organs and the body.[12]

Research with non-human animals provides an even more striking view of embryo models' potential. In 2022, Hanna's team grew mouse embryos for

[7] X Liu et al, 'Modelling Human Blastocysts by Reprogramming Fibroblasts into iBlastoids' (2021) 591 *Nature* 627.

[8] ibid; J Ping Tan, X Liu and JM Polo, 'Reprogramming Fibroblast into Human iBlastoids' (2024) 19 *Nature Protocols* 2298.

[9] H Devlin, 'Synthetic Human Embryos Created in Groundbreaking Advance' *The Guardian* (14 June 2023) www.theguardian.com/science/2023/jun/14/synthetic-human-embryos-created-in-groundbreaking-advance.

[10] B Oldak et al, 'Complete Human Day 14 Post-Implantation Embryo Models from Naive ES Cells' (2023) 622 *Nature* 562.

[11] Devlin (n 9).

[12] BAT Weatherbee et al, 'Pluripotent Stem Cell-Derived Model of the Post-Implantation Human Embryo' (2023) 622 *Nature* 584.

approximately half of a mouse's normal gestation period (eight days) using a kind of external uterus. Some of these embryo models passed through gastrulation, which is the key developmental milestone where the embryo begins to establish its body plan. Remarkably, the most advanced also progressed through organogenesis, forming complex, functional tissues including a primitive brain structure, the beginning of a vascular system, and even a beating heart.[13] In 2023, another group were able to trigger pregnancies in monkeys using monkey blastoid models similar to iBlastoids – though the pregnancies were ultimately short-lived, with none of the model embryos developing to term.[14]

These advances demonstrate the remarkable progress scientists have made in modelling embryonic development using stem cells. Such research is scientifically exciting, not least because it offers a pathway into studying what is sometimes called the 'black box period of human development' between 7 and 28 days of development.[15] The period between 14 and 28 days of development is particularly mysterious. In many jurisdictions, it is both legally permitted and practically feasible to study human embryos *in vitro* up to 14 days' development, while embryos from terminated pregnancies can be studied from roughly 28 days' development. However, we know little about what happens in the period between these two milestones. Opening the 'black box' of embryonic development could have a range of important benefits, ranging from improving infertility treatments, designing new contraceptives, and preventing developmental disorders.[16]

Those conducting research with embryo models have characterised their work as exciting *precisely because* of their potential to shed light on an 'inaccessible time window during early development [emphasis added].'[17] Speaking to *The Guardian*, Zernicka-Goetz has described the development of embryo models as a way to 'carry out experiments that would be otherwise impossible on natural human embryos.'[18] What is interesting, however, is that embryo models allow access to this developmental window not because they provide some new means for overcoming a technical obstacle to cultivating human embryos beyond 14 days (this technical barrier was overcome in 2016),[19] but rather because research with 'natural' human embryos is governed by the '14-day rule' – a widely-endorsed restriction on embryo research that limits investigations to the first fortnight of development. Embryo models provide a potential means for studying embryonic

[13] S Tarazi et al, 'Post-Gastrulation Synthetic Embryos Generated Ex Utero from Mouse Naive ESCs' (2022) 185 *Cell* 3290.

[14] J Li et al, 'Cynomolgus Monkey Embryo Model Captures Gastrulation and Early Pregnancy' (2023) 30 *Cell Stem Cell* 362.

[15] JB Hurlbut et al, 'Revisiting the Warnock Rule' (2017) 35 *Nature Biotechnology* 1029, 1031.

[16] Hurlbut and others (n 16); N Rivron et al, 'Debate Ethics of Embryo Models from Stem Cells' (2018) 564 *Nature* 183.

[17] Tarazi et al (n 13) 3302.

[18] P Ball, 'Are Human Embryo Models a Cause for Hope or Alarm?' *The Guardian* (1 July 2023) www.theguardian.com/science/2023/jul/01/are-human-embryo-models-a-cause-for-hope-or-alarm.

[19] S McCully, 'The Time Has Come to Extend the 14-Day Limit' (2021) 47 *Journal of Medical Ethics* e66.

development beyond the 14-day threshold because, in many (though not all) jurisdictions, they fall outside the scope of legal definitions of human embryos.[20] They are useful, in other words, in large part because they are considered a *model* of an embryo, not an embryo per se.

In most cases, it would presumably be more useful, scientifically, to culture 'natural' human embryos (rather than embryo models) beyond 14 days. The embryo models that have been created to date differ from 'natural' human embryos in known ways, and possibly also in other ways that we are not yet aware of. These differences must create at least some difficulties extrapolating from embryo models to 'real' human embryos. A natural, 'true' human embryo faces none of these limitations; their use would allow the study of embryonic development directly. The key obstacle that embryo models help overcome is, therefore, not *scientific*, but *regulatory*.

The obvious question raised by the above is whether an embryo model could ever mimic a 'natural' embryo in such a way that it ought, morally or legally, to be treated as one. Accordingly, there have been many media and scholarly discussions about when an embryo model would meet various definitions of a human embryo. The following section of this chapter reflects on how these definitional questions are relevant to the current legal and regulatory landscape. Next, we consider how much progress can be made by considering whether embryo models fit philosophical or legal definitions of 'human embryos', and whether restrictions on embryo research like the 14-day rule ought to apply to them. We ultimately suggest that definitional discussions about whether (or when) embryo models (should) count as human embryos can only get us so far; we need instead to consider whether an embryo model has any 'morally relevant features' that would make them an appropriate target for similar protections to those afforded to human embryos.

III. The Regulatory Question

As hinted at above, where embryo models fit within legal and regulatory systems has significant implications for whether and how easily research can be conducted using these entities. Research with human embryos is highly controversial and – accordingly – highly restricted. It was legally permitted in many jurisdictions only after significant public and political debate about the moral status of the embryo and the potential benefits of such research, and even then, only under

[20] There are some cases in which embryo models might have additional advantages over natural embryos. As Gyngell and colleagues point out, one possible advantage of using embryo models is that genetically identical embryo models can be generated in huge numbers, which may be useful for some forms of research where the genetic heterogeneity of natural embryos donated from IVF introduces undesirable variability. However, even in this case, one key advantage of the use of embryo models is that they may enable researchers to skirt legal and regulatory complexities related to human cloning. See C Gyngell et al, 'Stem Cell-Derived Embryo Models: Moral Advance or Moral Obfuscation?' (2024) Epub ahead of print. *Journal of Medical Ethics* jme.bmj.com/lookup/doi/10.1136/jme-2023-109605.

certain conditions. These include the 14-day restriction on in vitro embryo culture described above. They also include requirements, in many jurisdictions, that research with human embryos can proceed only after researchers secure a licence from a national embryo research licensing committee with the power to review proposals for scientific and ethical compliance, impose conditions on research, and revoke approvals if necessary.

In Australia (which is where the two authors of this chapter are based), embryo research includes (significant) restrictions. The Prohibition of Human Cloning for Reproduction Act 2002 (Cth) ('PHCR Act')[21] and the Research Involving Human Embryos Act 2002 (Cth)[22] ('RIHE Act') are the principal frameworks that regulate and prohibit certain practices such as human cloning and regulate research involving human embryos, including the use of excess assisted reproductive technology (ART) embryos and mitochondrial donation techniques, with strict and substantial penalties for non-compliance, including imprisonment.[23] The Acts were devised to address community concerns about the ethical and scientific developments regarding human reproduction and the use of human embryos in research activities.

Part 2 of the 'PHCR Act' provides a range of prohibited practices listed as 'offences' under the legislation.[24] From section 9-23C in Part 2 of the Act, these offences are broad ranging and include (but are not limited to) prohibitions in developing human embryo clones; the development of human embryos outside the body of a woman for more than 14 days (which is Australia's expression of the '14-day rule'); creating chimeric or hybrid embryos; and creating human embryos other than by fertilisation or developing such an embryo.

Similarly, Division 2 of the 'RIHE Act' provides a number of offences that pertain to the regulation and use of excess ART embryos for research that carry significant penalties including imprisonment.[25] Sections 10–12A of division 2 detail a range of offences, for example, for research involving embryos created by ART for use in ART in excess need of the woman for whom they were created and her spouse at the time the embryo was created.[26] Other offences include: the use of other embryos (such as hybrid embryos), certain activities involving the use of human embryos, and the use of embryos that are not an excess ART embryo for research (amongst other offences).

Given how stringently controlled research concerning 'natural' embryos is governed, the way we regulate embryo models will significantly impact the kind

[21] Prohibition of Human Cloning for Reproduction Act 2002 (Cth).

[22] Research Involving Human Embryos Act 2002 (Cth).

[23] For example, it is an offence under s 9 of the Prohibition of Human Cloning for Reproduction Act 2002 (Cth) to place a human embryo clone in the human body or the body of an animal, with a penalty of 15 years' imprisonment.

[24] See Pt 2, s 9-23C of the Prohibition of Human Cloning for Reproduction Act 2002 (Cth).

[25] Section 10B of the Research Involving Human Embryos Act 2002 (Cth) carries a penalty of imprisonment for 5 years.

[26] See Division 2, s 10.

of research that can be pursued. If embryo models are subjected to the same stringent restrictions as 'natural' embryos, they will offer very little new opportunities for studying human development. If, on the other hand, they are left entirely outside the scope of embryo research laws, they could dramatically expand what is possible in developmental biology. A middle-ground approach, regulating them separately but less restrictively than 'natural' embryos, could open new research avenues while still maintaining some oversight. Which of these constitutes the 'right' approach is not just a technical legal question but also an ethical one: it is about what degree and kinds of restrictions are appropriate to the kinds of things that embryo models are, and whether their differences from 'natural' embryos warrant differences in their treatment. The decisions we make about this will shape the future of human developmental science.

Below, we map out three broad kinds of regulatory approaches one could take to embryo models and explain why the appropriate choice of model turns on certain moral and philosophical questions.

A. Exclude Embryo Models from Embryo Research Regulation

The United Kingdom (UK) provides an important example for this approach. Unlike 'natural' embryos, embryo models can be cultured *in vitro* for any length of time, for any purposes, and without requiring a licence from the UK's Human Fertilisation and Embryology Authority.[27] In other words, embryo model research falls within a regulatory gap, with no enforceable restrictions on this research (though some voluntary, non-enforceable governance frameworks have been developed.)[28] Similarly, in Japan, embryo model research does not fall under the legal framework for fertilised embryos (though it is subject to ethics review at the institutional level.)[29] Such approaches open up avenues for scientific inquiry that are not otherwise available.

Excluding embryo models from the scope of embryo research regulation could also have an unanticipated consequence: it could raise the burden of justification for conducting research with 'natural' human embryos. Many jurisdictions and scientific organisations endorse a principle for embryo research known as the 'subsidiarity principle', according to which research on human embryos should be undertaken only if no suitable alternatives are available. For example, if the research objectives can be achieved using adult stem cells or animal models, then

[27] E Jackson, 'Regulating Embryo Models in the UK' (2024) 11 *Journal of Law and the Biosciences* lsae016.

[28] Cambridge Reproduction (n 6).

[29] T Sawai et al, 'Regulating Stem Cell–Based Embryo Model Research in Japan: Proposals, Debates, and Future Directions' (2025) 26 *EMBO Reports* 1682.

according to the subsidiarity principle human embryos should not be used.[30] Within Australia, this principle finds expression in the National Health and Medical Research Council's Ethical Guidelines on the use of Assisted Reproductive Technology in Clinical Practice and Research, which hold that ethics committees overseeing embryo research must be satisfied that 'the likely benefits of the proposed research cannot be achieved without using human embryos.'[31] Insofar as embryo models are treated as something *other* than human embryos, it would seem that – per the subsidiarity principle – research with 'natural' human embryos would become harder to justify, with embryo models preferred wherever their use is compatible with achieving scientific objectives.

Is this strategy for displacing 'natural' embryo research ethically desirable? That depends on the answer to an important question: do embryo models lack whatever feature(s) it is that have led us to restrict research with 'natural' embryos? Many commentators hold that the fundamental worry about embryo models is that highly accurate models might count, morally if not legally, as human embryos.[32] In such a case, it would be wrongheaded to prefer that they are used in research over natural embryos, and perverse to fail to extend them the same protections that we apply to natural embryos.

B. Include (Some) Embryo Models within the Scope of Embryo Research Regulation

In Australia, many kinds of embryo models *are* treated by the relevant regulatory body as human embryos; the National Health and Research Council considers its restrictions on human embryo research apply so long as an embryo model demonstrates 'organised development of the biological entity', understood in terms of the ability to develop 'up to, or beyond, the stage at which the primitive streak

[30] This principle is described, and critiqued, in G Pennings and A Van Steirteghem, 'The Subsidiarity Principle in the Context of Embryonic Stem Cell Research' (2004) 19 *Human Reproduction* 1060. Like many key features of embryo research regulation, it is consistent with the recommendations of the 1984 Warnock Report, which held that research with embryos should proceed only when no other research material is available. UK Department of Health and Security, 'Report of the Committee of Inquiry into Human Fertilisation and Embryology ('Warnock Report')' (Her Majesty's Stationery Office 1984) 64, wellcomecollection.org/works/pxgeeqnf.

[31] National Health and Medical Research Council, 'Ethical Guidelines on the Use of Assisted Reproductive Technology in Clinical Practice and Research' (National Health and Medical Research Council 2023) s 13.3 www.nhmrc.gov.au/about-us/publications/art.

[32] See eg P Ball, '"Embryo Models" Challenge Legal, Ethical and Biological Concepts' (*Quanta Magazine*, 2023) www.quantamagazine.org/embryo-models-challenge-legal-ethical-and-biological-concepts-20230613/; A Blasimme and J Sugarman, 'Human Stem Cell-Derived Embryo Models: Toward Ethically Appropriate Regulations and Policies' (2023) 30 *Cell Stem Cell* 1008; AM Pereira Daoud et al, 'Modelling Human Embryogenesis: Embryo-like Structures Spark Ethical and Policy Debate' (2020) 26 *Human Reproduction Update* 779; N De Graeff, L De Proost and M Munsie, 'Ceci n'Est Pas Un Embryon? The Ethics of Human Embryo Model Research' (2023) 20 *Nature Methods* 1863; KRw Matthews and D Moralí, 'National Human Embryo and Embryoid Research Policies: A Survey of 22 Top Research-Intensive Countries' (2020) 15 *Regenerative Medicine* 1905.

appears.'[33] Accordingly, an embryo model like the 'iBlastoid' model *does* count as an embryo under Australian regulation. Conversely, however, more primitive models do not. For example, an embryo model would not be regulated as an embryo if it lacks cell types found in 'natural' embryos that are necessary to form certain organs or extra-embryonic tissue (such as the placenta), and hence cannot demonstrate organised development of the biological entity.

While Australian regulators have adopted a relatively broad understanding of what an embryo is (particularly relative to the UK), it is possible to imagine a legal or regulatory framework that draws wider boundaries. For example, one could define an embryo model as an embryo if it does or could potentially develop neural tissue, even if it lacks some other cell types. Or one could regulate as an embryo any embryo model capable of passing through gastrulation, even if the resulting entity is not a complete, intact conceptus.

C. Regulate Research with Embryo Models Separately from Research with 'Natural' Embryos

The 2021 Guidelines of the International Society for Stem Cell Research recommend yet another approach. Like Australian regulators, the ISSCR distinguishes between two different kinds of embryo models: those that are 'integrated' and those that are 'non-integrated.'

Non-integrated models are those that 'are not intended to represent the integrated development of the entire embryo including its extraembryonic membranes' (eg, the placenta and yolk sac).[34] The ISSCR recommends such models are regulated only lightly; they do not require specialised scientific and ethics review.

By contrast, the ISSCR recommends that *integrated* embryo models – which do represent the development of the entire embryo, including extraembryonic membranes – be subject to specialised scientific and ethics review. Interestingly, however, the appropriate uses of integrated embryo models are circumscribed less tightly than appropriate uses of natural human embryos. Specifically, while the 2021 version of the ISSCR Guidelines maintain that *in vitro* culture of (natural) human embryos follow the 14-day rule, they recommend that integrated embryo models be 'maintained in culture for the minimum time necessary to achieve the scientific objective.'[35] This open-ended limit could, in principle, permit research on integrated embryo models that involve *in vitro* culture far beyond the 14-day limit. Integrated embryo models are thus treated as deserving of some intermediary

[33] National Health and Medical Research Council, 'Determining Whether an Embryo Model Is Regulated by the ERLC', www.nhmrc.gov.au/research-policy/embryo-research-licensing/commonwealth-and-state-legislation/determining-whether-embryo-model-regulated-erlc.

[34] International Society for Stem Cell Research, 'ISSCR Guidelines for Stem Cell Research and Clinical Translation' s 2.2.1, www.isscr.org/guidelines.

[35] ibid 2.2.2.

degree of protection that is greater than most cell and tissue cultures but nonetheless falls short of that afforded to 'real' human embryos.

Similarly, the voluntary Code of Practice for the Generation and Use of Human Stem Cell-Based Embryo Models (SCBEM), recently developed by a working group of UK experts, recommends that such research is evaluated by a specialised oversight committee, which would evaluate research proposals on a case-by-case basis. Like the ISSCR, the SCBEM Working Group that drafted this Code of Practice eschewed a fixed time limit for the development of embryo models, instead specifying that they should be 'experimented on for the minimum time needed to achieve the scientific objective proposed.'[36] This could, in principle, extend far beyond 14 days if this is necessary to achieve the proposed scientific objective; indeed, the SCBEM Code of Practice notes that embryo models could be developed to the point that they develop recognisable bodily structures such as a spinal cord or heartbeat, and encourages researchers to be sensitive to the discomfort that some members of the public may have regarding these developments.[37]

D. Which Approach Should We Take?

Having outlined these three approaches to embryo research regulation, we now consider which of them is the most appropriate or best reason to take. It is worth noting that they all involve some kind of value trade-offs. None is immune to seemingly reasonable objections.

The problems with the UK-style permissive approach are perhaps the most well-known and widely discussed.[38] The main concern with failing to regulate embryo model research is that if an embryo model mimics normal human embryogenesis closely enough, it could end up being similar enough to an actual embryo that it ought, morally, to be afforded the same protection. The fact that it was created by coaxing stem cells into the structure of an embryo, rather than through the fertilisation of human gametes, seems morally beside the point; much like how a child conceived via invitro-fertilisation (IVF) is clearly no less worthy of moral concern than a child conceived via natural reproduction, the fact that an embryo model was *created* in a different way to a normal embryo does not, by itself, seem relevant to how it should be treated. This would be an ethically worrying double-standard.

Aristotle's Principle of Equity holds, essentially, that we must treat like cases as like;[39] accordingly, to justify treating two people or things differently

[36] Cambridge Reproduction (n 6) 8.
[37] Cambridge Reproduction (n 6).
[38] See eg Jackson (n 27).
[39] A-H Chroust, 'Aristotle's Conception of Equity (Epieikeia)' (1942) 18 *Notre Dame Lawyer* 119.

from each other, we need to be able to point to some morally relevant difference between them. The worry with a UK-style permissive approach to embryo model regulation is that it might breach this principle of equality, and hence involve a morally objectionable double-standard, if embryo models are treated differently to natural embryos despite the lack of a morally relevant difference between them.

The middle-ground approaches proposed by the ISSCR and UK voluntary guidelines are somewhat more restrictive. Perhaps for this reason, they have not – to our awareness – attracted much criticism for involving objectionable double standards. However, such approaches still treat embryo models, including integrated ones, as worthy only of a lesser degree of protection than natural embryos. If the UK-style permissive approach raises a legitimate worry about double standards, then so too do these middle-ground approaches.

What about the restrictive approach, whereby some or all embryo models are regulated as embryos? The key moral concern is that there are good *prima facie* moral reasons not to interfere with potentially beneficial research unnecessarily. One such reason is a principled attachment to scientific freedom, and the associated belief that this freedom should be curbed only for good reason. Another (more explicitly consequentialist) concern is that a restrictive approach can be expected to impede the numerous beneficial applications of embryo model research. These include advancements for IVF, the potential to reduce miscarriage rates, and other improvements to human health and people's ability to pursue their reproductive goals. If we restrict embryo model research without good reason, we risk losing something valuable. It would be unethical to hinder scientific progress without sufficient moral justifications, particularly where this progress could promote human health and improve human lives.

In short, permissive approaches risk a morally unjustifiable double-standard in embryo research, with some entities that deserve protection not receiving it. But there are costs to being excessively conservative. If the protections afforded to natural embryos would serve no important purpose in relation to embryo models, erring on the side of excessive protection would itself be unethical.

How can we work out what level of protection is appropriate to embryo models? There are two broad kinds of approaches one could take. The first – which is common in discussions of embryo models that have taken place to date – is to try to determine whether (or which kinds of) embryo models should be considered, ontologically/definitionally, as embryos. The next section of this chapter considers this strategy, and finds it wanting.

The second strategy, which has seen much less attention, is to consider the moral purposes of embryo research regulations like the 14-day rule, then consider whether these moral purposes would be met or hindered if the restrictions are extended to embryo models. This is the approach that we recommend, and we explore its implications in the final section of this chapter. However, before that, we consider the definitional approach, and outline our objections to it.

IV. The Definitional Approach: (When) are Embryo Models Embryos?

The question of whether some or all stem cell-based embryo models fit the definition of a human embryo can be taken either as a legal/regulatory question, or as a philosophical/conceptual one. However, neither approach can give a satisfactory account of how human embryo models *should be treated* – for reasons we will now explain.

A. Legal Definitions of 'Embryo'

First, consider whether we can rely on existing legal definitions for human embryos, and simply determine whether stem cell-based embryo models fall within their scope.

Many countries have not yet considered how to categorise stem cell-based embryo models, and indeed, in many cases they seem to fall outside the remit of existing laws, policies, and regulations. The fact that embryo models are formed without using human reproductive materials means that they do not meet many countries' legal and regulatory definitions of human embryos, and are therefore exempt from these countries' often stringent restrictions.[40] This is the case (inter alia) in the UK, as discussed in Section III of this chapter.

Matthews and Morali have published an important survey of embryo research laws and policies across 22 top research-intensive countries. 6 of these countries (China, Brazil, France, Israel, Italy, and Turkey) did not explicitly define what constitutes a 'human embryo', making it unclear whether their embryo research laws extend to these entities. The remaining 16 countries explicitly defined what constitutes a 'human embryo', but these definitions varied widely. Countries such as Spain, South Korea, and Taiwan define an embryo specifically in relation to fertilisation, meaning that embryo models (which are created through the manipulation of stem cells) fall outside the scope of laws and policies governing embryo research.[41] Other countries' laws refer to the embryo's developmental potential, and so do not outright exclude embryo models from their regulation.[42] But even here, there is both ambiguity and variation.

For instance, as described above, Australia defines embryos in terms of any 'process that initiates organized development of a biological entity,' a threshold that the NHMRC understands to be met if an embryo model can develop up to or beyond the formation of the primitive streak at around 14 days' development.

[40] M Fabbri et al, 'Modeling Policy Development: Examining National Governance of Stem Cell-Based Embryo Models' (2023) 18 *Regenerative Medicine* 155.

[41] Matthews and Moralí (n 32).

[42] ibid.

Accordingly, in Australia, the iBlastoid model was understood to count as an embryo, though some more primitive embryo models – including a 'gastruloid' model created in 2023 – do not.[43]

By contrast, countries like Belgium and Japan define an embryo as a cell or set of cells capable of growing into a 'human being' (in the case of Belgium) or an 'individual' (in the case of Japan), definitions that Mathews and Morali take to suggest embryo models likely *do* meet the definition of embryo.[44] Others, however, have pointed out that the exact developmental threshold that needs to be achievable for a set of cells to count as a 'human being' or 'an individual' has not been specified, and could in fact be interpreted to mean that something is (legally) an embryo only if it has reproductive viability (ie, could be gestated and brought to term.)[45] The precise stage of development that needs to be achievable for an embryo or embryo-like entity to become a 'human being' is therefore uncertain – which renders such laws ambiguous.

In addition to their ambiguity, legal definitions cannot tell us what *conceptual* or *moral* category is appropriate to embryo models. The absurdity of relying on existing legal definitions can be illustrated by imagining that a complete, 'integrated' embryo model is flown between multiple jurisdictions. Imagine that it was created in Spain, where it would not count, legally, as an embryo, given that it was not created via fertilisation. If it were transported to Australia, it would become an embryo. If then flown to the United Kingdom, the same entity would presumably cease to be regarded as an embryo. If then flown to Belgium, it may or may not count as an embryo, depending on when one considers the life of a 'human being' to begin. After being flown to Brazil (which does not have an explicit legal definition of a 'human embryo'), its status as an embryo would become even more radically uncertain.

This international variability would not necessarily be cause for concern if each jurisdiction in question had deliberated on how fair their definitions of 'embryo' should stretch, and on whether embryo models should be caught within their scope. Variation that reflects cultural differences is not necessarily objectionable. But what seems to have occurred instead, is that different jurisdictions have defined (or failed to define) the legal category of 'human embryo' at a time where the possibility of coaxing stem cells into replicas of human embryos was unimaginable. These legal categories were not designed to deal with embryo model research. To rely on them now that stem cells can be coaxed into embryo-like structures would be unacceptably arbitrary. We can learn little about how these entities *should* be regulated by determining where they currently happen to fit in a legal landscape that was never intended to encompass them.

[43] National Health and Medical Research Council (n 33).
[44] De Graeff, De Proost and Munsie (n 32).
[45] Pereira Daoud et al (n 32).

V. Ontological Definitions of 'Embryo'

Another option is to adopt an *ontological*, rather than a legal, definition of an embryo. In other words, we would try to work out *exactly what it is that an embryo is*, then determine whether embryo models fit within this category. The main problem with such an approach is that we cannot guarantee that whatever ontological account of a 'human embryo' we adopt will track the features of an embryo that we find morally relevant. We explore this problem in relation to the two: biological definitions that include reference to fertilisation, and definitions that refer to an embryo's potential to become a human person.

A. Fertilisation

Consider the possibility of adopting a biological account of a 'human embryo', taken from the biological sciences. Some biological accounts of a 'human embryo' specify that an embryo is formed via sperm-egg fusion. Accordingly, some commentators and organisations who have adopted a biological definition of a human embryo argue that embryo models should *not* be regarded as human embryos.[46]

This may or may not be a plausible application of certain biological definitions of what a human embryo is. The difficulty is that a *biological category* does not, by itself, have moral significance. Indeed, it seems dubious in the extreme to think that how an embryo-like entity was created has moral implications for how it may be treated.

Imagine, for example, that an embryo model was created, implanted in a uterus, and grown to term, ultimately yielding a healthy child. It would seem absurd to say that this child (and the adult that they would ultimately become) lacks moral status, and can readily be enslaved or abused, since they did not begin life as a human embryo and hence fall outside of the biological category of 'human.' Equally, it would seem absurd to think that, over the course of its developmental progress, there would have been any point at which it deserved less moral consideration than the 'natural' embryo. An embryo's origins may be relevant to whether it is captured by (some) biological definitions of a human embryo – but these origins have no moral significance.

B. Potentiality

Another consideration is to ask whether embryo models have the same *potential* as a natural human embryo. For example, Rivron and colleagues agree that *how* an embryo is created is irrelevant, and propose a new, potentiality-based definition of

[46] Landecker and Clark (n 5); Cambridge Reproduction (n 6).

an 'embryo' that would encompass some embryo models. Specifically, they suggest that an embryo is any entity that 'has the potential to form a fetus.'[47] On their view, an embryo model can be considered to have met this threshold (and hence becomes an 'embryo proper' rather than a mere embryo model) once it has been demonstrated that the methodology used to create these models can successfully create living, fertile animals in multiple non-human species that are evolutionarily close to humans, such as pigs and monkeys.[48] In a related vein, Denker argues that we should define an embryo as a group of cells that has the active potential to form both a foetus and the extraembryonic tissues necessary for normal development; in effect, if the cells themselves carry the organisational instructions for making a new human individual, we should treat them as a human embryo.[49] Others argue that an embryo should be defined in terms of its ability to give rise to a live-born human being, rather than merely a foetus.[50]

What can we say about potentiality-based definitions of human embryos? One immediate worry is that they may be too narrow, in that they would exclude 'natural' human embryos that are also non-viable (eg, due to severe genetic abnormality.)[51] Non-viable embryos are, of course, covered by embryo research regulations like the 14-day rule. It seems arbitrary to exclude embryo models from these regulations' scope because they lack a feature that many natural human embryos also lack.

Potentiality-based definitions also raise the inverse concern that they may be too broad, in that they will include within their scope entities that seem clearly not to count as embryos. As Charo pointed out as early as 2001,[52] scientific advances are progressively expanding the category of things that possess some degree of potential to form a human being. Even before the advent of embryo models, the development of reproductive cloning techniques in the 1990s introduced the possibility that any adult somatic cell, given the right interventions, could develop into a genetically unique human. If potentiality alone is the criterion, then not only embryo models but also ordinary somatic cells would qualify for moral and legal consideration as embryos – which is, as Charo points out, an implausibly expansive conclusion.[53] A definition of 'embryo' that includes all somatic cells (including our skin cells, and many more besides) is absurd.

[47] NC Rivron et al, 'An Ethical Framework for Human Embryology with Embryo Models' (2023) 186 *Cell* 3548, 3555.

[48] ibid.

[49] H-W Denker, 'Embryoids, Models, Embryos? We Need to Take a New Look at Legal Norms Concerning the Beginning of Organismic Development' (2023) 30 *Molecular Human Reproduction* gaad047.

[50] I De Miguel Beriain, J Rueda and A Villalba, 'Re-Defining the Human Embryo: A Legal Perspective on the Creation of Embryos in Research' (2024) 25 *EMBO Reports*467.

[51] Pereira Daoud et al (n 32).

[52] R Alta Charo, 'Every Cell Is Sacred: Logical Consequences of the Argument from Potential in the Age of Cloning' [2001] *Cloning and the future of human embryo research* 82.

[53] ibid.

Some might object that natural embryos remain unique because of their autonomous developmental trajectory – that is, unlike adult somatic cells, they do not require extensive artificial intervention to develop into full organisms. However, as Piotrowska argues, this distinction is misleading.[54] No embryo, natural or synthetic, develops in a vacuum. All require external support and specific environmental conditions to actualise their developmental potential; an embryo that is never implanted into a uterus will never develop into a person. The necessity of an enabling environment undermines the claim that embryos possess a uniquely intrinsic potential that sets them apart from other cells. This renders untenable the idea that embryos have a special kind of intrinsic potential distinct from other cells, and that an embryo can be defined as an entity with a specific kind of potentiality.

Another, more general, concern about potentiality-based definitions is that appeals to potentiality have a shaky reputation in bioethics. It is sometimes argued that appeals to potentiality are absurd, since we routinely (and rightly) treat things according not to what they have the potential to become in the future, but rather in terms of what they currently are. For example: we might rightly hesitate to cut down a 100-year-old oak tree, but not to destroy an acorn;[55] we do not bequeath normal citizens with control of a country's armies, even if they are *potential* presidents or prime ministers or army chiefs of that country;[56] and we might rightly complain that a chef has entirely misunderstood our request if we order chicken at their restaurant and they serve us a fertilised chicken egg. In these examples, it seems clear that we would be making a conceptual and moral mistake if we treat an acorn, fertilised chicken egg, or regular citizen in light of their potential to become an oak tree, roast chicken, or army chief. Potentiality thus seems an unsatisfying basis for treating embryo models differently from natural embryos.

C. Purpose

Landecker and Clark point out that embryo models are created for research rather than reproduction, and suggest that this difference in purpose means they do not require the same stringent protections as natural embryos. The authors note:

> The purpose of embryo models is not to make human beings from in vitro entities. The purpose is to use them to explore human biology in ways that are not harmful to nascent or actual human persons.
>
> Concerns have been voiced that these embryo models could potentially cross the line between human embryo models and human embryos. This is reason enough to

[54] Piotrowska (n 3).

[55] K Devolder and J Harris, 'The Ambiguity of the Embryo: Ethical Inconsistency in the Human Embryonic Stem Cell Debate' (2007) 38 *Metaphilosophy* 153.

[56] P Singer and K Dawson, 'IVF Technology and the Argument from Potential' (1988) 17 *Philosophy & Public Affairs* 87.

continue to insist in both word and deed that the aim is to make a good model, not to make persons.[57]

However, this argument faces several difficulties.

The first difficulty is that purpose does not, in fact, provide a meaningful distinction between embryo models and 'natural' embryos. In some jurisdictions, embryos can be created explicitly for research. In these jurisdictions natural embryos are already being produced solely for scientific purposes, making embryo models no different in this respect than embryos that *are* covered by the 14-day rule and other protections. A similar problem arises for jurisdictions that *prohibit* creation of embryos for research. In these cases, the question is whether this prohibition should extend to embryo models. But the fact that embryo models are created for research cannot itself serve as the justification for exempting them – because if they were classified as embryos, their creation for research would be precisely what is prohibited.

One way to try to make sense of the purpose-based argument is by adapting the concept of potentiality. Because embryo models are not created for reproduction, it might be thought that regardless of their *biological* potential to develop into a foetus under the right conditions, they will in practice never be placed in these conditions – and hence have, in practice, no actual prospect of developing to the point of attaining significant moral status. But this argument, too, fails to distinguish embryo models from research embryos. Persson and Savulescu have argued that because research embryos are never intended for implantation, they lack 'actualisable potential' – the kind of potential that could lead to the development of a person.[58] The lack of actualisable potential applies to embryo models and research embryos alike.

There is also a deeper moral problem: the purpose for which an entity is created is not usually thought to determine the moral obligations we owe to it. We cannot exempt ourselves from animal welfare standards by breeding puppies with the explicit purpose of torturing them, nor can we skirt our moral and legal responsibilities to our children if we conceive them with the explicit goal of selling them into slavery. The moral status of an entity cannot be based on the intentions behind its creation.

VI. Morally Relevant Features

It is time to take stock. The most significant worry raised by embryo models is that they might come to resemble human embryos so closely that they morally ought

[57] Landecker and Clark (n 5) 1292.

[58] I Persson and J Savulescu, 'Actualizable Potential, Reproduction, and Embryo Research: Bringing Embryos into Existence for Different Purposes or Not at All' (2010) 19 *Cambridge quarterly of healthcare ethics: CQ: the international journal of healthcare ethics committees* 51.

to be afforded the same treatment as a natural embryo. The difficulty, however, is that we lack an adequate account of what an embryo is that we could apply to these new entities. Legal definitions of human embryos were not crafted with embryo models in mind, and scientific definitions do not necessarily pick out the features that motivated restrictions of human embryo research in the first place. Indeed, scientific definitions are simply not equipped to do moral work. The task of science is distinct from that of ethics, since it is dedicated to describing and explaining the natural world, rather than determining how we ought to act within it. As Albert Einstein put it,

> … science can only ascertain what is, but not what should be, and outside its domain value judgments of all kinds remain necessary.[59]

If we are to work out how to treat embryo models, we will need a different approach. One promising approach, proposed in papers by Piotrowska,[60] as well as Aach and colleagues,[61] is to shift the analysis away from the definitional question of whether embryos fit some plausible account of what an embryo is. Instead, they suggest that we assess whether an embryo model has what Piotrowska calls 'morally relevant properties',[62] and Aach and colleagues call 'moral status signifying features'.[63] This would involve, first, drawing up some list of features that ought to trigger moral concern (and, by extension, regulatory intervention.) While no exhaustive list has yet been produced, both sets of authors suggest that (for example) the emergence of sentience or the capacity for pain ought to trigger moral concern, regardless of whether the entity in question is a 'natural' embryo or an embryo model.

One very significant virtue of this proposal is that it would ensure moral consideration is given where it is actually due, rather than where historical or scientific definitions happen to have placed it. However, it is not without challenges. One such challenge lies in deciding what features belong on such a list. Some features, like pain perception, are likely to command broad agreement. Others are more controversial. Aach and colleagues tentatively suggest that having a recognisably human-like form might be morally relevant.[64] But the moral significance of an entity's outward appearance is questionable. Imagine a case where a human brain, complete with its owner's personality, memories, and cognitive capacities, is somehow transplanted into the body of a cow. It would be perverse to argue that, simply because of its new form, this individual with its human-like mind has lost its moral standing and is now fit for slaughter. Even in the realm of *cognitive* capacities, it is unclear what kinds of features ought to be considered morally relevant to a being's

[59] A Einstein, 'Science and Religion' [1940] *Nature* 605, 605.

[60] Piotrowska (n 3); M Piotrowska, 'Research Guidelines for Embryoids' (2021) 47 *Journal of Medical Ethics* e67.

[61] J Aach et al, 'Addressing the Ethical Issues Raised by Synthetic Human Entities with Embryo-like Features' (2017) 6 *eLife* e20674.

[62] Piotrowska (n 3) 166.

[63] Aach et al (n 61) s 4.3.

[64] ibid 12.

moral status.[65] While various lists of morally relevant features have been proposed, some will not ultimately pass muster. But this is not a fundamental flaw in the approach: the challenge of determining the right list of morally relevant features is merely a matter of detail, which can, with effort, presumably be overcome.

A more serious challenge is that drawing research boundaries on the basis of morally relevant features might *still* involve a kind of double standard, compared to how research with 'natural' human embryos is regulated. Consider the two possible 'morally relevant features' described above: sentience/pain perception, and a human-like form. A natural embryo at 14 days' development lacks both these characteristics. Most estimates for when a foetus becomes capable of pain perception sit at 20 weeks' development or later,[66] with the earliest reasonable estimates of which we are aware suggesting that there is a possibility of pain perception developing at 12 weeks (but no earlier).[67] If the possibility of pain perception is what justifies restrictions like the 14-day rule,[68] then arguably natural embryos should remain unprotected for much longer than 14 days. Similarly, while the point at which the embryo develops a 'human-like form' might be debatable, it would fall far later than 14 days – a point at which the embryo's body plan is only just beginning to be established.

Does this apparent inconsistency – applying a 'morally relevant features' test to embryo models, yet continuing to cap research on 'natural' embryos at 14 days – undermine the idea of tying research limits to pain perception or other morally relevant traits? No, it does not. If an embryo model lacks the capacities that motivate restricting research (such as the capacity for pain), there is no sound reason to foreclose the research. Indeed, as mentioned above, it would be unethical to curb such research without good reason, given its potential benefits. We should not reflexively cling to an arbitrary rule if the entity in question lacks the very features that rule is meant to protect.

If anything, the inconsistency should be resolved in the other direction: insofar as our existing 14-day rule for natural embryos does not track the morally relevant features of research embryos, it is itself morally arbitrary. The rule arguably stands on shaky ground, in part because it is largely a political compromise dating back to the Warnock Committee's work in the early 1980s. As Hare observed at the time, that committee never provided a robust moral justification for its chosen cut-off; its conclusions were reached by canvassing moral intuitions and finding a politically

[65] JJ Koplin, 'Human-Animal Chimeras: The Moral Insignificance of Uniquely Human Capacities' (2019) 49 *Hastings Center Report* 23.

[66] EC Brugger, 'The Problem of Fetal Pain and Abortion: Toward an Ethical Consensus for Appropriate Behavior' (2012) 22 *Kennedy Institute of Ethics Journal* 263; SJ Lee et al, 'Fetal Pain: A Systematic Multidisciplinary Review of the Evidence' (2005) 294 *JAMA* 947.

[67] SWG Derbyshire and JC Bockmann, 'Reconsidering Fetal Pain' (2020) 46 *Journal of Medical Ethics* 3.

[68] The importance of avoiding experimentation on humans capable of pain perception did, in fact, play a major justificatory role in the Warnock Committee's proposal for a 14-day rule, since such a threshold would fall before the beginning of neural development and hence rule out any possibility of sentience. UK Department of Health and Security (n 30) 65–66.

palatable compromise between them, rather than clarifying the philosophical and ethical principles underlying their positions or explaining the reasoning that supported them.[69] This leaves the 14-day rule open to criticism of moral arbitrariness, and the suggestion that it is overdue for rethinking.

Recent calls to extend the permissible window to 21 or 28 days signal a willingness – at least among some scientists and ethicists – to revisit the conclusions reached by the Warnock committee.[70] But if the 14-day limit is to be revised, we need a principled basis for deciding on a new threshold. This, in turn, demands clarity on what the morally significant properties (such as pain perception or anything else of genuine moral weight) of a human embryo or foetus are. The key philosophical task, then, is the same for both embryo models and natural embryos.

We are not defending any specific threshold here. Pain perception seems to us a serious moral consideration, but it arises much later in development than the 14-day or even the 28-day mark. There may, however, be other morally critical milestones earlier than this stage. We have levelled some objections to the idea that 'human form' alone should carry moral significance. Nonetheless, there may be other possible bases for an embryo's moral standing. It might also be the case that many people find the idea of experimenting on an embryo with human-like appearance uncomfortable, and that these public opinions have an appropriate role to play in shaping regulation. However, regardless of where the threshold is ultimately placed, we can see no good reason to apply a different threshold to natural human embryos and to embryo models that share their morally relevant features.

VII. Conclusion

The main point of this chapter has been that the current focus on categorising 'embryo models' versus 'natural embryos' is misguided. Rather than arguing over definitions, we should ask what moral harms these rules are trying to guard against and then measure both natural embryos and embryo models by those standards. In other words, what matters is whether the act in question (prolonged *in vitro* culture and experimentation on a certain set of entities) is morally right or morally wrong, not the language we use to describe it.

Progress on the question of how to regulate embryo models thus requires us to re-open debates about embryo moral status. While it might be hoped that these debates could be left behind us, the substantive moral issues underlying embryo research regulation were never really settled. The key text underpinning current

[69] RM Hare, 'Embryo Experimentation: Public Policy in a Pluralist Society' (1987) 7 *Bioethics News* 32; RM Hare, 'In Vitro Fertilisation and the Warnock Report' in R Chadwick (ed), *Ethics, Reproduction and Genetic Control*, 2nd edn (Routledge, 2006).

[70] JB Appleby and AL Bredenoord, 'Should the 14-day Rule for Embryo Research Become the 28-day Rule?' (2018) 10 *EMBO Molecular Medicine* e9437; S Chan, 'How and Why to Replace the 14-Day Rule' (2018) 4 *Current Stem Cell Reports* 228; Hurlbut et al (n 15).

regulations throughout much of the world – ie, the 1984 Warnock Report – sought a political compromise between different views on the moral status of human embryos. It did not articulate a robust philosophical justification for its recommendations. The shortcomings of the Warnock Report leave us without a well-established rationale for embryo research restrictions, and without meaningful moral guidance for synthetic embryos. The philosophical issues related to embryo moral status require revisiting.

In a 1987 discussion of the Warnock Report (reprinted in 2006), RM Hare raises the possibility that Warnock will '… prove to have been voicing … opinions typical of her own generation, which may in the twenty-first century come to seem archaic.'[71] Growing support for extensions to the 14-day rule suggest that he was right. The task before us is not to work out how to extend the existing framework to embryo-like entities that this framework was never designed to cover, but rather to replace the framework as a whole with one that is philosophically defensible.

[71] Hare (n 69) 84.

PART II

Life

4

An NHS Medical Devices Information System: Reconciling Patient Safety and Patient Choice?

JEAN McHALE

I. Introduction

Implantable medical devices have improved patients' quality of life and also have literally saved lives. From hip implants to cardiac pacemakers they are a critical part of clinical practice today. However, over the last two decades the use of some medical devices has been fraught with notable scandal and controversy. Across a number of European Union member states the PiP breast implant scandal arose when it was discovered that women had received breast implants made using industrial level silicone.[1] This led to very serious consequences as some of the implants ruptured and leaked.[2] This scandal ultimately resulted in heightened focus on the effectiveness of approval of medical devices at EU level, as we shall see below, followed by major reform of the existing EU law in the area.[3]

Further controversy concerned the use of metal on metal hip implants.[4] Advice was given by the National Institute for Healthcare and Clinical Excellence (NICE)

[1] See further C Greco, 'The Poly Implant Breast Prostheses Scandal: Embodied Risk and Social Suffering' (2015) 147 *Social Science and Medicine* 150; Department of Health, *Poly Implant Protheses (PiP) Breast Implants: Final Report of the Expert Group* (Department of Health, 2012); M Latham, '"If It Ain't Broke Don't Fix It": Scandals, Risk and Cosmetic Surgery Regulation in the UK and France' (2014) 22(3) *Medical Law Review* 384; V Martindale and A Menache. 'The PIP scandal: an analysis of the process of quality control that failed to safeguard women from the health risks' (2013) 106 *Journal of the Royal Society of Medicine* 173.

[2] See eg RD Berry, 'Rupture of PiP Implants' (2007) 60 *J Plast Reconstr Aesthet Surg* 967; A Lahiri and R Waters, 'Locoregional silicone spread after high cohesive gel silicone implant rupture' (2006) 59 *J Plast Reconstr Aesthet Surg* 885.

[3] See further discussion in JV McHale, 'Health law, Brexit and medical devices: A question of legal regulation and patient safety' (2018) 18(3-3) *Medical Law International* 195.

[4] C Heneghan, D Langton and M Thompson, 'Ongoing Problems With Metal on Metal Hip Implants' (2012) 344 *British Medical Journal* e1349; F Godlee, 'Serious risks from metal-on-metal hip implants' (2012) *British Medical Journal* 344.

in the United Kingdom to the effect that medical practitioners were to make sure that those individuals receiving such implants

> understand that less is known about the medium to long term safety and reliability of these devices or the likely outcome of revision surgery than for conventional hip replacements.[5]

Over time problems with these implants emerged, notably with DePuy implants.[6] DePuy is a company owned by Johnson & Johnson which had produced metal on metal hip implants. The roll out of DePuy implants had been undertaken after the laboratory tests had been performed on the devices, but not trials involving patients. Damage from the wear and tear of the hip implants had caused harm to patients, leading to the need for revision surgery. In 2018 it was reported that DePuy had paid the NHS an undisclosed sum of money in relation to monitoring and undertaking surgery on patients who had received defective hip replacements.[7] A third major controversy in the UK concerned the use of vaginal mesh. Vaginal mesh is a product originally used as a method for treating urinary stress incontinence or rectal prolapse suffered by women as a result of childbirth.[8] Further complications arising from its use were identified such as infections, chronic pain, and loss of sexual intimacy. The polypropylene which was used to produce the mesh was an 'unstable substance' which should not have been used.[9] Serious concerns regarding the impacts of vaginal mesh led to a patient petition to ban their use from 2011.[10] In England the use of vaginal mesh, along with the controversial medicine sodium valproate, was examined by an Independent Review established by the Government chaired by Lady Cumberlege which reported in 2020.[11] The Independent Review's Report 'First Do No Harm' highlighted major concerns regarding the manner in which such drugs and devices were prescribed/implanted and the need to identify and react where safety concerns were raised.

One method which has been suggested to facilitate patient safety regarding implantable medical devices is through the collation of relevant information through databases or registries. Collection of information enables device safety to be more effectively monitored and patients, clinicians and regulators to be informed if problems arise. While on its face this could be seen as a potentially

[5] National Institute for Clinical Excellence, *The Effectiveness of Metal on Metal Hip Resurfacing* (NICE, 2001).

[6] D Cohen, 'DePuy knew about hip implant's high failure rate three years before it was recalled' (2013) 346 *British Medical Journal* f626.

[7] H Osborne, 'Firm pays out to NHS over defective hip replacements' *The Guardian* (26 November 2018).

[8] J Gornall, 'How Mesh became a four letter word' (2018) *British Medical Journal* 363:k4137.

[9] This led to litigation in the United States, see further discussion in J O'Neill, 'Lessons from the vaginal mesh scandal: enhancing the patient-centric approach to informed consent for medical device implementation' (2021) 37 *International Journal of Technology Assessment in Health Care* 1.

[10] MHRA, *A summary of the evidence on the benefits and risks of vaginal mesh implants*, 28 October 2014.

[11] *First Do No Harm: The report of the Independent Medicines and Medical Devices Safety Review* (2020).

very straightforward solution to a problem, closer examination illustrates that in fact this is far more complex than might have been initially envisaged.

This chapter explores the establishment of an NHS medical devices information system in the form of the Medical Devices Outcomes Registry in the UK. This operates as part of an NHS Outcomes Registry Platform. It examines the challenges for its operation in reconciling questions of patient autonomy, privacy, the public interest and patient safety. The chapter begins by exploring the current legal regulation of implantable medical devices in the UK and how this can facilitate patient safety. It then critically evaluates how a Medical Devices Outcomes Registry came to be established. The chapter then unpacks the legal and regulatory issues which underpin the development and operation of this Medical Devices Outcomes Registry, its potential and also the challenges both short term and long term for its operation.

II. Legal Regulation of Implantable Medical Devices in the UK and Patient Safety

In order to understand the move towards an NHS medical devices Outcomes Registry we need to explore how medical devices are currently regulated in the UK. This is an area which was originally subject to EU law through the UK's implementation of the EU Medical Device Directives, Directive 90/385/EEC concerning implantable medical devices, Directive 93/42/EEC general medical devices and Directive 98/79/EC in vitro diagnostic devices into domestic law via statutory instrument.[12] This area was recently reformed at EU level with the existing EU Directives being replaced by two new EU Regulations. These are the general Medical Devices Regulation[13] and also a specific EU Regulation which concerns In Vitro Devices.[14] The focus of the subsequent discussion of this chapter is in relation to relevant issues concerning implantable medical devices, concentrating on those included under medium to high risk medical devices, Class IIb and Class III high risk medical devices. (Class IIb devices are devices such as non-biodegradable maxillofacial implants and Class III devices are devices such as pacemakers and breast implants.) In contrast to pharmaceutical regulation, medical devices are regulated through the device being given an approval mark, which in the EU is a conformity assessed 'CE' mark. Today in the UK post Brexit, with the exception of Northern Ireland, there is now also a UKCA mark (this refers to UK Conformity Assessed).[15]

[12] Medical Devices Regulation SI 2002 No 618.

[13] Regulation (EU) 2017/745 of the European Parliament and the Council of 5th April 2017 on medical devices amending Directive 2001/83/EC, Regulation (EC) No 178/2002 and Regulation (EC) No 1223/2009 and repealing Council Directives 90/ 385/ EEC and 93/42/ EEC.

[14] Regulation (EU) 2017/746 of the European Parliament and of the Council of 5 April 2017 on in vitro diagnostic medical devices and repealing Directive 98/79/EC and Commission Decision 2010/227/EU.

[15] See further S Mason, 'The Regulation of Medicinal Products and Medical Devices' in JM Laing and JV McHale (eds), *Principles of Medical Law*, 5th edn (Oxford University Press, forthcoming, 2025) paras 16:152–16.327.

The approval process of medical devices in EU law is not subject to central regulation at EU level. This is in contrast to the approach taken in relation to pharmaceuticals by the European Medicines Agency. Instead the approval of medical devices is a matter which is left to 'notified bodies' who are commercial companies situated in member states, with some oversight from what is known as a 'competent body' – a regulatory oversight body operational at member state level.[16] While medical devices regulation is still not adopting the pharmaceutical regulatory model, there is a movement towards collating information concerning medical devices centrally along with the processes for the notification of serious adverse events concerning medical devices.[17] This is facilitated by an EU level database – EUDAMED.[18] Medical devices are required to have unique identifiers in order that they can be tracked and traced.[19] In addition, there is to be provision of information to patients in receipt of such implantable devices who will be required to be given what is called an 'implant card.'[20]

Initially it was thought that the new EU Medical Devices Regulations would come into force during the period in which the UK was negotiating its exit with the EU, however their implementation was delayed.[21] Ultimately the new EU Medical Devices Regulation did not come into force until 26 May 2021 with the new In Vitro Device Regulation being in force from 26 May 2022. While the UK to date did not transplant these new EU law provisions wholesale into domestic law in Great Britain, as we shall see the UK Government has indicated its intention to undertake further reform of the law in the area, including in relation to safety matters concerning medical devices.[22] In the case of Northern Ireland however, EU law remains applicable due to the different arrangements under the Northern Ireland protocol.[23]

In terms of the safety of a medical device, one important question is how easy it is to identify which specific device has been implanted into an individual. As noted above, the new EU Medical Devices Regulation incorporates what is known as a 'unique device identifier' so that if problems were identified in specific medical devices these can be traced back to the specific patient.[24] This provision was not enacted into domestic law at the time of Brexit. However, in November 2024 the UK Medicines and Healthcare Regulatory Agency confirmed

[16] ibid, para 16:182.

[17] Regulation EU 2017/745 of the European Parliament and the Council of 5th April 2017 on medical devices amending Directive 2001/83/EC, Article 73.

[18] See health.ec.europa.eu/medical-devices-eudamed/overview_en.

[19] See further, Regulation EU 2017/745 (n 17), Articles 27 and 28.

[20] Regulation EU 2017/745 (n 17) Article 18.

[21] See eg discussion in McHale (n 3).

[22] Medicines and Healthcare Products Regulatory Agency, *Standard: Implementation of the future regulations* (updated 26 February 2025).

[23] The Medical Devices (Northern Ireland Protocol) Regulations 2021, SI 2021 No 905. See further M Quigley, L Downey, Z Mahmoud and JV McHale, 'The Shape of Medical Devices Regulation in the United Kingdom? Brexit and beyond' (2023) 5(2) *Law Technology and Humans* 21; see also Mason (n 15) paras 16:11–16:16.

[24] Regulation EU 2017/745 (n 17), Article 18.

that as part of a suite of legislative changes a unique device identifier would in fact be introduced into domestic law via UK statutory instruments.[25] In addition, again following the approach in the EU Regulation, all patients who have a device implanted into them in the UK are also to be provided with 'implant cards' which will provide them with information concerning the devices which have been implanted into them.[26] Other measures which will facilitate the safety of the device include an increase in the monitoring systems. The Medical Devices (Post-market Surveillance Requirements) (Amendment) (Great Britain) Regulations 2024 now places enhanced requirements on manufacturers regarding the reporting of safety issues such as suspected serious adverse reactions.[27] This includes a requirement to undertake regular reviews of post-market surveillance data.[28] It is clear it is important to be able to trace where problems may arise in relation to the safety of medical devices, and an NHS medical devices information system in the form of a Medical Devices Outcomes Register can be seen as an important part of this process.

III. Developing an NHS Medical Devices Outcome Registry

Given the history of concerns in relation to patient safety and medical devices, it was unsurprising that there has been a movement towards the development of medical device information systems and ultimately as we will see below an NHS Medical Devices Outcomes Registry. In this section we explore how this Registry ultimately came to be established. Medical device information systems have the potential for the outcomes of specific devices to be determined and patients to be rapidly identified and contacted should a problem with a particular device occur. In addition, they may also provide valuable information for research. Two main forms of information system have been identified in relation to the collection of data concerning medical devices, those of medical devices databases and registries. The Report of the Independent Review chaired by Lady Cumberlege defined these as follows:

- A database: … a structured set of data held in a computer, especially one that is accessible in various ways.
- A Registry: an organised system that continuously and consistently collects relevant data in conjunction with routine clinical care, evaluates meaningful outcomes and comprehensively covers the population defined by exposure to

[25] Medicine and Healthcare Products Regulatory Agency, *Standard: Implementation of the future regulations* (updated 26 February 2025).
[26] ibid.
[27] SI 2024 No 1368.
[28] ibid.

> a particular medical device(s) at a reasonably generalised scale (eg, national, regional, health system) with a primary aim to improve the quality of patient care.[29]

In the UK, calls for developments of such registries concerning the safety of medical devices long pre-dates recent controversies and reports such as that of the Independent Review. The creation of a register concerning audit of data regarding the use of mesh for severe urinary incontinence was originally recommended by the National Institute for Health and Care Excellence as far back as 2003.[30] However, it was more recent developments and controversies which have accelerated the adoption of such systems. For example, following the controversy concerning PiP implants the Keogh Review into the Regulation of Cosmetic Interventions recommended the creation of a Breast and Cosmetic Implant Registry in 2013.[31] This Breast and Cosmetic Implant Registry (BCIR) was finally established in 2016. The Registry was intended to hold all breast implant procedures which have been undertaken by NHS and private providers in England, Scotland and Northern Ireland. While this was one of a series of registries established on an ad hoc basis, more recent developments have been to move towards a major registry operating at national level.[32]

In 2017 the then UK Secretary of State for Health, Jeremy Hunt, expressed interest in the establishment of a national medical device registry. This was followed by discussions involving Sir Bruce Keogh (who was at that point Medical Director of NHS England) with an organisation called the 'Healthcare Quality Improvement Partnership', leading to a stakeholder meeting hosted by the Academy of Medical Royal Colleges which included a range of key stakeholders.[33] This resulted in a report proposing the establishment of a medical devices registry at national level.[34] The Think Tank Meeting Report emphasised two key justifications for the creation of such a national registry, those of ensuring the safety of the device in question and of ensuring its efficacy. In relation to safety it noted that a medical devices registry can be viewed as a comprehensive dataset of 'who, where, how and why' the device was implanted.[35] The stated intention was that such a registry would enable clinical issues to be identified and identify where the device had performed poorly.[36] A further advantage of such a registry identified in the Report was that it

[29] *First Do No Harm* (n 11) para 2.88.
[30] *First Do No Harm* (n 11) para 2.85.
[31] Department of Health, *Review of the Regulation of Cosmetic Interventions Final Report* (2013), Recommendation 21.
[32] This particular registry was subsequently moved to the Outcome Registries Platform in March 2024 See digital.nhs.uk/data-and-information/clinical-audits-and-registries/breast-and-cosmetic-implant-registry#:~:text=The%20registry%20records%20the%20details,complications%20relating%20to%20specific%20implants.
[33] Healthcare Quality Improvement Partnership, *Proposals for a medical devices registry: Full Report* (2020).
[34] ibid p 1.
[35] ibid p 4.
[36] ibid p 4.

could be constructed to make available comparative data which would enable the efficacy of devices overall to be assessed and also enable post market surveillance.[37] A long-standing issue regarding the monitoring and safety of medical treatment relates to the question of innovative procedures and off-label use of medicines.[38] The Report highlighted the related challenges concerning 'off label' use of medical devices – use of a device outside the original purpose for which it was approved. This included the identification of the manner in which such devices are used, and the Report suggested it would be 'ideal' if they were included in a new registry.[39]

The subsequent Report of the Independent Review chaired by Lady Cumberlege extensively considered the question of medical device databases and registries.[40] One of the issues examined in the Cumberlege Report was the use of mesh in relation to stress urinary incontinence (SUI) and pelvic organ prolapse (POP). Here the Cumberlege report was not only concerned with a registry for the device itself but also with the question of the safety of the surgical procedures including those involving a particular device. The Report was of the view that surgical procedures for treatment of SUI and POP should be included on a national database and that:

> To move towards one hundred percent compliance across the NHS and private sector requires the collection of this data to be mandated by the Secretary of State for Health and Social Care. As this mandate or direction overrides a patient's right to opt out of their personal data being shared it is only reasonable that the data collected for the database is the least necessary to fulfil its legitimate purpose.[41]

Thus it was seen that collation of information on a such a database was a matter of patient safety which critically should override the views of any one specific individual as to whether this information should be stored to mandate compliance. In contrast the Report stated that in relation to a Registry

> The registry, as we have defined it, is a repository of more complex information necessary for evaluating long term outcomes and patient safety. It requires patient consent under GDPR {General Data Protection Regulation}. If that consent is explicitly given and the activities of the Registry are transparent and adequately explained to the patient in advance (of each surgical procedure) it would allow Registry administrators when required, to contact the patients. The information collected by Registries is not just clinically coded but will also often include patient sensitive information including PROMs {Patient Reported Outcome Measures} and PREMs {Patient Reported Experience Measures}. They therefore have to be individually designed by patients and clinicians working together.[42]

[37] ibid p 4.

[38] See further J Miola, 'Bye Bye Bolitho: The Curious Case of the Medical Innovation Bill' (2015) 15(2–3) *Medical Law International* 124; J Miola, 'Postscript to the Medical Innovation Bill: clearing up loose ends' (2019) 11(1) *Law, Innovation and Technology* 17; JV McHale, 'Falling between the gaps post the Declaration of Helsinki: innovative medical treatment in England – the case for comprehensive legal regulation' (2019) 11(1) *Law, Innovation and Technology* 93.

[39] See n 33 above at p 4.

[40] See n 11 above.

[41] ibid para 2.89.

[42] ibid para 2.96. See also discussion of the General Data Protection Regulation below.

The Report noted that at that time there were few Registries and a number of those which were in existence had followed controversies such as metal on metal hip implants leading to the National Joint Register[43] and the Breast and Cosmetic Implant Register following the PiP breast implant scandal.[44] It commented that

> A database of implanted devices and linked specialist registries will allow long-term follow up of patients and provide information on both device safety and patient reported outcomes, including those that become apparent after several years …[45]

The Government in its response to the Report of the Independent Review stated that they had accepted its recommendation in relation to the creation of a Medical Devices Information System.[46] In its policy document 'How a medical device information system might work in practice' the Department of Health and Social Care stated that the intention was to be able to 'intervene earlier to prevent harm before it happens'.[47] It was seen as important for patients to be able to be traced if an implantable device was recalled or in the event of other safety issues arising.[48] The intention was that a medical device information system should develop over time in collaboration with existing and future registries. It was to be operated by NHS Digital, an organisation already concerned with data analysis and dissemination. The intention was that the information system would be able to share relevant data while at the same time 'protecting the details of sensitive information which would be restricted to those who absolutely need it for legitimate purposes.'[49]

The Medicines and Medical Devices Act 2021 provides a broad regulatory structure with provision for the enactment of related statutory instruments post-Brexit in relation to medicines and devices. Specific reference is made under section 19(1) of the Medicines and Medical Devices Act 2021 for the Secretary of State to establish

> … one or more information systems for purposes relating to—
> (a) the safety and performance, including the clinical effectiveness, of medical devices that are placed on the market;
> (b) the safety of individuals who receive or are treated with a medical device, or into whom a medical device is implanted;
> (c) the improvement of medical device safety and performance through advances in technology.

[43] *First Do No Harm* (n 11) para 2.93. See www.njrcentre.org.uk/. The National Joint Register is itself currently hosted by the Health Information Partnership.
[44] ibid para 2.94.
[45] ibid para 2.115.
[46] Department of Health and Social Care *Government response to the Report of the Independent Medicines and Medical Devices Safety Review* Published 26 July 2021 at para 8.1.
[47] Department of Health and Social Care Policy Paper (Withdrawn) 'How a medical device information system might work in practice' (updated 18 July 2024).
[48] ibid.
[49] ibid.

Section 19 of the 2021 Act then goes on to provide that the regulations can specify matters such as what information concerning medical devices should be included in these registers and how such information will be used and disclosed,[50] along with the information which can be provided to NHS England where it is undertaking work concerning the registers.[51] There is provision for the regulations to state who will be required to provide information, to whom, how and when.[52] The Government's response to the Independent Review in 2021 stated that as well as developing regulations

> over £11m has been set-aside for a package of work in 2021/22 involving partners across the healthcare system to scope, test and cost options for MDIS and other medical devices patient safety workstreams, as well as complete a business case for a 5-year programme of work.[53]

However, progress in its development did not prove as fast as might have been hoped. The House of Commons Health and Social Care Select Committee in its document 'Follow up on the IMMDS report and the Government's response'[54] in January 2023 expressed concern regarding the fact that at that time data collection and the monitoring of long-term impacts had still not been undertaken.[55] The Independent Review team itself wrote to the Select Committee stating that

> This absence of data means that the system did not – and still does not – track patient-outcomes measured with direct patient input or direct trends of concern. That represents a serious risk to patient safety'.[56]

In addition the Independent Review team commented that though the Secretary of State had in his response to the Review committed to a compliance rate of 100 per cent in relation to one of the existing registries – that of the National Joint Registry – in fact the compliance rate was some 15 per cent.[57]

In setting up what was to eventually become the Medical Devices Outcomes Registry as noted above NHS England made reference to the Independent Review's First Do No Harm Report and also to the recommendations of the Independent Inquiry into the Issues raised by Paterson.[58] The criminal case of *R v Paterson* concerned Ian Paterson, a breast surgeon who was charged and convicted of some 17 counts of wounding with intent under section 18 of the

[50] Medicines and Medical Devices Act 2021, s 19(2)(a) and (c).
[51] Medicines and Medical Devices Act 2021, s 19(2)(d) and (dd).
[52] Medicines and Medical Devices Act 2021, s 19(3).
[53] See n 46 at p 9.
[54] Sixth Report of Sessions 2022–23 HC 689, 20 January 2023.
[55] ibid para 16.
[56] ibid para 18.
[57] ibid.
[58] *Report of the Independent Inquiry into the Issues raised by Paterson*. Chairman the Right Reverend Graham James, February 2020, HC 31.

Offences Against the Person Act 1861 in relation to nine women and one man.[59] He was also convicted of three other unlawful wounding offences. The charges related to patients being given exaggerated or inaccurate information regarding possible cancer risks from treatment resulting in them deciding to go ahead with surgery. Concerns were also raised in relation to Paterson's practice of undertaking what was known as 'cleavage saving mastectomies' which involved retaining some breast tissue. This in turn led to the risk of cancer subsequently re-occurring.

The Report of the Independent Inquiry into the Issues Raised by Paterson commented on the lack of comprehensive consultant performance data[60] and recommended that

> there should be a single repository of the whole practice of consultants across England, setting out their practising privileges and other critical consultant performance data, for example, how many times a consultant has performed a particular procedure and how recently. This should be accessible and understandable to the public. It should be mandated for use by managers and healthcare professionals in both the NHS and independent sector.[61]

The Government in its response stated that it accepted this recommendation 'in principle'.[62] It went on to state that the collation of data nationally had improved since Paterson. A scheme had been launched by the NHS known as 'ADAPt' with aims including that of a 'move towards a common set of standards for data collection, performance measure methodologies and reporting systems across the NHS and the independent sector.'[63]

NHS England subsequently indicated in 2022 that it would be operating an 'Outcome Registries Programme'.[64] This was introduced with the aim of addressing recommendations in the 'First Do No Harm' Report and the Paterson Report. This demonstrates that the decision to insert a device and the effectiveness of that decide itself is integrally linked to the competence of the practitioner implanting it. This new platform is to ultimately include over 37 clinical registries. Three of the registries began operation on the platform in March 2024 – a breast implant registry, a cochlear implants registry and a major trauma registry.[65] There will also be provision made for information to be submitted in the future where devices do not fall within a specific existing registry. Others are to follow in due course. While as we have seen above such databases and registers can be seen as a very important means of monitoring and identifying safety concerns regarding medical devices and also to ensure the safety of

[59] *R v Paterson* [2017]. Sentencing remarks of Mr. Justice Jeremy Baker, see www.judiciary.gov.uk/wp-content/uploads/2017/05/r-v-paterson-sentencingremarks-mr-justice-jeremy-baker-201705.

[60] See pp 131–32.

[61] ibid p 218.

[62] Department of Health and Social Care, *Policy paper Government response to the independent inquiry report into the issues raised by former surgeon Ian Paterson* (16 December 2021).

[63] ibid.

[64] Jackie Gray, *Summary of Outcomes and Registries Directions 2024 issued to NHS England by the Secretary of State for Health and Social Care in March 2024* (NHS England, 16 May 2024).

[65] T Lovell, 'Patient Groups oppose NHSE plans for unified clinical registry platform' (*Cyber Security News, Digital Health Net*, 3 July 2024).

practitioners who were implanting those devices. But their development, as we shall see in the following section of this chapter, has been the subject of debate.

IV. Medical Devices Outcomes Registry: Legal and Ethical Issues

As noted above, the creation of a medical devices registry can be seen as a means of addressing patient safety concerns regarding medical devices. They can highlight what may be systemic failures in relation to the use of such devices – whether of the device itself and/or the procedure which led to the implantation of this device. At the same time their establishment can give rise to legal and ethical issues. These are explored in this section. Such information systems will inevitably involve the collation of certain patient data. But on what basis should that information be obtained, stored and subsequently disseminated? One argument is that patients should provide fully informed consent for the use of their information to be stored subsequently in databases and in device registers. It can be argued that this is in line with respect for individual decision-making autonomy – and also consequently individual privacy. It may be also seen as a means of facilitating patient trust in the operation of the medical device database or register itself. Concerns have however been raised as to the appropriateness of a standard 'informed consent' model for storage of patient information in a registry or in a database and whether in fact the public interest is best served by for example automatic inclusion of such information.

Comparisons here can be drawn with two existing areas where there has been debate over the nature and scope of consent. The first concerns the use of information for health administrative purposes such as audit; the second relates to use of information for research purposes in the context of genetic databases.[66] Use of patient information needs to be seen from a patient confidentiality and also a right to privacy perspective. The confidentiality of patient information remains protected in English law through the equitable remedy of breach of confidence. It was held by Lord Goff that

> a duty of confidence arises when confidential information comes to the knowledge of a person (the confidant) in circumstances where he has notice, or is held to have agreed, that the information is confidential, with the effect that it would be just in all the circumstances that he should be precluded from disclosing the information to others.[67]

Being an equitable remedy, this is discretionary in nature. In determining whether there was a breach of confidence the courts balance the public interest in maintaining patient confidentiality with the public interest in disclosure of information.[68]

[66] See further ES Dove and MJ Taylor, 'Confidentiality, Privacy and Data Protection', paras 12:16–12:40 in JM Laing and JV McHale (eds), *Principles of Medical Law* 5th edn (Oxford University Press, forthcoming 2025).

[67] See *Attorney General v Guardian Newspapers (No 2)* [1990] AC 109.

[68] *W v Egdell* [1990] 1 All ER 835.

Patient information is also safeguarded through the human right to privacy under Article 8 of the ECHR.[69] In addition, as confirmed in *Bloomberg LP v ZXC* there are today separate actions in relation to the misuse of private information.[70] In relation to the misuse of private information that is an action in the law of tort[71] and in relation to breach of confidence that remains an equitable remedy. In relation to an action for misuse of information the basis of the action is first: is there a reasonable expectation of privacy which is an objective test, this is determined on a case-by-case basis.[72] Here there is to be a 'threshold of seriousness', although its scope, as Dove and Taylor comment, remains an uncertain issue.[73] Second, the balancing test as to whether the expectation of privacy is outweighed by other considerations such as other conflicting rights.

Moreover, although personal patient information is safeguarded, the right to privacy in the form of Article 8 of the ECHR itself is not an absolute right. Instead it is a qualified right and it is qualified with reference to factors such as the rights and freedoms of others and the broader public interest. Finally, personal health information is also protected through data protection law. Use of personal data remains regulated in domestic law through a structure which was introduced through EU law concerning data protection. This initially was driven by Directive 95/46/EC and was then subsequently followed by the EU General Data Protection Regulation – more commonly known as GDPR.[74] Although the UK is no longer a member of the EU, this regulatory approach remains as this was implemented into domestic law prior to the UK leaving the EU in the Data Protection Act 2018 and it remains part of retained EU law. The patient has various control rights regarding their personal information. These include access rights and rights concerning deletion of information.[75] However as we shall see below, in some situations control of personal data may be limited due to the operation of specific statutory provisions enabling the collation or dissemination of that information.

[69] *Campbell v MGN* [2004] 2 AC 457 HL. Today in the light of *Campbell* it has been stated in relation to the duty of confidence by Dove and Taylor (n 66 at para 12:33) that 'It might now be said that a duty of confidence – insofar as personal information is concerned – may exist whenever a person knows or ought to know that a "person of ordinary sensibilities" in the position of the person to whom the information relates would have a reasonable expectation that the information will not be used or disclosed without their prior authorization or a lawful basis.'

[70] *Bloomberg LP* v *ZXC* [2022] UKSC 5 in E Dove and M Taylor, 'Confidentiality and Data Protection' in JM Laing and JV McHale (eds), *Principles of Medical Law*, 5th edn (Oxford University Press, forthcoming 2025) paras 12:47–12:54.

[71] *Vidal-Hall and Others v Google* [2015] EWCA Civ 311.

[72] See further *Prismall v Google UK Ltd* [2024] EWCA Civ 1516 and see discussion of that case in ES Dove and MJ Taylor, '*Prismall v Google UK Ltd* [2024] EWCA Civ 1516; Misuse of Private Information in the Medical Context' (2025) 33 *Medical Law Review* 1.

[73] ibid p 7.

[74] Regulation (EU) 2016/679 of the European Parliament and of the Council of 27 April 2016 on the protection of natural persons with regard to the processing of personal data and on the free movement of such data, and repealing Directive 95/46/EC (General Data Protection Regulation).

[75] Data Protection Act 2018, Ch 3.

Can such medical device information systems be seen as analogous to research databases or to audit processes, or indeed both? In the past, in relation to storage and use of information in genetic databases, questions arose as to the scope of consent.[76] One approach is to initially see as necessary the respect of individual rights concerning control of their personal information for storage and use. The question then arises as to whether, if it is intended to use that information for other perhaps related purposes, further consent should be required. Should information be collected for audit purposes then it can be assumed that individuals will not need to give specific or indeed generic consent at the outset, rather that such use may simply be deemed to be legitimate subject to eg requisite safeguards such as anonymisation etc.[77] Is however the use of anonymisation itself a means of legitimising use of patient information in medical device registries without the need for patient consent? The Court of Appeal in the case of *R v Department of Health ex p Source Informatics Limited* took the approach that where patient information was anonymised this would not be seen as a breach of confidence.[78] Nonetheless, this approach has been questioned. It can be argued that anonymisation itself does not address the question of an individual right to privacy to control the use of their personal information.[79] Moreover, anonymisation is different from information which is totally delinked – some information links will inevitably be needed to ensure the validity of the information. Nonetheless, as we shall see below, statutory provisions which have currently been used in relation to the Medical Devices Outcomes Registry are in place to authorise the use of information and requiring information which is disclosed initially to be anonymous.

A pertinent analysis is provided by Schofield and Brednoord et al examining the issue of consent in relation to medical device registries through the particular perspective of breast implant registries. Writing in 2013 Scofield, discussing the then National Breast Implant register, commented that one option was to ask for consent initially but then also have further consent at that time to ask consent for other use, such as for the future use of the data in research studies.[80] She suggested that there needed to be consideration of how ethical principles such as respect for individual autonomy through the process of consent can be considered alongside broader principles of public health ethics. These can be particularly sensitive questions bearing in mind the information concerned – as here in the context of breast implants. Alternatively Schofield suggests that

[76] See further eg discussion in M Otlowski, 'Developing an Appropriate Consent Model for Biobanks: In Defence of 'Broad' Consent' in J Kaye and M Stranger, *Principles and Practice in Biobank Governance* (Routledge, 2009).

[77] See General Medical Council, *Confidentiality: Good Practice in Handling Information* (2017) and the discussion regarding disclosure of patient information for audit purposes from para 98.

[78] See *R v Department of Health ex p Source Informatics Limited.* [2000] 1 All ER 786 CA.

[79] See D Beyleveld and E Histed, 'Betrayal of Confidence in the Court of Appeal' (2000) *Medical Law International* 227; see also Dove and Taylor (n 66) at paras 12:55–12:64.

[80] B Schofield, 'The Role of Consent and Individual Autonomy in the PIP Breast Implant Scandal' (2013) 6(2) *Public Health Ethics* 220.

> an opt-out strategy to consent could be considered in the case of the breast implant registry. This strategy would assume that all required surveillance data can be collected on all women undergoing breast implant surgery unless they opt-out after having been informed of the option to do so. An opt-out strategy would still preserve individual autonomy.[81]

The perceived advantage of not requiring specific consent is that this may be likely to facilitate greater uptake. As Bredenoord et al also note commenting on the situation of a breast implant register may reduce the prospect of selection bias which can result where consent is refused and improve data outcomes.[82] They also comment that this can be seen as a moral duty derived from principles such as beneficence, reciprocity and solidarity. Overall however, they do not see an opt out for medical device registries in general as justifiable.[83] While they recognise that information could be given to patients in general about the existence of registries, they note that in practice for the registry to be most effective patients would need to be followed up and there would also need to be links to the medical records of those patients. This they argue is a privacy issue and thus use of such information would in fact need patient consent. Second, as they comment, some individuals may be particularly sensitive regarding this form of personal information being included in a register in this form. Third, they note that if something problematic is identified there needs to be the prospect of re-contacting the individual. However, they go on to suggest that

> a thick opt-out procedure for medical device registries might be suitable in cases where inclusion does not involve burdens (or low), when it does not involve a sensitive subject and when the data are stored anonymously (or at least not directly linked to the medical record). An opt-out is suitable when public health benefits are large and potential intrusion on privacy low. Otherwise, inclusion should be sought by means of an opt-in.[84]

The question is then, whether inclusion of information in a registry or database without consent may be seen as a disproportionate infringement of individual privacy.

Following the Healthcare Quality Improvement Partnership Report and the Independent Review Report, the approach which has been taken in the establishment of an NHS medical devices information system in the form of the Medical Devices Outcomes Registry has been to collate such information in such a registry without the need for patient consent. The Health and Social Care Act 2012 enables information, including confidential health information, to be disclosed for certain NHS purposes.

[81] ibid p 222.

[82] AL Bredenoord, NAA Giesbertz and JJM van Delden, 'Consent for Medical Device Registries, Commentary on Schofield, B. (2013) The Role of Consent and Individual Autonomy in the PIP Breast Implant Scandal' (2013) 6(2) *Public Health Ethics* 226 at 227.

[83] ibid p 228.

[84] ibid p 228. The authors use the term 'thick opt out' for opt out procedures they see as justifiable in the light of autonomy and public trust because of fulfilling criteria of raising people's awareness of research, provision of adequate information to those individuals along with situations where there is a genuine possibility that individuals can object.

Section 254 of the Act enables the Secretary of State to direct that NHS England 'establish and operate a system for the collection or analysis of information of a description specified in the direction'.[85] This is where it is 'necessary or expedient' in relation to the duties of the Secretary of State in relation to healthcare or adult social care. A Direction has now been produced in relation to the operation of the Medical Devices Outcomes Registry.[86] This confirms that the existing ability of patients to opt out of collection of their personal data under the existing 'National Data Opt Out' system will not apply in the context of information submitted to the Registry.[87] In relation to the transparency of the data collected there is a legal requirement to publish the information collected. This will take the form of publications twice a year.[88] It is stated that this will be 'anonymous, aggregate and small number suppressed, so that individuals (patients or clinicians) cannot be identified'.[89] Information from the Registry can also be disseminated back to those organisations who provided patient information if, for example, they have requested this.[90] Thus for example information will be able to be disseminated by NHS England to hospitals, for the purposes of the direct care of patients. This will be subject to NHS England having a lawful basis to disclose and the organisation having a lawful basis to process that information. Data collection is to take place on a 24 hour a day basis and across all days in the year.[91] It will involve collation of information both from NHS hospitals and from independent providers. In contrast to the initial collation of information for the Registry where there is then subsequent dissemination of the data by NHS England, that information will be subject to the National Data Opt-Out Policy.[92] However there is not a requirement for specific individual patient consent before being disclosed. There remains the question as to whether patients who object to the storage and use of their information in medical device registries could subsequently bring an action complaining in relation to the use of the information. An action in relation to breach of confidence appears unlikely to be successful as there is express legal authority for disclosure of the information derived from statute, and it is also uncertain as to whether a successful action could be brought under the Tort of misuse of private information.[93] One issue here it is suggested will be as to the extent to which disclosure of information may be justified under the exceptions to the right to privacy which themselves include the broader public interest including the health of others.

[85] Health and Social Care Act 2012, s 254(1).

[86] As required under the Health and Social Care Act 2012, s 259(1)(a). See further NHS England, 'Data Provision Notice: Outcomes and Registries Programme: Medical Devices Outcomes Registry' V. 3.0 28 March 2025. This replaces DAPB3103 Surgical Devices and Implants Core Data Set.

[87] NHS Digital *National Data opt-out operational policy guidance document*. Version 4 (2020).

[88] ibid and in relation to the duty placed on NHS England to publish all data collected, see the Health and Social Care Act 2012, s 260.

[89] ibid.

[90] ibid and for the statutory basis of this action see the Health and Social Care Act 2012, s 261(1)(d).

[91] ibid.

[92] ibid.

[93] See eg *Prismall v Google UK Ltd & Anor* [2024] EWCA Civ 1516.

A further practical and also ethical issue which has arisen is that of combining a large number of different datasets from disparate registries etc into one National Registry Platform, including the devices register. Its creation was met with concerns from the Haemophilia Society and the Anthony Nolan Charity regarding what they saw as lack of both engagement and of transparency in this exercise. They were strongly of the view that the National Haemophilia Registry should operate outside the NHS.[94] These particular concerns can be seen in the context of the backdrop of the Infected Blood Inquiry and the question of trust of individuals and families impacted by the infected blood scandal.[95] The chair of the Infected Blood Inquiry Brian Langstaff had called for the UK Government to stop plans to include the National Haemophilia Database in the National Outcomes Register.[96] Further concerns have related to the data security where multiple data sources are held in a single register.[97] Section 258(1) of the Health and Social Care Act 2012 makes provision for consultation of representatives of persons whose information is collected under a direction. Moreover, patient groups and also the Federation of Clinical Registries (who are a group of clinicians involved in the management of clinical registries) expressed objections in relation to the failure of consultation with regards to the Outcomes Register.[98] At the end of 2024 the National Medical Director for Secondary Patient Care and Quality, Stella Vig, stated that NHS England was

> working with stakeholders to develop a new strategy for clinical audits and registries, which will direct future work on clinical audit, quality improvement and patient safety to bring further benefits to patients.[99]

This was to develop a National Clinical Audit and Registries Strategy which would go to consultation in 2025. The question now is as to how this will develop and whether the future developments will ensure the trust of patients and stakeholders.

V. Concluding Thoughts

The establishment of medical device information systems can provide very important clinical information regarding the efficacy of medical devices and also potentially the success rates and consequent safety of those practitioners undertaking those

[94] Lovell (n 65).
[95] See www.infectedbloodinquiry.org.uk/.
[96] ibid.
[97] See further A Scroxton, 'NHS experts raise warning over patient data breach risk in registries project' (*Computer Weekly.com*, 25 June 2024) and A Scroxton, 'Fresh concerns over NHS England registries procurement' (*ComputerWeekly.com*, 11 November 2024).
[98] T Lovell, 'NHSE to consult on clinical registry data plans following opposition' (*Digital Health*, 9 December 2024) www.digitalhealth.net/2024/12/nhse-to-consult-on-clinical-registry-data-plans-following-opposition/.
[99] ibid.

implants. However as we have seen such major information storage inevitably gives rise to questions of patient consent and the privacy and confidentiality of their own personal information. Many of these issues raised concerning consent and storage of information in a medical device registry involve concepts and theoretical discussions which are not new such as autonomy, privacy and solidarity, which has arisen for example in relation to such things as biobanks.[100] The tensions between the legitimacy of use and storage without patients' knowledge and consent where this is seen for 'administrative' or 'audit' purposes and as being different from the storage of other information again resonate across other areas. What is critical is that medical devices databases and registries should not be simply seen as a means of tracking safety of devices and identifying clinicians who may be putting patients at risks. Those devices are implanted in people. The people receiving these implants have interests in those databases. This is both in terms of the use of their own information included in that database but also because this implant is in their body and they themselves have a stake in knowing the safety of products implanted into them. They are not merely a subject – or even a standard participant – they are an active player in this process.

Medical devices information systems will work best and most effectively if they are accompanied by trust. Trust and the implanting of medical devices have in the past not been easy bedfellows, as discussed above. It is essential that the future operation of medical device information systems is rooted in respect for the individual patient implanted with this device and with transparency regarding that device and the use of that patient's information. Positive steps are already being made to open up patient access to their own information regarding the medical devices with which they are implanted with the indications that the UK Government will implement the unique device identifier and the implant card. A centralised NHS medical devices information system can be seen to have a notable advantage of centralising protections facilitating standards and in turn supporting patient safety.[101] In this regard, the gradual movement of registries to the NHS Medical Devices Outcomes Registry is to be welcomed.

The question of patients being able to choose whether they are happy with information being collated in a huge registry system of this form however needs to be the subject of more detailed engagement. The reaction of certain patient groups in relation to the inclusion of their information in the NHS Outcomes Registry Platform in the future, as noted above, shows that it is important that trust is maintained in the system. While the decision in late 2024 to now undertake consultation of patient groups and stakeholders regarding its operation is to be welcomed, it is a matter of great concern that it appears that extensive planning and

[100] See eg B Prainsack and A Buyx 'A solidarity based approach to the governance of research biobanks', (2013) 21(1) *Medical Law Review* 71.

[101] See eg discussion of the problems of divergent standards from a US perspective in E Parasidis and DB Kramer, 'Compulsory Medical Device Registries Legal and Regulatory Issues' in IG Cohen, T Minssen, WN Price II, C Robertson and C Shachar, *The Future of Medical Device Regulation* (Cambridge University Press, 2022) 17.3.

implementation of the Registry went ahead without certain groups being involved from the outset. An effective medical device information system is likely to have a radical and positive impact on patient health in the long term. Its creation should be seen as an opportunity for ongoing reflection as to the use and control of patient information and its relationship with patient safety and public health.

5

Parents, Children and Open-source Artificial Pancreas: Morality in the Era of Healthcare Financialisation

GILES BIRCHLEY*

I. Introduction

Type 1 diabetes usually manifests in childhood: an estimated 1.5 million young people globally,[1] and 35,000 children in the UK[2] have type 1 diabetes. The body requires a hormone, insulin, to manage the transfer of sugar from the blood to the cells to stay alive. Type 1 Diabetes Mellitus occurs due to damage to the insulin producing cells in the pancreas, and requires lifelong insulin therapy to regulate blood sugar levels, avoid coma and eventual death.[3] Artificial pancreas – a system that automatically monitors blood glucose and titrates an insulin infusion to keep blood glucose in a healthy range – was first innovated by people with diabetes and parents of children with diabetes. Commercial devices appeared some years later. Commercial artificial pancreas has been adopted by some universal healthcare systems, notably New Zealand[4] and the United Kingdom (UK). In the latter the National Health Service (NHS) responded to a recommendation from the National Institute for Health and Care Excellence (NICE) that commercial versions of the technology be made available to all young people living with diabetes. The NHS

* Acknowledgements: This work was in part supported by the UKRI Trustworthy Autonomous Systems (TAS) Hub Node in Functionality [Grant Number EP/V026518/1].

[1] GA Gregory, TIG Robinson, SE Linklater, F Wang, S Colagiuri, C de Beaufort, KC Donaghue and International Diabetes Federation Diabetes Atlas Type 1 Diabetes in Adults Special Interest Group, 'Global incidence, prevalence, and mortality of type 1 diabetes in 2021 with projection to 2040: a modelling study' 2022 10(10) *Lancet Diabetes Endocrinol* 741.

[2] Diabetes UK, 'High Quality Care for Children and Young People with Type 1 Diabetes' 2016, see www.diabetes.org.uk/about-us/about-the-charity/our-strategy/position-statements/high-quality-care-for-children-and-young-people-with-type-1-diabetes-in-the-uk.

[3] American Diabetes Association, 'Standards of Care in Diabetes – 2023 Abridged for Primary Care Providers' 2023 41(1) *Clin Diabetes* 4.

[4] Kids Health/Hauora Taitamariki 'Diabetes Technology' 2024, see www.kidshealth.org.nz/diabetes/diabetes-technology.

began a five-year rolling out of commercial closed loop systems to patients in April 2024. Parents now face a choice of waiting for commercial devices through the NHS, or adopting open-source systems. Open-source adopters need to follow a technical process, following instructions that are freely available online, to combine equipment that can be obtained in most countries for a few hundred US dollars, and in the UK, freely on the NHS.

While the advent of commercial devices means that open-source artificial pancreas is not the only option available, the wide distribution of open-source software, and the apparent parity between the safety and efficacy profile of commercial and open-source systems, means that its continued use raises questions about what skills and characteristics are needed to use it safely. Despite these questions, the idea that commercial devices are inherently safer or more dependable has died hard in the face of successive failures of device regulation.[5] In part such an assumption rested on the belief that user safety is part of an unwritten contract between commercial medical device manufacturers and their users. Yet, notwithstanding universal healthcare funding of artificial pancreas in some countries – which allows access to only a small minority of people globally – the commercial model, by excluding all those who cannot afford it, in many ways inherently shows a disregard for general health and wellbeing.

Technological advances have been accompanied by innovations in business practice. While healthcare businesses once ostensibly balanced the production of social goods with the production of profit, the influence of neoliberal economics meant increasing focus upon the interests of shareholders of these businesses, to the exclusion of the interests of patients, in what was first described in the pharmaceutical industry by William Lazonick as a process of 'financialisation'.[6] The model is now widespread within the wider healthcare industry,[7] and there are signs that healthcare investors see (and have long seen) artificial pancreas as an area ripe to grow profits.[8] Even the limited provision of commercial devices in universal healthcare systems, while hugely impactful to those patients who benefit, should further be seen in the context of state health spending being viewed in increasingly extractive terms by the commercial sector, whose behaviour is characterised by

[5] S Macleod, 'The independent medicines and medical devices safety review: regulatory reform and remedies' 2023 5(2) *Law, Technology and Humans* 5.

[6] O Tulum, A Andreoni and W Lazonick, 'From Financialisation to Innovation in UK Big Pharma: AstraZeneca and GlaxoSmithKline' (Cambridge University Press, 2022); W Lazonick, 'The Financialization of the U.S. Corporation: What Has Been Lost, and How It Can Be Regained' 2013 36(2) *Seattle U L Rev* 857.

[7] B Hunter and SF Murray, 'Deconstructing the financialization of healthcare' 2019 50(5) *Development and Change* 1263–87.

[8] Anon, 'North America and Europe Artificial Pancreas Systems Market Is Anticipated to Grow Significantly to Reach US$ 250 Million By 2026 – Comprehensive Research Report By FMI' (*Biospace*, 12 May 2022), see www.biospace.com/north-america-and-europe-artificial-pancreas-systems-market-is-anticipated-to-grow-significantly-to-reach-us-250-million-by-2026-comprehensive-research-report-by-fmi.

unrestrained exploitation of financial contracts[9] and prices[10] paid by state funded bodies.

In such conditions the emergence of alternative, non-profit driven technologies arising from open-source software more generally means that parents and professionals will recurrently have to make decisions about the trustworthiness of new open-source technologies vis their commercial alternatives, while society will have to judge the fitness of parents and professionals to make these judgments when they affect children.[11] While artificial pancreas has attracted varied commentary, little attention has been paid to the adoption of artificial pancreas by parents. This chapter therefore returns to the topic of open-source artificial pancreas, reviewing briefly the legal background to parental decisions to use do-it-yourself technologies, and the moral and ethical questions the choice between open-source and commercial technology raises. I argue that the issues raised by the use of open-source artificial pancreas go far beyond simple black and white questions of what sort of character parents should have, and what parents of that character should be allowed to do, instead raising epistemic issues about the nature and politics of knowledge, choice and expertise, in an era when rampant financialisation that has seen the commodification of a huge range of public goods. My analysis thus looks to the wider economic and social spheres that place parents in the position where doing the best for their child may require significant personal knowledge and resources and what is right may not be clear. I begin this analysis by considering the background to how and why artificial pancreas emerged, surveying open-source as a technological platform in itself, before considering artificial pancreas technology in particular, including the commercial and grassroots development of artificial pancreas.

II. Background: Diabetes, Distress and Artificial Pancreas

Since the commercial production of insulin began in the 1920s,[12] management of Type 1 diabetes has been through multiple daily finger prick tests to measure blood sugar, followed by injectable doses of insulin based on the measurement. This regime is demanding to manage. Numerous factors affect blood sugar levels

[9] B Clover, N Kituno and J Serle, 'Suing trust for £56m is "last resort", says Lloyds Bank' (*Health Service Journal*, 18 April 2023); I Kotecha and M Hellowell, 'Dealing With The Legacy Of PFI – Options For Policymakers' (London: Centre for Health and Public Interest, 2018) www.chpi.org.uk/reports/dealing-with-the-legacy-of-pfi-options-for-policymakers.

[10] B Kenber, 'A bitter pill to swallow: How price-hiking drug companies exploit the National Health Service' 2018 86(3) *Medico-Legal Journal* 123.

[11] See eg A Nada, J Chan, A Meehan, B Collett, S Benki-Nugent, RA Bly, S Gollakota, J Bonilla-Velez and ER Gallagher, 'An Open-Source Smartphone Otoacoustic Emissions Test for Infants' 2025 155(3) *Pediatrics* e2024068068.

[12] CC Quianzon and I Cheikh, 'History of insulin' 2012 2(2) *J Community Hosp Intern Med Perspect.* 18701.

and attempting to control these is intellectually and temporally demanding for diabetics and/or their carers, taking around two hours, in aliquots of minutes at a time, every day[13] to maintain recommended blood sugar levels. The intensity of these demands mean that fewer than one in five diabetics are able to meet these recommended blood glucose levels.[14] This leads to constant fluctuations in blood sugar, which is associated with a range of physical[15] and mental[16] pathologies. Whenever blood sugar levels are poorly controlled by insulin therapy, diabetics experience mood swings, poor quality of life and ultimately, a reduced lifespan. Type 1 Diabetes usually manifests in childhood. Effective management is challenging and burdensome for both children and parents. A United States (US) study suggested 'Diabetes distress' is a complex mix of emotions and behaviours associated with the challenges of living with diabetes. It is common in children and, significantly, parents of children, with diabetes.[17] This reflects the immense difficulties in managing routines and family dynamics in the face of a disease that affects all aspects of family life.[18]

Recent developments in technology have made the possibility of improved blood sugar control a reality. First developed as a large and unwieldy collection of machines in 1963[19] the so-called 'artificial pancreas' was a combination of devices that monitors blood sugar in real-time, and a feedback loop that used this information to vary the rate of a continuous infusion of insulin[20] to maintain blood glucose in narrow limits.[21] A modern artificial pancreas is a fusion of four technologies: a blood glucose measurement system using non-venous sampling; fast acting analogues of glucose regulating hormones, primarily insulin; a hormone delivery system, and; an algorithm that can accurately predict fluctuations in blood glucose during both to the slow changes in insulin levels while patients are at rest and the rapid changes that occur after food

[13] DM Lewis, 'Do-It-Yourself Artificial Pancreas System and the OpenAPS Movement' 2020 49(1) *Endocrinol Metab Clin North Am.* 203.

[14] ER Hankosky, D Schapiro, KB Gunn, EB Lubelczyk, J Mitroi and DR Nelson, 'Gaps Remain for Achieving HbA1c Targets for People with Type 1 or Type 2 Diabetes Using Insulin: Results from NHANES 2009–2020' 2023 14(6) *Diabetes Ther* 967.

[15] NH White, 'Long-term Outcomes in Youths with Diabetes Mellitus' 2015 62(4) *Pediatr Clin North Am* 889.

[16] E van Duinkerken, FJ Snoek and M de Wit, 'The cognitive and psychological effects of living with type 1 diabetes: a narrative review' 2020 37(4) *Diabet Med* 555.

[17] SR Patton, N Kahhan, JS Pierce, M Benson, LA Fox and MA Clements, 'Parental diabetes distress is a stronger predictor of child HbA1c than diabetes device use in school-age children with type 1 diabetes' 2023 11 *BMJ Open Diabetes Research & Care* e003607.

[18] S Simpson, P Hanna and CJ Jones, 'A systematic review of parents' experiences of raising a child with type 1 diabetes' 2021 21(1) *British Journal of Diabetes* 43.

[19] C Cobelli, E Renard and B Kovatchev, 'Artificial pancreas: past, present, future' 2011 60(11) *Diabetes* 2672; BW Bequette, 'Challenges and Recent Progress in the Development of a Closed-loop Artificial Pancreas' (2012) 36(2) *Annu Rev Control* 255.

[20] Systems utilising Glucagon in addition to Insulin have been proposed but still face safety questions and technical barriers. See MK Åm, IA Teigen, M Riaz, AL Fougner, SC Christiansen and SM Carlsen, 'The artificial pancreas: two alternative approaches to achieve a fully closed-loop system with optimal glucose control' (2024) 47 *J Endocrinol Invest* 513.

[21] Cobelli et al (n 19).

is eaten[22] to maintain blood sugars in healthy limits. The potential of combining these technologies was long recognised, and development was accelerated at key points by charitable and government funding.[23] Yet commercial development was slow to follow, and 50 years after the first working protype, diabetes type 1 patients were increasingly frustrated with waiting for long-promised commercially available devices. Yet by this time the technological environment was ripe for the open-source development of the technology by these patients.

III. Open Source Technologies: A Vital Part of Artificial Pancreas Development

Open-source software and other technologies are those published under licences that allow free use and sharing of that technology. Open-source software is written by enthusiasts in semi-cooperative projects using decentralised version control systems, such as GitHub, that allow many users to simultaneously work on code. Open-source software is often modular in nature, where portions of code address specific and distinct issues. These modular sections of code are often combined in an 'open-source stack' of interoperative, publicly available tools that together allow complex tasks to be undertaken. Because open-source software is free, it is widely used and, given the extra costs that would be entailed by writing new software from the ground up, open-source is fundamental to keeping most commercial development competitive (one study estimated its value to the global economy at $8.8 trillion USD).[24] Open-source software is therefore critical infrastructure, playing a vital part in modern technologies – from phones[25] to artificial intelligence.[26] Some open-source licences, such as GNU General Public License (GPL),[27] require commercial users to make any code they use that incorporates open-source freely available (although there are instances where proprietary projects have been found to be abusing these licence terms).[28] However the majority of open-source projects use licences, such as the Massachusetts Institute of Technology license (MIT),[29] that allow commercial

[22] D Dermawan and K Purbayanto, 'An overview of advancements in closed-loop artificial pancreas system' (2022) 8(11) *Heliyon* e11648.

[23] Cobelli et al (n 19).

[24] M Hoffmann, F Nagle and Y Zhou, 'The Value of Open Source Software' (2024) *Harvard Business School Working Paper* 24–038, see www.hbs.edu/faculty/Pages/download.aspx?name=24-038.pdf.

[25] N Gandhewar and R Sheikh, 'Google Android: An emerging software platform for mobile devices' (2010) 1(1) *International Journal on Computer Science and Engineering* 12.

[26] Billigence, 'H2O.ai', see billigence.com/h20-ai/.

[27] Free Software Foundation, 'GNU General Public License' *(Free Software Foundation*, 2007) see www.gnu.org/licenses/gpl-3.0.en.html.

[28] See eg A Robertson, 'Trump's social network has 30 days to stop breaking the rules of its software license' (*The Verge*, 22 October 2021) www.theverge.com/2021/10/22/22740354/trump-truth-social-network-spac-mastodon-license-software-freedom-conservancy.

[29] B Balter, 'Open source license usage on GitHub.com' (*Github blog*, updated 20 December 2021) github.blog/open-source/open-source-license-usage-on-github-com/.

users to use open-source within their software while keeping their code closed, meaning it does not have to be publicly readable and accessible.[30] Open-source algorithms, licensed under MIT, for use within artificial pancreas were first developed in 2013.[31]

As the 2010's began, grassroots activists, frustrated with slow commercial development of artificial pancreas found one another through the novel technologies of social media.[32] The first DIY artificial pancreas adapted commercial devices using open-source software. Parents, aware nocturnal hypoglycaemic episodes were a common event thought to account for 6 per cent of deaths of those with diabetes type 1,[33] developed 'Nightscout'[34] to allow remote monitoring of their child's glucose levels overnight. This open-source software allowed patients and parents to read data from continuous glucose monitoring devices and upload it to the cloud so it could be read remotely by a smartphone. Others developed an open-source algorithm, 'OpenAPS',[35] that could use this continuous glucose monitoring information to predict future blood glucose levels and prompt users to adjust the baseline rate of insulin delivery accordingly.[36] This created a so-called 'open-loop' artificial pancreas. An open-source 'closed-loop' – where the insulin rate could be automatically titrated by the algorithm – followed after further software development reverse engineered commercial insulin pumps to circumvent safety features that prevented third party use.[37] In 2015 open-source artificial pancreas was made public, after overcoming initial blocks from regulators who prohibited free distribution of the OpenAPS code on the grounds that it was a Class III medical device.[38] Professionals often responded with concern when their patients arrived at clinic using a technology they could not confirm was safe.[39] Open-source artificial pancreas users responded to this challenge both by being gatekeepers to the steps that new users must pass through to competently use the technology, and by initiating increasingly sophisticated research.[40]

[30] M Forcada, 'Open Source Machine Translation Technology' in Sin-Wai (ed), *Routledge Encyclopedia of Translation Technology* (Taylor & Francis, 2023) 160.

[31] C Davis, 'The routinization of lay expertise: A diachronic account of the invention and stabilization of an open-source artificial pancreas' 2024 54(4) *Social Studies of Science* 626.

[32] See n 13 above.

[33] Juvenile Diabetes Research Foundation Continuous Glucose Monitoring Study Group, 'Prolonged nocturnal hypoglycemia is common during 12 months of continuous glucose monitoring in children and adults with type 1 diabetes' 2010 33(5) *Diabetes Care* 1004.

[34] The Nightscout Project, 'Nightscout #WeAreNotWaiting' (2025) www.nightscout.info/.

[35] D Lewis and #OpenAPS community, 'OPENAPS.ORG' (2024) openaps.org/.

[36] J Kesavadev, S Srinivasan, B Saboo, M Krishna and G Krishnan, 'The Do-It-Yourself Artificial Pancreas: A Comprehensive Review' (2020) 11 *Diabetes Ther* 1217.

[37] See n 13 above.

[38] See n 31 above.

[39] W Palmer, SAW Greeley, LR Letourneau-Freiberg and RN Naylor, 'Using a do-it-yourself artificial pancreas: Perspectives from patients and diabetes providers' (2020) 14(5) *Journal of Diabetes Science and Technology* 860.

[40] D Lewis, S Leibrand and #OpenAPS Community, 'Real-world use of open source artificial pancreas systems' (2016) 10(6) *Journal of Diabetes Science and Technology* 1411; J Zabinsky, H Howell,

As gatekeepers, the OpenAPS community warn that 'this is not a 'set and forget' system'.[41] The community attempts to educate and train its users in order to guard against both professional concerns about user competence,[42] and regulatory concerns about the distribution code that is classed as a 'medical device'. The algorithm is available as modules, but users must engage with the open-access community to learn the skills to put their modules together and put them to use in a working system.[43] Throughout, users are required to engage with the community and offer help to those less experienced than themselves. Meanwhile, as community initiated research has demonstrated the safety and efficacy of the technology, eventually culminating in the first randomised controlled trial.[44] Studies on complex biological simulations suggest open-source artificial pancreas is safe and effective,[45] although real-world studies have taken opposing views about the safety of open-source artificial pancreas.[46] Whether open-source systems are ultimately judged more or less safe depends on the answers more rigorous real-world trials will produce.[47] There is nevertheless some clinical consensus that such open-source systems are both highly responsive to user needs, have full user-centric feature sets, and can thus be acceptable when the best interests of the patient outweigh their inevitable risks.[48]

In 2017, the Medtronic 670G became the first commercial system to be available to people with type 1 diabetes. Yet, open-source retained an appeal.

A Ghezavati, DM Lewis, A Nguyen and JC Wong, 'Do-it-yourself artificial pancreas systems for type 1 diabetes reduce hyperglycemia without increasing hypoglycemia' 2020 69(S1) *Diabetes* 988-P.

[41] #OpenAPS community, 'Welcome to OpenAPS's documentation!' (2017) 30b2443b openaps.readthedocs.io/en/latest/index.html.

[42] EG Wilmot and T Danne, 'DIY artificial pancreas systems: the clinician perspective' 2020 8(3) *The Lancet Diabetes & Endocrinology* 183.

[43] See n 31 above.

[44] M Burnside, D Lewis, H Crocket, R Wilson, J Williman, C Jefferies, R Paul, BJ Wheeler and M de Bock, 'CREATE (Community deRivEd AutomaTEd insulin delivery) trial. Randomised parallel arm open label clinical trial comparing automated insulin delivery using a mobile controller (AnyDANA-loop) with an open-source algorithm with sensor augmented pump therapy in type 1 diabetes' (2020) 19(2) *Journal of Diabetes and Metabolic Disorders* 1615.

[45] C Toffanin, M Kozak, Z Sumnik, C Cobelli and L Petruzelkova, 'In Silico Trials of an Open-Source Android-Based Artificial Pancreas: A New Paradigm to Test Safety and Efficacy of Do-It-Yourself Systems' (2020) 22 *Diabetes Technol Ther* 112.

[46] See n 44 above; J Künzler, T Züger, C Stettler, MW Laimer and A Melmer, 'Comparing the technical reliability and insulin dosing of a "do-it-yourself artificial pancreas" with a commercial hybrid closed-loop system in a "shadow-mode" scenario: An exploratory study' (2023) *Diabetes Obes Metab* 1; K Braune, S Hussain, R Lal, S Leibrand, DM Lewis and S O'Donnell, 'Breaking a feedback loop: A reassessment of an investigator initiated OS-AID study' (2024) 26(1) *Diabetes, Obesity and Metabolism* 400.

[47] M Lei, B Lin, P Ling, Z Liu, D Yang, H Deng, X Yang, J Lv, W Xu and J Yan, 'Efficacy and safety of Android artificial pancreas system use at home among adults with type 1 diabetes mellitus in China: protocol of a 26-week, free-living, randomised, open-label, two-arm, two-phase, crossover trial' (2023) 13 *BMJ Open* e073263.

[48] K Braune, RA Lal, L Petruželková, G Scheiner, P Winterdijk, S Schmidt, L Raimond, KK Hood, MC Riddell, TC Skinner, K Raile and S Hussain, 'Open-source automated insulin delivery: international consensus statement and practical guidance for health-care professionals' (2022) 10(1) *The Lancet Diabetes & Endocrinology* 58.

The longstanding problems with the lack of responsiveness to user requests for features remained amongst many commercial manufacturers,[49] and commercial systems remain less advanced and feature rich than open-source systems.[50] Despite concerns about adverse events with both commercial[51] and open-source systems,[52] It seems increasingly likely that, given the unavoidable risks of insulin management of type 1 diabetes, the risk profile of open-source and commercial systems are similar.[53] However, few would suggest that open-source systems are for everyone, and commentators urge that potential users are informed of the high technical bar they face in using these systems. Hammond argues 'We need to be able to support those who are able to use OpenAPS systems effectively, while cautioning those who may not be suited to such systems, for whom alternative interventions may be more beneficial.'[54] This notwithstanding, self-management of type 1 diabetes inherently requires engagement with complex technologies and a good awareness of blood sugar management, and many users of open-source consider it an incremental step from earlier self-management technologies like finger prick tests.[55]

IV. Parents, Artificial Pancreas Technology, and the Law

In the development of open-source artificial pancreas, parents played a leading role, with the so-called 'D-Dads', a group of fathers of diabetic patients, developing key innovations.[56] 20 per cent to 30 per cent of users of open-source artificial pancreas are parents and young people.[57] Within the UK, the government's roll-out of the commercial systems aims to give access to all children under 18 years as a priority group.

Unlike commercial systems, open-source systems have not been approved by a regulator, indeed US and French regulators have both issued statements warning

[49] RA Lal, M Basina, DM Maahs, K Hood, B Buckingham and DM Wilson, 'One year clinical experience of the first commercial hybrid closed-loop system' (2019) 42(12) *Diabetes Care* 2190.

[50] See n 48 above.

[51] AM Ferguson and AC Lin, 'Themes, Rates, and Risk of Adverse Events of the Artificial Pancreas in the United States Using MAUDE' (2024) 52 *Ann Biomed Eng* 2282; JS Krouwer, 'An Analysis of 2019 FDA Adverse Events for Two Insulin Pumps and Two Continuous Glucose Monitors' (2022) 16(1) *J Diabetes Sci Technol* 228.

[52] M Cafrey, 'FDA Issues Warning on Do-It-Yourself Artificial Pancreas' (*American Journal of Managed Care*, 19 May 2019) www.ajmc.com/view/fda-issues-warning-on-do-it-yourself-artificial-pancreas.

[53] See n 42 above.

[54] P Hammond, 'Open source artificial pancreas systems: to use or not to use' (*Primary Care Diabetes Society*, 7 January 2019) www.pcdsociety.org/resources/details/open-source-artificial-pancreas-systems-use-not-use.

[55] See n 31 above.

[56] J Kesavadev, B Saboo, MB Krishna and G Krishnan, 'Evolution of Insulin Delivery Devices: From Syringes, Pens, and Pumps to DIY Artificial Pancreas' (2020) 11 *Diabetes Ther* 1251.

[57] See n 48 above; D Lewis and the #OpenAPS community, 'Frequently Asked Questions' (*Openaps.org*, 2024) openaps.org/frequently-asked-questions/.

of safety implications,[58] the former following an adverse event.[59] This creates a quandary for clinicians who, as we have already discussed, may feel uncertain about the safety of devices when they encounter patients in clinic.[60] English law contains mixed messages about whether patients who show an interest in artificial pancreas should be informed about open-source options. The *Montgomery*[61] judgment ruled that patients needed to be informed of any treatments, alternatives, and attendant risks, that a reasonable – and that particular – patient would attach significance to when making a decision. The subsequent judgment in *McCullough*[62] however, ruled that what counted as a reasonable alternative treatment was ultimately a matter of medical expertise, and therefore determined by the standard set in the venerable case of *Bolam*,[63] in other words, what a reasonable body of medical opinion would agree was a reasonable alternative. Roberts argues that the current guidance from the UK's medical regulator, the General Medical Council (GMC), does not prevent the discussion of unapproved medical devices with patients.[64] Although the question has never been tested in court, current law suggests it remains a matter of professional judgement whether open-source artificial pancreas is discussed among the alternative options for parents and children.

In the case of any decision to both share information, recommend a device or adopt a particular technology, clinicians and parents face further issues.[65] Medical treatment must be the result of a partnership between clinicians and parents because '*choice of treatment is in some measure a joint decision*'.[66] While this partnership implies that clinicians are open about the options available, decisions about children must make the child's welfare or best interests (standards the courts treat as synonymous)[67] as the paramount consideration.[68] Guidance on the best interests/welfare of the child can be gained through reference to the welfare checklist,[69] but best interests is an open-textured standard that is deliberately under-specified to allow its application to a wide range of situations. This results in a culturally sensitive, but unpredictable test, which is particularly pertinent where the decision concerns a technology to which clinicians are only gradually becoming accustomed and for which parental interest and enthusiasm will vary wildly. Parents' enthusiasm should by law be tempered by their responsibilities

[58] JTF Roberts, V Moore and M Quigley, 'Prescribing unapproved medical devices? The case of DIY artificial pancreas systems' (2021) 21(1) *Medical Law International* 42.

[59] See n 52 above.

[60] See n 39 above.

[61] *Montgomery v Lanarkshire Health Board* [2015] UKSC 11.

[62] *McCulloch v Forth Valley Health Board* [2023] UKSC 26.

[63] *Bolam v Friern Hospital Management Committee* [1957] 1 WLR 582.

[64] See n 58 above.

[65] A fuller discussion of legal liability can be found in R Dickson, J Bell, A Dar, L Downey, V Moore and M Quigley, '#WeAreNotWaiting DIY artificial pancreas systems and challenges for the law' (2022) 39(5) *Diabet Med* e14715.

[66] *Re J* [1991] Fam 33 at 42 per Donaldson MR.

[67] *In Re B (A Minor) (Wardship: Sterilisation)* [1988] AC 199 at 206.

[68] Children Act 1989, s 1(1): 'the child's welfare shall be the court's paramount consideration'.

[69] Children Act 1989, s 1(3).

towards their child, so that they cannot adopt a particular technology purely out of their own enthusiasm for, for example, open-source software.[70] There are some grounds to consider open-source technologically superior, given that it is more responsive to user needs and has a wider range of features.[71] Although neither commercial nor open-source appear to be inherently safer, open-source has higher time, knowledge and commitment costs in successfully using the technology than commercial systems. Thus, whether the use of an open-source system by any given parent is in the best interests of any given child will inevitably require a judgement of the character of that parent. Should the parent and the clinician disagree, then the matter would need to be tested in court; once again, such a legal case has yet to appear before the courts.

All types of parent-led care for a child with type 1 diabetes are time-consuming and difficult. Whether it is appropriate for parents to use complex technologies without direct supervision is not in itself a novel question.[72] Norms of what a parent is expected to manage have inevitably followed what it is considered normal for adult patients to self-manage, despite the differences between self-management and parental management. History suggests what constitutes appropriate technology for home use is fluid and evolving. For example, portable blood glucose testing was developed in 1965,[73] when the notion of self-care faced resistance from professionals.[74] Such resistance now seems anachronistic – especially because trials eventually showed that patient self-monitoring led to better management.[75] In the case of open-source artificial pancreas, we are some way from such categorical agreement. Yet, whether, given that simpler commercial devices have been approved for roll-out to young people in the UK, it continues to be reasonable for parents to use the more intellectually demanding open-source alternative remains a fluid question.

V. Commercial or Open-source Artificial Pancreas in a Welfare State: Why not Wait?

The UK Government's aspiration to supply commercial artificial pancreas systems for all young people is certainly laudable, however it is likely some parents will adopt open-source artificial pancreas. The five-year roll out period for the

[70] *Gillick v West Norfolk and Wisbech Area Health Authority* [1986] AC 112, 170.

[71] See n 48 above.

[72] KC Glass and FA Carnevale, 'Decisional challenges for children requiring assisted ventilation at home' (2006) 18(3) *HEC Forum* 207.

[73] SF Clarke and JR Foster, 'A history of blood glucose meters and their role in self-monitoring of diabetes mellitus' (2012) 69(2) *British journal of biomedical science* 83.

[74] LS Levin and EL Idler, 'Self-care in health' (1983) 41(1) *Annual review of public health* 181.

[75] SA Mazzuca, F Vinicor, SJ Cohen, JA Norton, NS Fineberg, SE Fineberg, WC Duckworth, TW Kuebler, EE Gordon and CM Clark Jr, 'The diabetes education study' (1988) 3 *J Gen Intern Med* 1.

technology means that not all people with diabetes who want to use commercial systems are able to do so when they want to do so. While children are a priority group, even a short wait can amount to a very long time in the life of a child with a demanding disease to manage. Moreover, although the current NHS plan intends to make artificial pancreas available to all children with type 1 diabetes, with no mention of restrictions, at a local level at least some individual NHS Trusts are attaching stricter conditions to this access. For example an internal document from one NHS Trust seen by the author indicates strict criteria that young people and parents should fulfil before being considered, including being assessed as motivated to self-manage to a safe and acceptable level.[76] Limiting eligibility for publicly funded commercial artificial pancreas to families whose children have well-managed diabetes, who are adept at insulin management and are fully engaged with professional management of their diabetes, excludes those whose children have difficulties controlling their diabetes, despite this group of people being most at risk of deleterious outcomes.[77] Moreover there are a range of subtypes of diabetes, the classification of which is still in its infancy, and goes far beyond the longstanding differentiation into type 1 and type 2 diabetes.[78] Different subtypes are of varying difficulty to manage. In such a context, demonstrating good motivation when conventional efforts to manage diabetes are not effective is not a simple diagnostic task but a complex, and value replete, assessment of the presentation and characteristics of the family by a professional. Given the susceptibility of such assessments to prejudices and (un)conscious biases, it is likely that some parents of children with hard-to-manage diabetes will fail to qualify for commercial systems where they are available, even if they are well-motivated.

A further issue is that, while there are a number of commercial options, the current device landscape presents problems for parents. All current options have limitations on the age of the child who can be treated, that are made more restrictive by the limited technology ecosystems with which they are compatible. For example, the commercial CamAPS FX algorithm can be used with children from 12 months old, the youngest child the equipment with which it can be combined is currently licensed for is four years old. The Medtronic MiniMed 670G is licensed for two year-olds, but can only be combined with the Guardian 4 sensor, which is licensed for children aged seven and over. While these problems will undoubtedly be solved over the coming years, they highlight the dangers of closed technology ecosystems that prevent interoperability with a wide range of devices. While there are some moves toward making commercial devices intraoperable,[79] opponents of

[76] Details of the source have been omitted because many NHS Trusts are likely to be doing the same, and it could bring this particular NHS Trust into disrepute if it is singled out here.

[77] A Quintal, V Messier, R Rabasa-Lhoret and E Racine, 'A critical review and analysis of ethical issues associated with the artificial pancreas' (2019) 45(1) *Diabetes & metabolism* 1.

[78] AJ Deutsch, E Ahlqvist and MS Udler, 'Phenotypic and genetic classification of diabetes' (2022) 65(11) *Diabetologia* 1758.

[79] E Renard, 'Certified Interoperability Allows a More Secure Move to the Artificial Pancreas Through a New Concept: Make-It-Yourself' (2020) 14(2) *J Diabetes Sci Technol* 195.

intraoperability argue that retaining closed technology ecosystems helps to make devices more secure from cyberattack.[80] We will consider in due course the wider context of such claims. In the meantime, we must note that restricting interoperability also clearly serves the interests of the businesses that market commercial artificial pancreas. It does so because it restricts a user's choices to a small number of compatible devices, reducing any downward cost pressures from competition. While those NHS patients qualifying for artificial pancreas may be unaffected by this restriction, those patients who source commercial artificial pancreas privately sorely need price reductions because costs are high. For example, based on quotes from private providers that include three months of consumables,[81] after the cost of private outpatient clinics – between £1,200–£1,700 (GBP) – the cheapest package is the Omnipod,[82] with startup costs of £1,125, plus £1,908 annual costs for a continuous glucose monitor. The newer Medtronic 780G[83] has an initial cost of £6,536.50. These startup prices are much greater than the costs of open-source artificial pancreas, equipment for which is usually easily available on the NHS,[84] or for a few hundred US dollars in other countries.[85]

VI. Morality, Markets and Artificial Pancreas

Few commentators on open-source artificial pancreas focus on children,[86] yet by identifying gaps in the wider discourse we can nevertheless find issues which are pertinent to our focus on the justifiability of choosing open-source artificial pancreas. There are clearly many issues that can be discussed in relation to the technology – bioethical analysis[87] – which does not explore open-source – highlights the need to protect patient privacy, to respond to patient reported outcomes, to ensure patient education, to be aware of the stigmatising effects of wearable technology, and to ensure equitability of access to the technologies. Any choice of themes is somewhat arbitrary, yet the ultimate analysis of goods within any issue is the result of a complex tension between individual actions and a wider context. Indeed, the wider context, being outside individual control, can in many ways feel akin to immutable facts of nature. This tension exposes distinctions between the

[80] E Lee, Y-D Seo, S-R Oh and Y-G Kim, 'A Survey on Standards for Interoperability and Security in the Internet of Things' (2021) 23(2) *IEEE Communications Surveys & Tutorials* 1020.

[81] The London Diabetes Centre, private correspondence, 21 March 2024.

[82] Dexcom Inc, 'Meet Dexcom G6 and Omnipod 5' (*Dexcom*, 2024) www.dexcom.com/en-GB/integrations-and-connectivity/insulin-pumps/omnipod-5-new.

[83] Medtronic, 'MiniMed 780G System' (*Medtronic*, 2025) www.medtronic-diabetes.com/en-gb/minimed-780g-system-info.

[84] TS Crabtree, A McLay and EG Wilmot, 'DIY artificial pancreas systems: here to stay?' (2019) 36 *Pract Diab* 63.

[85] See n 57 above.

[86] An exception is: Dickson et al (n 65).

[87] See n 77 above.

often-conjoined concepts of ethics and morality. Ethics – derived from the Greek *ethos* (ἦθος) is translated as 'nature' or 'character', and the Latin *mores*, is translated as 'custom'. Generally speaking, it is far easier to impugn the ethics of an individual character or choice, rather than recognise the much greater difficulties that arise from that individual's moral place within an established culture or context. Since the question of whether to choose open-source or commercial artificial pancreas is one that arises from the grander moral challenges that form the background to technological innovation, this analysis places more emphasis on the *moral* than the *ethical*. My discussion thus first turns to a consideration of the lack of equitability of diabetic healthcare worldwide and how this narrows the scope of claims that open source artificial pancreas technology improves equitability, before moving on to discussions of the downsides of technological progress, cybersecurity, and only in the last turn to the *ethical* question of individual autonomy in parental choices to adopt artificial pancreas technology.

VII. Equitability

The equitability of artificial pancreas is a frequent concern of many commentators.[88] Braune et al[89] suggest that open-source is ethically superior to commercial systems because it provides more equitable access to the information that users need to develop their own systems, thus empowering users outside a relatively small population in affluent countries. However, the claim of improved equitability, while it may be true in the limited sense that the information on how to create open-source artificial pancreas is theoretically accessible to the 70 per cent or so of the world's population who can access the internet,[90] must be placed in a structural context that may makes contributions of artificial pancreas to inequity less meaningful.

It is undeniable that inequality, and I assert without argument, inequity, dominate the wider context of diabetic healthcare. Diagnosis of type 1 diabetes in young people is rising globally, and morbidity and mortality are high in this age group.[91] Countries with low income per capita, low educational attainment and high birthrates have high levels of diabetic mortality,[92] almost certainly because of low levels of diagnosis and the inaccessibility of treatment.[93] Less than half of health facilities

[88] ibid; see n 48 above.

[89] See n 48 above.

[90] World Bank Group, 'Individuals using the Internet (% of population) 1960–2023' (*World Bank*, 2025) data.worldbank.org/indicator/IT.NET.USER.ZS.

[91] K Zhang, C Kan, F Han, J Zhang, C Ding, Z Guo, N Huang, Y Zhang, H Ningning and X Sun, 'Global, Regional, and National Epidemiology of Diabetes in Children From 1990 to 2019' (2023) 177(8) *JAMA Pediatr* 837.

[92] B Gong, W Yang, Y Xing, Y Lai and Z Shan, 'Global, regional, and national burden of type 1 diabetes in adolescents and young adults' (2024) *Pediatr Res* doi.org/10.1038/s41390-024-03107-5.

[93] World Health Organisation and Integrated African Health Observatory (2023) 'Diabetes, A Silent killer in Africa', www.scribd.com/document/720935621/iAHO-Diabetes-Regional-Factsheet; AJ Adler,

in Low and Middle Income Countries (LMIC) have stocks of insulin[94] and costs of insulin are higher on average in these countries than in higher income countries,[95] meaning only 63 per cent of LMIC households can afford them.[96] These statistics make clear the vast disparities in global health resourcing that prevent many people with diabetes, including children, from accessing treatment. Moreover, such disparities place in proper context the potential for open-source artificial pancreas to widen accessibility to the technology. The insulin analogues used in artificial pancreas can cost six times as much as regular insulin in LMIC, prices far in excess of the estimated costs of production at profit.[97] This reflects a recent history[98] of inflated insulin prices (especially in the USA). While domestic insulin prices in the US have reduced thanks to governmental action,[99] without radical reductions of price of insulin analogues in LMIC[100] there is little sense that open-source artificial pancreas has any relevance for most children with diabetes globally. Certainly, there is little scope for open-source artificial pancreas to reduce inequities without affordable insulin analogues.

Even narrowing the scope to countries, like the UK, with universal healthcare provision, socioeconomic inequalities mean people with diabetes have a far higher incidence of morbidity and mortality.[101] In these instances, existing inequalities may be compounded by open-source artificial pancreas. There are ample concerns that the skills and motivation required of those using open-access means that open-access technologies exclusionary.[102] The very real differences between individual skills and talents, responsibilities and opportunities raises concerns of a

C Trujillo, L Schwartz, L Drown, J Pierre, C Noble, T Allison, R Cook, C Randolph and G Bukhman, 'Experience of living with type 1 diabetes in a low-income country: a qualitative study from Liberia' (2021) 11 *BMJ Open* e049738.

[94] R Atun, JI Davies, EAM Gale et al, 'Diabetes in sub-Saharan Africa: from clinical care to health policy' (2017) 5 *Lancet Diabetes Endocrinol* 622.

[95] D Beran, IB Hirsch and JS Yudkin, 'Why are we failing to address the issue of access to insulin? a national and global perspective' (2018) 41 *Diabetes Care* 1125; M Ewen, D Beran and H-J Joosse, 'Insulin prices profile' (Amsterdam: Health Action International, 2016) haiweb.org/wp-content/uploads/2016/04/ACCISS-Prices-report_FINAL-1.pdf.

[96] CK Chow, C Ramasundarahettige, W Hu, et al, 'Availability and affordability of essential medicines for diabetes across high-income, middle-income, and low-income countries: a prospective epidemiological study' (2018) 6 *Lancet Diabetes Endocrinol* 798.

[97] M Ewen, J Huibert-Jan, D Beran and R Laing, 'Insulin prices, availability and affordability in 13 low-income and middle-income countries' (2019) 4 *BMJ Global Health* e001410.

[98] AG Aaron, IG Cohen and EY Adashi, 'Lawsuits Over the Price of Insulin – State Efforts for Insulin Access' (2024) 184(1) *JAMA Intern Med* 9.

[99] J Burns and L Seegert, 'Clearing up confusion on drug price rules and revisions' (*Association of Healthcare Journalists*, 13 January 2025) healthjournalism.org/blog/2025/01/clearing-up-confusion-on-drug-price-rules-and-revisions/.

[100] Medecins Sans frontières, 'Eli Lilly, Novo Nordisk, and Sanofi must make insulin pens available at $1 each' (*MSF News and Stories*, 12 November 2024) www.doctorswithoutborders.org/latest/eli-lilly-novo-nordisk-and-sanofi-must-make-insulin-pens-available-1-each.

[101] A Scott, D Chambers, E Goyder and A O'Cathain, 'Socioeconomic inequalities in mortality, morbidity and diabetes management for adults with type 1 diabetes: A systematic review' (2017) 12 *PloS One* e0177210.

[102] C Farrington, 'Hacking diabetes: DIY artificial pancreas systems' (2017) 5(5) *The Lancet, Diabetes & Endocrinology* 332.

'digital divide'[103] between people with diabetes. Such a scenario suggests the more technically adept, digitally connected, and time-rich patients and parents will join the open-source community, leaving those who are less skilled to (at best) languish on waiting lists waiting for commercial systems that may be less responsive to their needs.[104] Some have concluded that inherent 'structural inequalities are weaved in this [open-source artificial pancreas] movement'.[105]

VIII. Progress Traps and Vulnerability to Withdrawal

Ultimately, where accessibility was not at issue, the experiences of parents, children and young people with both commercial and open-source artificial pancreas are generally good. Parents reported decreases in the burden of managing their child's diabetes and positive impacts on their feelings of freedom and flexibility.[106] Nevertheless, while young people in one study mentioned they frequently 'almost forgot about diabetes',[107] artificial pancreas does not eliminate all problems of diabetes management. Users must regularly interact with the technology to change consumables, change the site of invasive monitoring and to give the algorithm information about carbohydrate intake.[108] The burden of constant problematising of food intake can result in significant mental ill-health, especially a higher prevalence of eating disorders in people with diabetes.[109] Moreover, to the extent reduction of cognitive burdens addresses the impacts of constant problematisation, Quintal et al[110] note this creates something akin to what Wright called a 'progress trap',[111] where the benefits of a technology make it more or less unthinkable to relinquish. Artificial pancreas provides the benefits of simplifying the

[103] See n 42 above.
[104] See n 48 above.
[105] B Jansky and H Langstrup, 'Device Activism and Material Participation in Healthcare: Retracing Forms of Engagement in the #WeAreNot- Waiting Movement for Open-source Closed-loop Systems in Type 1 Diabetes Self-care' (2022) 18 *BioSocieties* 498.
[106] K Braune, S O'Donnell, B Cleal, D Lewis, A Tappe, I Willaing, B Hauck and K Raile, 'Real-World Use of Do-It-Yourself Artificial Pancreas Systems in Children and Adolescents With Type 1 Diabetes: Online Survey and Analysis of Self-Reported Clinical Outcomes' (2019) 7(7) *JMIR Mhealth Uhealth* e14087; KK Hood, WH Polonsky, SA MacLeish, CJ Levy, GP Forlenza, AB Criego, BA Buckingham, BW Bode, DW Hansen, JL Sherr, SA Brown, DJ DeSalvo, SN Mehta, LM Laffel, A Bhargava, LM Huyett, TE Vienneau and TT Ly, 'Psychosocial Outcomes with the Omnipod® 5 Automated Insulin Delivery System in Children and Adolescents with Type 1 Diabetes and Their Caregivers' (2023) *Pediatric Diabetes* 1.
[107] KR Howard, KP Garza, M Feldman and J Weissberg-Benchell, 'Parent, child, and adolescent lived experience using the insulin-only iLet Bionic Pancreas' (2024) 49(6) *Journal of Pediatric Psychology* 413, at 415.
[108] Although there are advanced algorithm settings that can adjust for more limited information, for users who wish to experiment with unannounced meals see: #OpenAPS community, 'Autotune' (*OpenAPS*, 2017) openaps.readthedocs.io/en/latest/docs/Customize-Iterate/autotune.html.
[109] AP Winston, 'Eating Disorders and Diabetes' (2020) 20 *Curr Diab Rep* 32.
[110] See n 77 above.
[111] R Wright, *A Short History of Progress* (Canongate Books, 2009) 6.

management of type 1 diabetes relative to less technological systems. But this means that any withdrawal of access to artificial pancreas will have dramatic hardships on the child and their family, making it extremely arduous to give up these advantages, whatever drawbacks might emerge with the technology in the interim. This perspective suggests differing risks for commercial and open-source devices based on the way such devices are vulnerable to being withdrawn. Depending on the country, access to commercial devices relies on stable healthcare system spending priorities, insurance coverage or personal wealth. While open-source artificial pancreas systems are more resilient to these risks, the risks are internalised to the family in open-source systems, so that access to artificial pancreas relies on members of the family having the appropriate skills and time. Changes to the family makeup, for example, the estrangement, death or incapacity of a parent, may have bring significant additional hardships and anxiety to the child because they may be accompanied by a gradual inability to maintain the open-source system.

IX. Cybersecurity

Maintenance is a major issue within both mature open-source and commercial software technologies. The increasing integration of new technologies to the internet-of-things creates security problems for the users of medical devices, many of which are far from secure.[112] In a recent case, a monitor widely employed in hospitals was found to contain security backdoors which allow the third party exfiltration of data and execution of code.[113] Such problems may be widespread: one study identified 661 distinct software vulnerabilities in a wide range of medical devices.[114] Early open-source advocates championed the idea that the eyes of a multitude of volunteer open-source developers were a more rapid and efficient way of finding errors and vulnerabilities in software than smaller commercial development teams.[115] However open-source's reliance on volunteer coders can be spectacularly exploited. In one – widely reported – example, an anonymous maintainer added malicious code to an open-source JavaScript module, a vulnerability that was not spotted by others in the community for two weeks.[116] For

[112] AS Wilner, H Luce, E Ouellet, O Williams and N Costa, 'From public health to cyber hygiene: Cybersecurity and Canada's healthcare sector' (2021) 76(4) *International Journal* 522.

[113] M Kan, 'Chinese-Made Patient Monitor Contains a Secret Backdoor' (*PC Mag*, 31 January 2025) uk.pcmag.com/security/156508/chinese-made-patient-monitor-contains-a-secret-backdoor.

[114] L Bracciale, P Loreti and G Bianchi, 'Cybersecurity vulnerability analysis of medical devices purchased by national health services' (2023) 13 *Scientific Reports* 19509.

[115] ES Raymond, *The Cathedral & the Bazaar: Musings on Linux and Open Source by an Accidental Revolutionary* (O'Reilly Media, 2001).

[116] M Heller, 'Compromised NPM package highlights open source trouble' (*Techtarget*, 28 November 2018) www.techtarget.com/searchsecurity/news/252453398/Compromised-NPM-package-highlights-open-source-trouble. For similar examples see C Sharma, 'Tragedy of the digital commons' (2023) 101(4) *North Carolina Law Review* 1129.

critics this is an example of a 'tragedy of the commons',[117] where the free nature of open-source software leads to individuals and companies consuming open-source products without contributing to their maintenance as a common resource, leading to a long-term decline in quality. Certainly, many vital areas of open-source infrastructure are reliant on one or two hard-pressed individuals. Eghbal quotes one maintainer describing the pressure of supporting others who use their code as 'annihilating'.[118] Ultimately this can manifest in under-maintained code that is vulnerable to the sorts of malicious behaviour seen above. This is clearly a concern for the long-term viability of open-source artificial pancreas – what happens when the volunteer coders cease to give the time and effort to support others and maintain the software? Yet commercial software is also vulnerable to its own tragedies. These occur where maintenance of commercial software is de-prioritised in a drive for increased profitability.[119] Examples abound,[120] but a spectacular case is the 2022 ransomware incident that arose from vulnerabilities in code maintained by 'Advanced', a major commercial software provider to the NHS and other healthcare providers. Like many successful companies, Advanced had been repeatedly bought and sold by private equity funds for some years prior to the incident. Equity funds seek to raise the efficiency of investments over a few years, rapidly increasing profitability before selling the company on and harvesting dividends to their investors. In Advanced's case this behaviour came at the cost of egregious neglect of software maintenance. Advanced's most affected software, 'Staffplan', had not been updated for 11 years,[121] suggesting that basic cybersecurity was of little importance to short term investors. As one expert noted, months of delays in restoring function and security to their software after the incident took place suggested Advanced's owners '... have under-invested in it, under-documented it, and probably been frustrated by the age of the application ...'[122]

Despite these issues, the language of 'security vulnerability' disguises more positive effects. Vulnerabilities give opportunities to reverse engineer devices for positive reasons. It was a vulnerability that allowed open-source artificial pancreas[123] to communicate with insulin pumps, at a fraction of the cost of, and some two years before the advent of, commercial artificial pancreas. In some countries, including the UK and Europe, device manufacturers sell newer pumps

[117] ibid Sharma.
[118] N Eghbal, 'Working in Public: The Making and Maintenance of Open Source Software' (*Stripe Matter Incorporated*, 2020) 15.
[119] H Krasner, 'CISQ Consortium for Information & Software Quality TM: The cost of poor software quality in the US: A 2020 report' (*CISQ*, 2021) www.it-cisq.org/cisq-files/pdf/CPSQ-2020-report.pdf.
[120] J Wolff, *You'll See this Message when it is Too Late: The Legal and Economic Aftermath of Cybersecurity Breaches* (MIT Press, 2018).
[121] E Targett, 'Care home software won't be fully restored until 2023 despite backups' (*The Stack*, 16 September 2022) www.thestack.technology/staffplan-rebuild-advanced-ransomware/.
[122] Anon, 'Advanced confirms attack was LockBit 3.0 ransomware, legitimate creds used' (*The Stack*, 13 October 2022) www.thestack.technology/advanced-data-breach-credentials-ransomware-post-incident-summar/.
[123] See n 13 above.

with a special Bluetooth protocol[124] implemented, allowing the open-source AndroidAPS to communicate with the pumps. However, in others, including in the US, vulnerabilities in newer insulin pumps have been closed without enabling legitimate protocols to allow open-source compatibility. Open-source users in the US have no option but to use older second-hand pumps that are out of warranty. The difference between the responses is apparently explained, at least in the case of the US, by the regulatory environment. The US Food and Drug Administration have incentivised device intraoperability since around 2018. However, manufacturers have been allowed to loosely interpret the incentives to apply to 'in-house intraoperability' rather than to intraoperability with the wider ecosystem of available, third party devices.[125] Thus the lack of intraoperability, at least in the US, appears to be motivated by commercial opportunism and enabled by current regulation. It seems clear then that any individual benefits derived from artificial pancreas are frustrated by systemic factors at work here, and indeed, these factors may pose risks for the long-term viability of artificial pancreas. Given the work of contextual factors in the availability, existential salience and security of artificial pancreas, the space for determinative choices by individual parents appears to be very narrow. We shall consider the opportunities and challenges for autonomous choices now.

X. Autonomy, Choice and Epistemology

Open-source artificial pancreas technology is often seen as a paradigm case of patient-empowerment,[126] including by patient-activists themselves.[127] Commentators recall that people with diabetes have a long history of innovation in the face of hostile professionals,[128] or fear that patients who are not active innovators in their own care will become 'dumb patients',[129] reliant on the precarious bone fides of experts for their wellbeing. In such circumstances a decision to join the open-access community may be rewarded with widespread approval and support by that community.

[124] Bluetooth SIG, 'Speciofications: Insulin Delivery Service 1.0.1' (*Bluetooth SIG*, 2025) www.bluetooth.com/specifications/specs/insulin-delivery-service-1-0-1/.

[125] H Look, 'The inside scoop on 'Third Party Control' for ACE Pumps' (*Tidepool*, 1 February 2023) www.tidepool.org/blog/the-inside-scoop-on-third-party-control-for-ace-pumps.

[126] See n 56 above; AR Hatch, JT Gordon and SR Sternlieb, 'The Artificial Pancreas in Cyborg Bodies' in N Boero and K Mason (eds), *The Oxford Handbook of the Sociology of Body and Embodiment* (Oxford University Press, 2019).

[127] S Riggare, 'E-patients hold key to the future of healthcare' (2020) 54 *British Journal of Sports Medicine* 1065; T Omer, 'Empowered citizen 'health hackers' who are not waiting' (2016) 14 *BMC Med* 118.

[128] See n 13 above.

[129] NJ Fox, 'Personal health technologies, micropolitics and resistance: A new materialist analysis' (2017) 21(2) *Health* 136.

While young people with diabetes and their parents overwhelmingly experience artificial pancreas positively,[130] it would be a mistake, despite the types of narratives identified above, to endorse a broad and unreflective view of empowerment as 'self-sufficiency'. Yet, to the extent that generalisations can be made, it has been argued that the values of information-technologists combine revolutionary disruption, hyper-capitalism and 'a profound faith in the emancipatory potential of the new information technologies'.[131] This 'Californian ideology'[132] is said to have widely permeated western societies.[133] One of the fallouts from such a widespread viewpoint is that we can become blind to the differences between people and the wider contextual and cultural factors that might interfere with their technological emancipation. Scenarios where the ideal patient rationally pursues a libertarian vision of self-care have increasingly been viewed as flawed within the bioethical and legal discourse.[134] Autonomy within these disciplines is more widely seen as contingent on supportive relationships and contexts. The contextual factors we have explored above sharply reframe the 'choice' between open-source and commercial artificial pancreas that is offered to people with diabetes and their parents. Parents wanting artificial pancreas for their child face radical restrictions of inequity which limit any choice to a small subset of parents who can access and effectively make use of the technology. Those who would choose commercial artificial pancreas face further restrictions to this consumer choice due to the lack of widespread interoperability between devices. For the same reason parents who favour open-source artificial pancreas are often dependent on others within the open-source community being able to find and exploit vulnerabilities in commercial devices. Potentially these parents are incentivised by the widespread approval of adoption among the open-source community. Ultimately all parents make choices that are coloured by the social matrix and the coercive effects of managing type 1 diabetes, which make any solution that reduces the burden of management an offer that is welcomed with open arms.

The fact that the choice between open-source and commercial artificial pancreas is ultimately enabled by the free availability of open-source information, which the user must internalise and use, has been the source of much attention by the open-source community, who incorporate new users in a stepwise fashion, requiring them to develop the knowledge to build the open-source artificial pancreas themselves. Such steps are commendable, yet the very nature of informedness is fraught with uncertainty about the very notion of 'sufficient information' when dealing with any complex technical project. Manufacturers of commercial artificial

[130] See n 107 above.

[131] R Barbrook and A Cameron, 'The Californian ideology' (1996) 6(1) *Science as Culture* 44, at 45.

[132] ibid.

[133] JC York, *Silicon Values: The Future of Free Speech Under Surveillance Capitalism* (Verso, 2021).

[134] J Nedelsky, 'Reconceiving autonomy: Sources, thoughts and possibilities' (1989) 1 *Yale JL & Feminism* 7; S Conly, 'Against autonomy: justifying coercive paternalism' (2014) 40(5) *Journal of Medical Ethics* 340; N Stoljar, 'Informed consent and relational conceptions of autonomy' (2011) 36(4) *Journal of Medicine and Philosophy* 375.

pancreas systems actively protect their technologies from scrutiny by the public, and this limits the degree users can be informed. At the other end of the spectrum, open-source, while ostensibly readable by anyone, limits how much each user can become knowledgeable because of the complex and technical nature of the code, which will be fully understandable by few. In his discussion of the way the internet has expanding accessible knowledge, Lynch argues that near instant access to vast amounts of information creates a paradox where 'our digital form of life seems to both expand and inhibit our knowledge, simultaneously.'[135] Drawing a distinction between 'knowledge' and 'understanding', Lynch observes that knowing is an embodied experience that cannot be broken down into stages and steps to be followed, because 'it involves a type of discernment or acuity that can't be discursively codified.'[136] Thus, despite the foundational 'Californian ideology' belief that increasing the accessibility of information can emancipate anyone who is willing to learn, what we can actually *know* is ultimately restricted by *who* we are. In such a situation the knowledge needed to access open-source artificial pancreas limits choice because people's differing talents and experiences but also their stresses and their opportunities. Whether we are able to be 'knowers' will ultimately be a test of character that cannot in every case be readily discerned beforehand, even by the would-be knower themselves.

XI. Parents as Users of Open-source Artificial Pancreas for Children

While open-source artificial pancreas offers more features, more control, and a degree of protection from the depredations of an increasingly financialised healthcare infrastructure,[137] it will not be appropriate in all cases. Some parents may be experienced coders and engineers and have full confidence in their own abilities. Yet most parents must learn in the hope that they can develop sufficient skills and enough understanding to implement the technology successfully. The wider context throws into question the idea that many parents will be making a 'choice' between open-source and commercial artificial pancreas. Delays in access to – or limited or non-availability of – commercial systems in many countries will mean many parents face the unbearable situation of either continuing with a high

[135] MP Lynch, *The Internet of Us: Knowing More and Understanding Less in the Age of Big Data* (Liveright, 2016) 179.

[136] ibid 169.

[137] M Zechner, L Näre, O Karsio, A Olakivi, L Sointu, H Hoppania and T Vaittinen, 'Profit making and ailment: the marketisation and financialisation of care' in *The Politics of Ailment* (Policy Press, 2023) 43; S Friel, A Schram, N Frank, M Arthur, B Townsend and H Gajurel, 'Financialisation: a 21st century commercial determinant of health equity' (2024) 9(9) *The Lancet Public Health* e705; BM Hunter and SF Murray, 'Deconstructing the financialization of healthcare' (2019) 50(5) *Development and Change* 1263.

burden of disease, suboptimal blood glucose control and the potential for overnight fatality, or trying to gain knowledge of an open-source system that may be beyond their abilities. The OpenAPS community recognise this and have carefully curated information and support to increase the chances that new users can develop the knowledge they need. Yet these users must face the risks on their own. Ultimately, no matter how supportive the community, the burden is devolved onto the individual. In such a situation, the best interests of the child can only be known contingently, contextually and ultimately, partially. A thorough examination suggests it is not parental recklessness or bad faith that is the ethical problem but instead flaws in the moral context in which these decisions happen, a context that we have collectively constructed where the goods of human cooperation are not equitably shared or maintained.

Ultimately the moral solution to these problems begins with tighter regulation of commercial suppliers, and incentivisation of open-source developers to ensure maintenance of the open-source infrastructure. The advantages of open source could be cemented with policy that legislated for interoperability, and that offered support for user-centred open-source design and coding, and maintenance of existing code. Such funding could be channelled through new strands of existing research funding schemes, which would aim to bring financial security to open-source coders and maintainers where projects were recognised as key infrastructure. While the UK's interventions to make artificial pancreas available to children and families is welcome, doing so by investing in the commercial model seems irrational. Suppliers were, afterall, insufficiently motivated by profit for 50 years to bring artificial pancreas to market. Only when grassroots, open-source innovation developed and distributed the technology did commercial manufacturers move in to extract value. Rewarding these manufacturers is ultimately a short-term fix that props up an increasingly inequitable system. As such it seems less like the largesse of a functioning social contract, than a welfare state repurposed on shoring up extractive commercial healthcare. A less myopic approach would reform the relationship between grassroots developers and universal healthcare, releasing long-term funding for grassroots development and maintenance. Such an approach could develop ways to close the skills gap so that more – perhaps all – parents could benefit, for example through the governmental sponsorship of non-profit entities in the third sector who could partner with parents to aid their use of the technology. Such a vision is radical, but would allow open-source technologies to be the foundation of truly empowering universal healthcare.

XII. Conclusion

We have seen that the answers to questions about the justifiability of parental use of open-source artificial pancreas are mired in questions of context. Undoubtedly open-source artificial pancreas is more affordable, although health inequities will prevent its benefits being more widespread for the vast majority of people with diabetes, for whom even basic treatment is scarce. For those who are able to access the technologies required, the community has worked hard to make open-source artificial pancreas inclusive and as full-featured as possible. Many of the initial concerns with the technology are dissipating and – although conclusive trials have yet to conclude – there is clearly a strong case that children would benefit from this technology. The advent of commercial systems makes more pointed the balance between risks and benefits for children of parents who opt for open-source systems.

Implementing and using open-source artificial pancreas involves mastery of certain skills, and whether parents are able to do so will depend on a range of factors, many of which may only become obvious after the success or failure of their attempt. The supportive community is vulnerable to the deactivation of the minority of users who have resources to help and support others, and open-source systems in some jurisdictions face challenges from commercial interests who have blocked interoperability. At the same time the relentless financialisation of healthcare throws into question the long-term trustworthiness and reliability of commercial systems, which may be vulnerable to price hikes and neglect. It is time to reign in these interests, and both regulate for interoperability while partnering with grass-roots open-source maintainers, developers and non-profits to allow the benefits of open-source to be made secure and shared more widely.

Although universal healthcare in some countries may make these concerns less immediate, the scope and longevity of the social contract on which universal healthcare depends appears uncertain. Such a context makes ever more acute the division between bioethical discussion that focuses on the moral and that which focuses on the ethical. Indeed, a focus on the decisions of individual autonomous parents taking responsibility for their child's health and wellbeing using open-source artificial pancreas suggests this apparently paradigm case of patient empowerment is largely prompted by exogenous factors. Ultimately it is context that has the most dramatic effects on the permissibility of parental use of open-source artificial-pancreas with their diabetic children. Given the individualistic perspective of the law and ethics focuses attention on individual actions, the coercive role of contextual factors means we must urgently reframe the terms of the discussion to account for this.

6

Neuroethics, Governance, and the Brain

NATHAN HIGGINS, STEPHANIE K SLACK, JOHN GARDNER AND ADRIAN CARTER

I. Introduction

Globally, the burden of disease posed by neurological and psychiatric disorders is significant. Recent estimates suggest 'disorders of the nervous system' affect 3.4 billion people globally (43.1 per cent of the population), surpassing cardiovascular diseases and musculoskeletal disorders as the top contributor to global disability-adjusted life year (DALY) counts.[1] Neurotechnologies hold great promise as novel tools for diagnosing, treating and preventing disorders of the nervous system.[2] Parallel developments in artificial intelligence (AI) have equipped neurotechnologies with enhanced capabilities to monitor or modulate neural activity in powerful new ways.[3]

Neurotechnology innovation has attracted considerable investment from governments and the private sector. National-level brain initiatives in the US, EU, Japan, Korea, Canada and China have invested well over $6 billion USD in neuroscience research since 2013.[4] In the private sector, medical neurotechnologies now lead the market in venture capital investment. Capital investments in medical neurotechnology climbed to $1.3 billion in 2023, with three in five of the largest investments going toward large, multi-site pivotal trials. There is also an expanding market of direct-to-consumer (DTC) neurotechnology products. Wearable monitoring devices such as smartwatches and headsets, non-implantable neurostimulation devices, and mental health apps for cognitive training and behavioural management allow users to monitor and influence cognition or behaviour without

[1] JD Steinmetz et al, 'Global, Regional, and National Burden of Disorders Affecting the Nervous System, 1990–2021: A Systematic Analysis for the Global Burden of Disease Study 2021' (2024) 23 *The Lancet Neurology* 344.

[2] DS Hain et al, *Unveiling the Neurotechnology Landscape: Scientific Advancements, Innovations and Major Trends* (UNESCO Publishing, 2023).

[3] D Valeriani, F Santoro and M Ienca, 'The Present and Future of Neural Interfaces' (2022) 16 *Frontiers in Neurorobotics*.

[4] Hain et al (n 2).

the need for a physician or clinical researcher.[5] The market for DTC neurotechnologies is projected to swell to $24.2 billion by 2027.[6]

A. Ethics and Governance of Neurotechnology Innovation

Neurotechnological innovation has long promised to revolutionise our understanding and treatment of disorders of the nervous system.[7] However, there is also concern about ethical, legal, social and cultural issues that might arise as these novel interventions are further studied. For example, the promise of mental health apps is that they will reduce costs for providers and expand access to healthcare services; but some have worried that inequalities in access to healthcare may be exacerbated if these apps do not meet the needs of diverse communities.[8] Others have drawn attention to new ethical tensions raised by post-trial access; if ongoing access to implantable devices is not provided, depriving participants of the health gains achieved during the trial may lead to profound disruptions to their agency and autonomy.[9] Finally, there is general concern about potential infringements to mental privacy or freedom of thought raised by the collection and storage of 'neural data'.[10]

These concerns have sparked discussions about the appropriate governance of neurotechnologies. Human rights organisations, expert consortiums, and advocacy groups have begun to develop guidance for the responsible research and innovation of neurotechnologies.[11] UNESCO is currently developing the first global soft governance instrument for neurotechnologies, and several instruments have already been published.[12] Some soft governance tools prescribe decision-making practices or codes of conduct for professionals within a particular specialty (eg, clinical investigators working with implantable devices). Other instruments have instead outlined

[5] M Ienca, P Haselager and EJ Emanuel, 'Brain Leaks and Consumer Neurotechnology' (2018) 36 *Nature Biotechnology* 805.

[6] Hain and others (n 2).

[7] R Bhidayasiri, 'The Grand Challenge at the Frontiers of Neurotechnology and Its Emerging Clinical Applications' (2024) 15 *Frontiers in Neurology*; C Cinel, D Valeriani and R Poli, 'Neurotechnologies for Human Cognitive Augmentation: Current State of the Art and Future Prospects' (2019) 13 *Frontiers in Human Neuroscience* 13.

[8] R Yao et al, 'Inequities in Health Care Services Caused by the Adoption of Digital Health Technologies: Scoping Review' (2022) 24 *Journal of Medical Internet Research* e34144.

[9] F Gilbert, 'Self-Estrangement & Deep Brain Stimulation: Ethical Issues Related to Forced Explantation' (2015) 8 *Neuroethics* 107.

[10] Hain et al (n 2).

[11] M Pham et al, 'Developing Ethical Guidelines for Implantable Neurotechnology: The Importance of Incorporating Stakeholder Input' in NV Thakor (ed), *Handbook of Neuroengineering* (Springer Nature Singapore, 2023).

[12] We define 'soft' law governance to refer to guidelines, principles, or codes of conduct designed to influence actions and decision-making without being legally enforceable, and 'hard' law governance to refer to legally-binding, formalised governmental rulemaking procedures that follow standardised processes. See also R Hagemann, J Huddleston and AD Thierer, 'Soft Law for Hard Problems: The Governance of Emerging Technologies in an Uncertain Future' (Social Science Research Network, 5 February 2018).

high-level priorities or norms to guide all those involved in research, innovation, and clinical practice. A recent scoping review by our research group identified 51 soft governance tools for the responsible innovation of neurotechnologies.[13]

Neurotechnologies intended for medical use are also subject to hard governance, often via national regulatory mechanisms aimed at ensuring the safety and quality of medical devices. Medical device regulation was initially introduced in the US and elsewhere in the late 1970s to oversee what were then relatively simple devices. The development of increasingly complex neurotechnologies has required regulatory agencies such as the US Food and Drug Administration (FDA) and the European Medicines Agency (EMA) to adjust regulation. This has included reviewing safety risk classifications and ambiguous definitions (eg 'intended medical purpose') that had allowed some device manufacturers to evade medical device regulatory review.

Soft law governance frameworks have also been influential in shaping new hard governance for the regulation of neurotechnologies. For example, within the past five years, governance initiatives and lobbying efforts have influenced policy reforms specifically aimed at regulating neurotechnologies. Spain, France, Chile, Mexico, and the states of Colorado and California have recently codified into law new 'neurorights', a controversial category of novel rights designed to protect certain coveted properties of the human mind, such as cognitive liberty, mental integrity, and neural data privacy.[14]

In this chapter, we aim to contribute to discussions around effective, global neurotechnology governance. This is a timely discussion as UNESCO has embarked on a multi-disciplinary consultation process to develop a set of international guidelines for neurotechnology research and innovation, with the final report expected in 2025. We begin with a review of the current state of neurotechnology in research and health practice, followed by a summary of established and emerging neurotechnology governance. We then draw on case studies to critically examine approaches to neurotechnology governance, spotlighting several 'critical issues'. We conclude by offering some suggestions for how principles of responsible research and innovation (RRI) might be incorporated into soft and hard governance frameworks.

II. Overview of Neurotechnologies

There are numerous definitions of neurotechnology. Much of the definitional divergence is due to how 'technology' is conceptualised.[15] For the purposes of this chapter,

[13] LJ Robertson, NL Higgins, MJ Maier, J Gardner and A Carter, 'Ethical Governance Strategies for the Responsible Innovation of Neurotechnologies: A Scoping Review' (In press) *Journal of Bioethical Inquiry*.

[14] D Borbón and J Alberto Ramírez-Gómez, 'Between Politics and Scholarship: The (Un)Settled Debate over Neurorights' (2024) 6 *Frontiers in Political Science* 1335561.

[15] We recognise that sometimes neurotechnologies are said to include digital innovations that aim to facilitate the treatment, or the prediction and diagnosis, of psychiatric disorders usually via continuous

we have adopted a definition of 'neurotechnology' that aligns with definitions typically used in international governance instruments. In its draft guidance on neurotechnology governance, published in 2024, UNESCO defined 'neurotechnologies' as 'devices and procedures used to access, monitor, investigate, assess, manipulate, and/or emulate the structure and function of neural systems of human beings and other animals'.[16,17]

A. Neuromodulation

Deep brain stimulation (DBS) is the most widely used implantable brain stimulation system in clinical practice. The electroceutical effects of DBS on neuronal activity are thought to 'mimic' the therapeutic effects of ablative neurosurgical techniques of the twentieth century. Microelectrodes ('leads') are positioned deep within the brain via stereotactic neurosurgery, and are connected to a battery-powered pulse generator implanted below the patient's collarbone. DBS was approved by the FDA in 1997 for Parkinson's disease and essential tremor and later for epilepsy in 2004 and dystonia in 2013. DBS has more recently been explored in intractable psychiatric disorders, such as treatment-resistant depression and OCD.[18] It is estimated that DBS has been used to treat over 200,000 patients globally.[19]

remote, and AI enabled, monitoring and analysis of an individual's behavioural – and sometimes physiological – data. These tools also may raise challenges for the regulation and responsible research and innovation that may be similar and distinct to those we discuss in this chapter.

[16] UNESCO, First Draft of the Recommendation on the Ethics of Neurotechnology (2024), 4. unesdoc.unesco.org/.

[17] We have applied a slightly amended version of this definition. Some taxonomies focus narrowly on those technologies that directly alter or measure brain activity. A close analysis of these technologies shows that defining what qualifies as 'direct' is contestable. Pharmacological agents are often excluded from definitions of neurotechnology, despite the fact that they can be used with some precision to directly modulate neurophysiological processes. We also recognise that society often regards health 'technologies' as machines or devices that diagnose, prevent, or treat health conditions; however, there does not appear to be any good reason why a novel drug synthesised in a laboratory that acts directly on neural activity shouldn't qualify as a 'neurotechnology'. Finally, while our discussion will foreground human applications of these technologies, we recognise and support the need for engagement with neurotechnology ethics and governance as they pertain to animal research. See also L Marx, 'Technology: The Emergence of a Hazardous Concept' (2010) 51 *Technology and Culture* 561.

[18] MP Dandekar et al, 'Deep Brain Stimulation for Treatment-Resistant Depression: An Integrative Review of Preclinical and Clinical Findings and Translational Implications' (2018) 23 *Molecular Psychiatry* 1094; M Naesström, P Blomstedt and O Bodlund, 'A Systematic Review of Psychiatric Indications for Deep Brain Stimulation, with Focus on Major Depressive and Obsessive-Compulsive Disorder' (2016) 70 Nordic Journal of Psychiatry 483.

[19] V Vedam-Mai et al, 'Proceedings of the Eighth Annual Deep Brain Stimulation Think Tank: Advances in Optogenetics, Ethical Issues Affecting DBS Research, Neuromodulatory Approaches for Depression, Adaptive Neurostimulation, and Emerging DBS Technologies' (2021) 15 *Frontiers in Human Neuroscience* 644593.

Several approaches to implantable modulation of the central nervous system do not require open brain surgery as DBS does. For example, Vagus Nerve Stimulation (VNS) can be an effective treatment of drug-resistant epilepsy, depression, and cluster headaches.[20] It involves implanting a metallic coil around the Vagus nerve. Electrical impulses are delivered to the coil at regular intervals, and stimulation parameters can be set by an external magnetic wand. Spinal Cord Stimulation (SCS) is a commonly prescribed treatment for severe, intractable chronic pain.[21] Electrical impulses are delivered to the dorsal columns of the spinal cord, influencing neurotransmitter release and ablating afferent pain signalling.

At the cutting-edge of implantable neuromodulation is 'closed loop' stimulation. Closed-loop systems continuously monitor disease 'biomarkers', with the feedback from these biomarkers used to make real-time adjustments to stimulation parameters.[22] Closed-loop DBS has been used in advanced Parkinson's disease since 2013, and several feasibility studies have identified neural biomarkers of clinical depression to deliver focal stimulation of target brain regions.[23] Closed-loop SCS and VNS systems are also in development, with several recent studies showing superior symptom relief over conventional open-loop stimulation.[24]

Research interest in non-implantable neurostimulation devices has been increasing significantly. Transcranial Magnetic Stimulation (TMS) therapy involves placing a magnetic coil over the scalp to induce a magnetic field in the underlying cerebral cortex.[25] Recent studies show that TMS guided by functional magnetic resonance imagining (fMRI) or electroencephalography (EEG) can be used to administer personalised, indication-specific neurostimulation.[26] Transcranial direct-current stimulation (tDCS) is a more affordable and portable method of non-invasive neurostimulation that involves placing low-current electrodes on the scalp. A recent clinical

[20] R Carron et al, 'Latest Views on the Mechanisms of Action of Surgically Implanted Cervical Vagal Nerve Stimulation in Epilepsy' (2023) 26 *Neuromodulation: Technology at the Neural Interface* 498.

[21] CC de Vos and K Meier, 'Spinal Cord Stimulation for the Treatment of Chronic Pain' (2024) 20 *Nature Reviews Neurology* 447.

[22] F Hell et al, 'Deep Brain Stimulation Programming 2.0: Future Perspectives for Target Identification and Adaptive Closed Loop Stimulation' (2019) 10 *Frontiers in Neurology* 314.

[23] A Priori et al, 'Adaptive Deep Brain Stimulation (aDBS) Controlled by Local Field Potential Oscillations' (2013) 245 *Experimental Neurology* 77; AS Widge, 'Closing the Loop in Psychiatric Deep Brain Stimulation: Physiology, Psychometrics, and Plasticity' (2024) 49 *Neuropsychopharmacology* 138.

[24] N Mekhail et al, 'Durability of Clinical and Quality-of-Life Outcomes of Closed-Loop Spinal Cord Stimulation for Chronic Back and Leg Pain: A Secondary Analysis of the Evoke Randomized Clinical Trial' (2022) 79 *JAMA Neurology* 251; GM Winston et al, 'Closed-Loop Vagal Nerve Stimulation for Intractable Epilepsy: A Single-Center Experience' (2021) 88 *Seizure – European Journal of Epilepsy* 95.

[25] SL Cohen et al, 'A Visual and Narrative Timeline of US FDA Milestones for Transcranial Magnetic Stimulation (TMS) Devices' (2022) 15 *Brain Stimulation: Basic, Translational, and Clinical Research in Neuromodulation* 73.

[26] AT Hill et al, 'TMS-EEG: A Window into the Neurophysiological Effects of Transcranial Electrical Stimulation in Non-Motor Brain Regions' (2016) 64 *Neuroscience & Biobehavioral Reviews* 175.

trial of home-based tDCS for depression reported high efficacy, acceptability and safety.[27]

High-frequency focused ultrasound delivers precise, irreversible thermoablation of aberrant brain tissues that is receiving growing attention.[28] High-frequency focused ultrasound can target deep brain structures without general anaesthesia, and is considered a lower risk, albeit permanent, and less 'invasive' procedure than DBS as it does not require neurosurgery.[29] Low-intensity focused ultrasound (LIFU) is also being explored for a range of psychiatric conditions, including PTSD, anxiety disorders, depressive disorders, OCD, and schizophrenia.

B. Brain-computer Interfaces

Brain-computer interfaces (BCIs) are multi-component device systems that decode neural activity into external commands, enabling direct communication between the brain and devices. They often function to bypass impaired natural neural pathways, often due to disease or injury. BCIs have been trialled in humans since the late 1990s, but research has expanded substantially over the past decade.[30] Following several impressive demonstrations of BCIs restoring communication and movement in patients with paralysis, Nature Electronics named 2023 'the year of the brain-computer interface'.[31]

Several BCI start-up companies, most notably Elon Musk's Neuralink, and Australia-based Synchron, have received Breakthrough Device Designation from the FDA.[32] Neuralink successfully implanted devices using the company's R1 surgical robot in January and September 2024 as part of its PRIME study. Synchron will have implanted 10 patients by the end of its COMMAND feasibility study and is preparing to commence a pivotal clinical trial in the US. Both companies have demonstrated that BCIs can enable patients to send emails,

[27] RD Woodham et al, 'Home-Based Transcranial Direct Current Stimulation Treatment for Major Depressive Disorder: A Fully Remote Phase 2 Randomized Sham-Controlled Trial' (2025) 31 *Nature Medicine* 87.

[28] VS Bachu et al, 'High-Intensity Focused Ultrasound: A Review of Mechanisms and Clinical Applications' (2021) 49 *Annals of Biomedical Engineering* 1975.

[29] R Asher et al, 'Neuroethical Implications of Focused Ultrasound for Neuropsychiatric Illness' (2023) 16 *Brain Stimulation* 806.

[30] KM Patrick-Krueger, I Burkhart and JL Contreras-Vidal, 'The State of Clinical Trials of Implantable Brain–Computer Interfaces' (2024) *Nature Reviews Bioengineering*, see www.nature.com/articles/s44222-024-00239-5.

[31] SL Metzger et al, 'A High-Performance Neuroprosthesis for Speech Decoding and Avatar Control' (2023) 620 *Nature* 1037; FR Willett et al, 'A High-Performance Speech Neuroprosthesis' (2023) 620 *Nature* 1031.

[32] E Musk and Neuralink, 'An Integrated Brain-Machine Interface Platform With Thousands of Channels' (2019) 21 *Journal of Medical Internet Research* e16194; TJ Oxley et al, 'Motor Neuroprosthesis Implanted with Neurointerventional Surgery Improves Capacity for Activities of Daily Living Tasks in Severe Paralysis: First in-Human Experience' (2021) 13 *Journal of NeuroInterventional Surgery* 102.

manage finances, and play video games using trained mental imagery translated into computer command.

C. Neuromonitoring

There are currently a variety of neuromonitoring techniques for investigating the structure and function of the nervous system. Functional magnetic resonance imaging (fMRI) measures blood oxygenation level-dependent (BOLD) signals, that reflect changes in the relative concentration of oxygenated and deoxygenated haemoglobin. fMRI provides a spatial resolution typically in the range of 2–3 mm at standard field strengths, with higher resolution possible using ultra-high-field (eg, 7T) scanners. fMRI is commonly used for pre-surgical evaluation, such as mapping brain function before epilepsy surgery, but its role as a standalone diagnostic tool remains limited.

Cutting-edge applications of fMRI for research purposes have revealed the powerful potential of these tools. AI-assisted fMRI has emerged as an important tool to assist communication in patients with disorders of consciousness.[33] Some exploratory fMRI studies have successfully recreated images shown to participants,[34] and decoded and translated sub-vocalised speech into readable text.[35]

Electroencephalography (EEG) captures numerous brain processes occurring simultaneously and are often used in BCIs. To observe the brain's response to a specific stimulus, researchers conduct multiple trials and average the results, allowing random brain activity to cancel out to identify an event-related potential (ERP) associated with the stimulus. Machine learning algorithms may then classify the detected ERP pattern to determine the user's intent (e.g., moving a mechanical arm).[36]

Similar to EEG, electrocorticography (ECoG) measures neural activity of neurons in the cortex of the brain. ECoG involves a craniotomy, with electrodes implanted directly into the surface of the brain. ECoG provides excellent temporal resolution similar to EEG and improved spatial resolution, but the resolution is still limited by electrode grid spacing. Electrocorticography (ECoG) carries greater risks, however due to superior spatial and temporal resolution it yields much lower error rates when used as part of BCIs for restoring speech and movement.[37]

[33] S Leinders et al, 'Using fMRI to Localize Target Regions for Implanted Brain-Computer Interfaces in Locked-in Syndrome' (2023) 155 *Clinical Neurophysiology* 1.

[34] Y Takagi and S Nishimoto, 'High-Resolution Image Reconstruction With Latent Diffusion Models From Human Brain Activity'.

[35] J Tang et al, 'Semantic Reconstruction of Continuous Language from Non-Invasive Brain Recordings' (2023) 26 *Nature Neuroscience* 858.

[36] M Risetti et al, 'On ERPs Detection in Disorders of Consciousness Rehabilitation' (2013) 7 *Frontiers in Human Neuroscience* 775.

[37] KJ Miller, D Hermes and NP Staff, 'The Current State of Electrocorticography-Based Brain–Computer Interfaces'.

III. Neurotechnology Ethics and Governance

Neurotechnologies as medical devices are subject to review by medical regulation authorities.[38] The regulation of medical devices can be generally broken down into the regulation of clinical trial research, and the regulation of market entry of new medical devices. Our review will centre on medical device regulations in the US and the EU where the majority of clinical neurotechnology research takes place.[39]

A. Clinical Trial Regulation

In general, regulatory bodies must review and approve clinical trials of medical devices before they can commence. Responsible persons must apply to the relevant regulatory body with details of the device's technical specifications, therapeutic purpose, and evidence of safety and tolerability.

In the US, investigators on trials of medical devices must first obtain an Investigational Device Exemption (IDE) from the FDA.[40] Clinical trials involving 'significant risk devices', such as implants or life-sustaining devices that pose serious risks to a subject's health, will require both FDA approval via an IDE, as well as ethics review by an investigational review board. This can be either a medical device with no prior approvals being explored in human participants for the first time, or a device with a prior authorisation in a new treatment condition or patient population. Every clinical trial must undergo review by an Institutional Review Board (IRB), responsible for reviewing and the trial protocol to ensure the protection of participants rights, safety, and welfare. IRBs are also responsible for overseeing long-term compliance with FDA regulations to ensure ethical and regulatory standards are upheld.

Not all medical device trials in the US require an IDE. Studies of 'non-significant risk' devices may only require IRB review. 'Non-significant risk' trials include, for example, studies of diagnostic (rather than treatment) medical devices that meet certain conditions (eg, do not involve sampling of body materials). For clinical trials of significant-risk neurotechnologies specifically, the FDA has recently released guidance on IDE applications for trials of implanted BCIs.[41]

[38] This overview of neurotechnology regulation ('hard governance') will focus on neurotechnologies as medical devices rather than commercial products. Commercial products must be marketed and sold in accordance with various local consumer protection laws. See also Walter G Johnson, 'Catching Up with Convergence: Strategies for Bringing Together the Fragmented Regulatory Governance of Brain-Machine Interfaces in the U.S.' (Social Science Research Network, 2020).

[39] IE Harmsen et al, 'Clinical Trials for Deep Brain Stimulation: Current State of Affairs' (2020) 13 *Brain Stimulation* 378.

[40] Code of Federal Regulations (CFR), 21 CFR 820.30.

[41] Food and Drug Administration, Implanted Brain-Computer Interface (BCI) Devices for Patients with Paralysis or Amputation – Non-Clinical Testing and Clinical Considerations: Draft Guidance for Industry and Food and Drug Administration Staff (FDA 2019).

The document offers guidance to investigators on information to include in IDE submissions, such as non-clinical testing and clinical study design, risk management, biocompatibility, sterility, and MR-compatibility.

In the EU, clinical trials of all medical products must request authorisation under Regulation 536 / 2014 in order to protect the safety of trial participants while ensuring the reliability of clinical trial data. Regulation 536 / 2014 repealed Directive 2001/20/E in January 2022, replacing the previous requirement for separate applications for each EU member state with a single application for approval in all member states. It is also worth noting here that an EU 'Directive' is a legislative act that lays out goals EU member states must meet, whereas a 'Regulation' must be followed in full and applies uniformly to all EU member states.

With respect to clinical trial approval, there are notable differences between the US's IDE approval pathway and the EU's 536 / 2014 regulation for clinical investigations. In the US, an IDE is only required for clinical trials involving 'significant risk devices' with an 'intended medical purpose'. Regulation 536 / 2014, on the other hand, stipulates that EU member states must subject all medicinal products to the same clinical trial approval process, albeit with 'less stringent rules' for medical products that 'pose only very limited additional risk' or have prior authorisations.

Clinical trials of medical devices in the EU are also subject to Medical Device Regulation (MDR), introduced in 2017.[42] The MDR lays out requirements for clinical investigations of medical device conducted for the purpose of demonstrating European conformity (conformité européenne, CE). Article 62 of the MDR requires that EU member states also designate accredited notified bodies to assess of 'pilot stage clinical investigations' of medical devices.[43] Clinical trial evidentiary requirements are most stringent for non-CE marked devices that involve 'invasive or burdensome' procedures, and least for clinical investigations of CE-marked medical devices when the study aims to further evaluate the device 'within the scope of its intended purposes'.[44] Some implantable components, such as screws, plates, and pins, are exempted from having to conduct a pre-market clinical investigation.[45]

B. Market Access of Medical Devices

A successful clinical trial of a medical device will often be followed by a larger, multi-centre pivotal trial aimed at gathering evidence to support an application for market access. As with regulatory oversight of clinical trials, review processes

[42] Regulation (EU) 2017/745, Article 5.

[43] Relevant for medical devices are electromagnetic compatibility (EMC), low voltage directive (LVD), and restriction of hazardous substances (RoHS).

[44] Regulation (EU) 2017/745, Article 74.

[45] Regulation (EU) 2017/745, Article 61.

for market authorisation in the US and EU are tiered according to the risk classification of the device. In general terms, manufacturers of devices with higher risk classifications are required to produce clinical data of a greater quality and quantity to support their application.

In the US, around three-quarters of Class I ('low risk') and a small proportion of Class II ('moderate risk') devices are exempt and do not require substantial evidence of safety and effectiveness for market approval.[46] Most Class II and Class III ('high risk') devices[47] will undergo review by one of two pathways: the pre-market notification (PMN) or the pre-market authorisation (PMA) pathway. The FDA reviews several thousand PMN (or '510(k)') applications every year requiring only that the manufacturer demonstrate 'substantial equivalence' to a previously approved device (called a 'predicate device').[48] The more costly and lengthy PMA pathway is reserved for first-of-their-kind Class III devices without a predicate device. The FDA only processes between 30 and 40 PMA applications every year, with manufacturers typically expected to provide extensive safety and efficacy data from randomised controlled clinical studies.[49]

In the EU, the MDR risk classification also has three tiers (I, II & III), with higher risk classes being subject to greater scrutiny of clinical trial data by the Notified Body of the EU member state. To be legally marketed in the EU, medical devices must obtain a CE mark, confirming compliance with EU standards. Manufacturers must also maintain a quality management system (QMS) and a post-market surveillance system proportionate to the risk class of the device. To be approved for placement on the EU market the Notified Body must determine that the therapeutic benefits of the medical device outweigh the risks. In a notable departure from the previous Medical Device Directive (MDD), Annex XVI of the MDR has expanded its scope to cover a range of non-medical devices that do not have an 'intended medical purpose'. Instead of demonstrating therapeutic benefit, manufacturers of devices without an 'intended medical purpose' must prove that the device 'performs' as claimed. The EU's regulation of non-medical devices in this way constitutes a significant regulatory shift and has had implications for neurotechnology devices used in research (which we will later discuss).[50]

The transition from MDD to MDR – which came into force in 2017 – has impacted medical device regulation in the EU. Some have argued that the

[46] N Naghshineh et al, 'Demystifying the U.S. Food and Drug Administration: Understanding Regulatory Pathways' (2014) 134 *Plastic and Reconstructive Surgery* 559.

[47] Class I ('low risk of illness or injury') devices are lowest risk and are not intended to help support or sustain life (eg, EEG headsets). Class II ('moderate risk') devices are designed to perform as indicated without causing injury or harm to patient or user (eg transcranial magnetic stimulator). Class III is reserved for devices that 'support or sustain human life, are of substantial importance in preventing impairment of human health, or present a potential, unreasonable risk of illness, or injury' (eg, DBS).

[48] M Moynahan, 'Neuromodulation: Regulatory Considerations', *Neuromodulation* (Elsevier, 2018).

[49] GA Van Norman, 'Drugs, Devices, and the FDA: Part 2: An Overview of Approval Processes: FDA Approval of Medical Devices' (2016) 1 *JACC. Basic to translational science* 277.

[50] E Steindl, 'Consumer Neuro Devices within EU Product Safety Law: Are We Prepared for Big Tech Ante Portas?' (2024) 52 *Computer Law & Security Review* 105945.

introduction of Notified Bodies has created unnecessary obstacles and delays in medical device innovation.[51] Under the MDR, all medical devices approved in the EU before the implementation of the MDR in 2021 are considered 'legacy devices' and must meet conformity under the new MDR before the end of 2027 and 2028 (depending on risk class). EU devices must have their CE mark renewed every five years; no such requirement exists for FDA-approved medical devices.[52] The MDR also has more stringent post-market surveillance requirements; manufacturers must maintain a quality management system, register for a Unique Device Identification (UDI) for tracing and monitoring, and implement a post-market surveillance system proportionate to the device's risk class. Finally, it may become more difficult to demonstrate equivalence to previously marketed devices, as the MDR requires comprehensive access to technical and clinical documentation, which will often require a letter of authorisation from the manufacturer of the equivalent device.[53]

C. Neuroethics and Neurorights

Ethicists have long been concerned with ethical issues related to mental health, cognitive decline, and dying. However, it was only in 2002 that ethicists, scientists and legal academics came together to argue for the need for a separate discipline dealing with the 'unique' ethical issues raised by neuroscience research made possible by neurotechnological innovations, such as DBS and fMRI. Discussions were focused primarily on issues such as legal responsibility following traumatic brain injury or dementia, implications for selfhood, and the appropriateness of cognitive enhancement. There has been much debate over whether neuroscience necessitated a new branch of ethical deliberation called 'neuroethics'.[54] In 2006, the field was formalised through the formation of the Neuroethics Society, and the later International Neuroethics Society in 2011.

In its first 15 years, neuroethics research primarily focused on the theoretical exploration of the ethical implications of developments in neuroscience and technology. However, early neuroethics scholarship was criticised as overly focused on 'speculative' ethics that did not adequately attend to the practical capacities and limitations of current and emerging neurotechnologies.[55] The field has since embarked on an 'empirical turn'. Whilst not completely eschewing its commitment

[51] C Bublitz and S Ligthart, 'The New Regulation of Non-Medical Neurotechnologies in the European Union: Overview and Reflection' (2024) 11 *Journal of Law and the Biosciences* lsae021.

[52] M Fink and B Akra, 'Comparison of the International Regulations for Medical Devices–USA versus Europe' (2023) 54 *Injury* 110908.

[53] ibid.

[54] A Roskies, 'Neuroethics for the New Millenium' (2002) 35 *Neuron* 21.

[55] Emerging Issues Task Force, International Neuroethics Society, 'Neuroethics at 15: The Current and Future Environment for Neuroethics' (2019) 10 *AJOB Neuroscience* 104; G Lázaro-Muñoz et al, 'Neuroethics at 15: Keep the Kant but Add More Bacon' (2019) 10 *AJOB neuroscience* 97.

to theoretical ethical scholarship, the field has become increasingly focused on ensuring the ethical research and use of neuroscience research and technology.

Interdisciplinary scholars have provided ethical principles, guidance and recommendations for scientists, clinicians, and developers for the research and use of neurotechnology. This research made important contributions including the management of incidental findings in neuroimaging research, the conduct of studies seeking to understand and treat people with disorders of consciousness, and ethical recruitment of psychiatric patients to experiential trials of DBS (to name a few).[56]

Since 2017, the field of neuroethics has been largely preoccupied by debates over proposed human rights ('neurorights') aimed at addressing ethical issues in neuroscience research.[57] Later that year neurorights were popularised by a piece in the journal Nature authored by a consortium of 25 neuroethics scholars (the 'Morningside Group) and, beginning in 2019, advocacy by the Neurorights Foundation.[58]

While there is no agreement of what neurorights are, the Neurorights foundation proposes protections for the following: a right to personal identity, right to free-will, right to mental privacy, equal access to mental augmentation, protection from algorithmic bias.[59] Some form of 'neurorights' has now been adopted in several South and Central American nations despite having received relatively little critical engagement by human rights law experts. Next, we discuss some of the critical issues raised by such forms of neurotechnology governance.

IV. Critical Issues in Neurotechnology Governance

There are several critical issues relating to neurotechnology governance. In general terms, these critical issues reflect the considerable enthusiasm surrounding the purported therapeutic and research potential of neurotechnologies, and their potential to impact and measure brain functions that are deeply implicated in human identity and well-being. This enthusiasm has inadvertedly promoted some unsupported assumptions about what neuroscience research can reveal about the mind, the brain and behaviour.

In this section we will focus on three critical issues: neuroexceptionalism, global ethical pluralism, and balancing regulation and innovation. The issue of

[56] NA Scott, TH Murphy and J Illes, 'Incidental Findings in Neuroimaging Research: A Framework for Anticipating the next Frontier' (2012) 7 *Journal of empirical research on human research ethics: JERHRE* 53; A Peterson, S Aas and D Wasserman, 'What Justifies the Allocation of Health Care Resources to Patients with Disorders of Consciousness?' (2021) 12 *AJOB Neuroscience* 127; P Rabins et al, 'Scientific and Ethical Issues Related to Deep Brain Stimulation for Disorders of Mood, Behavior, and Thought' (2009) 66 *Archives of General Psychiatry* 931.

[57] M Ienca and R Andorno, 'Towards New Human Rights in the Age of Neuroscience and Neurotechnology' (2017) 13 *Life Sciences, Society and Policy* 5.

[58] R Yuste et al, 'Four Ethical Priorities for Neurotechnologies and AI' (2017) 551 *Nature* 159.

[59] M Ienca, 'On Neurorights' (2021) 15 *Frontiers in Human Neuroscience* 701258.

neuroexceptionalism in governance extends from perennial debate in neuroethics over the 'uniqueness' (or lack thereof) of ethical tensions posed by neurotechnology innovation. Uncritically accepting that issues at the neuro-level are 'unique' by their very nature could lead governance frameworks to unjustifiably reinforce the brain's perceived 'special status'. The critical issue of global ethical pluralism underscores a broader issue in soft governance: the design of governance frameworks often prioritises the values of the Global North while marginalising perspectives from the Global South and other underrepresented communities. Finally, the interplay between soft governance and hard regulation raises concerns about overregulation and underregulation, which we examine by drawing from several case studies.

A. Critical Issue 1: Neuroexceptionalism

On 2 April 2013, US President Barack Obama took to the stage at the White House, announcing a bold new research funding programme called the 'BRAIN' initiative to a room full of the nation's leading scientists. During his address, Obama remarked:

> As humans, we can identify galaxies light years away, we can study particles smaller than an atom. But we still haven't unlocked the mystery of the three pounds of matter that sits between our ears … So there is this enormous mystery waiting to be unlocked, and the BRAIN Initiative will change that by giving scientists the tools they need to get a dynamic picture of the brain in action and better understand how we think and how we learn and how we remember. And that knowledge could be – will be – transformative.[60]

Underpinning these remarks is neuroexceptionalism. Neuroexceptionalism is the assumption that 'matters concerning the neurolevel are somehow exceptional, ie, relevantly different to others'.[61] At first pass, there may not seem to be anything problematic about neuroexceptionalism in neurotechnology governance. Obama is correct about the vast complexity and enduring mystery of the human brain. After all, how could a funding programme specifically orientated toward neuro-innovation *not* regard the brain as 'relevantly different' in some sense? Neuroexceptionalism becomes problematic when it is treated as a scientific fact, obscuring critical epistemic assumptions about neuroscientific inquiry and its object – for our purposes, the human nervous system.

In this section, we argue that some neurotechnology governance, particularly soft governance, has accepted a strong form of neuroexceptionalism that relies on a misleading account of the relationship between brain and behaviour. This

[60] B Obama, 'Remarks by the President on the BRAIN Initiative and American Innovation' (White House, 2 April 2013) obamawhitehouse.archives.gov/the-press-office/2013/04/02/remarks-president-brain-initiative-and-american-innovation.

[61] JC Bublitz, 'Novel Neurorights: From Nonsense to Substance' (2022) 15 *Neuroethics* 7, 8.

form of neuroexceptionalism mistakes or exaggerates how neurotechnology is 'relevantly different' to other technologies. We also explore in this section whether it is appropriate (or perhaps even necessary) to adopt a weak form of neuroexceptionalism when developing neurotechnology governance.

Most governance tools that assume neuroexceptionalism do not do so explicitly. However, neuroexceptionalism may become evident in the normative significance assigned to 'neural data', by the descriptions of the effects of neurotechnologies on the brain, or by the 'uniqueness' of the ethical issues these technologies raise.

For example, soft governance instruments that give special treatment to neural data often argue that it is more sensitive, intimate, or exploitable compared to other kinds of personal data (including personal health data). Neural data has been linked more closely to fundamental human faculties, such as identity and self:

> Neural data … is therefore capable of revealing enormously sensitive information about the people from whom it was collected, including identifiable information about their mental health, physical health, and cognitive processing.[62]
>
> Brain data … could provide access to highly intimate information that is proximal to one's identity. Such data is sensitive because it contains information about the organ that generates the mind.[63]

We disagree that special treatment should be afforded to neural data because it is more proximal to identity.[64] We are not convinced that monitoring, collecting or storing neural data is *ipso facto* more ethically concerning simply because it intuitively feels more intrusive to 'get inside someone's head'. Other kinds of data, such recordings of private conversations, or health records containing diagnostic information (eg HIV-positive status), are arguably just as personal if not more so. These data already provide robust insights into our identities and intimate experiences, often revealing more about us than neural data could. Sensitive health data is already protected under professional standards regarding patient confidentiality and existing laws, such as the US Health Insurance Portability and Accountability Act (HIPPA), or the European Union's General Data Protection Regulation (GDPR). There is scope for these regulations to provide sufficient protections of neural data collected or analysed by medical devices within medical or research settings.

Calls for special protections for neural data often appeal to neuroimaging studies that have been able to decode personal information from participants. Indeed, fMRI studies have been able to recreate images shown to participants[65]

[62] Neurorights Foundation, 'Safeguarding Brain Data: Assessing the Privacy Practices of Consumer Neurotechnology Companies' (2024) www.perseus-strategies.com/wp-content/uploads/2024/04/FINAL_Consumer_Neurotechnology_Report_Neurorights_Foundation_April-1.pdf.

[63] S Goering et al, 'Recommendations for Responsible Development and Application of Neurotechnologies' (2021), *Neuroethics* 7.

[64] D Susser and LY Cabrera, 'Brain Data in Context: Are New Rights the Way to Mental and Brain Privacy?' (2024) 15 *AJOB neuroscience* 122; Bublitz (n 61).

[65] Takagi and Nishimoto (n 34).

and decode sub-vocalised speech and translate this into readable text.[66] However, proponents of special protections for neural data overlook key facts. These studies are conducted in tightly controlled lab settings that do not translate to the real world, and the algorithms used to predict personal information only do so slightly better-than-chance.[67] They are not 'reading minds' any more than other forms of cognitive prediction, such as lie detectors or digital phenotyping.

Some soft governance instruments claim that neurostimulating devices modulate neural activity in a manner that is different in kind, and thus normatively distinct, from other modes of altering mental states or behaviour. The means by which these devices act on the brain is often understood as more 'immediate' and 'magnitudinous' than other brain-altering interventions. Consider for instance UNESCO's recent 'Draft Recommendations on the Ethics of Neurotechnology':

> Neurotechnology is unique in terms of the immediacy and magnitude of its potential to allow access to and modification of neural processes and mental states.[68]

It is the case that neurostimulating devices have direct neurophysiological effects (i.e., high-frequency electrical modulation of neuronal activity). However, many electroceutical applications have weak or imprecise effects on the symptoms of brain illnesses and mental phenomena more generally. Neurostimulation is not universally the most 'magnitudinous' means of modulating neural processes or targeting mental phenomena. Some psychotherapeutic, cognitive, or behavioural approaches target mental processes with marked effectiveness,[69] while psychopharmaceuticals can have more significant and irreversible impacts on mental states.[70]

Consider also that many forms of human torture have significant and enduring effects on one's mental state without introducing a neuromodulating substance into the body or applying neurostimulation, acting only via the body's somatosensory pathways (eg, pain in the periphery) and processed by top-down perceptual/cognitive centres. While it may be the case that neural devices act 'directly' on the neural tissue, it is not clear this should warrant distinct normative consideration than those that do so more substantially, even if less directly.

[66] Tang and others (n 35).

[67] A Wexler, 'Separating Neuroethics from Neurohype' (2019) 37 *Nature Biotechnology* 988; A Wexler and R Thibault, 'Mind-Reading or Misleading? Assessing Direct-to-Consumer Electroencephalography (EEG) Devices Marketed for Wellness and Their Ethical and Regulatory Implications' (2019) 3 *Journal of Cognitive Enhancement* 131.

[68] UNESCO, First Draft of the Recommendation on the Ethics of Neurotechnology (2024) 7.

[69] P Cuijpers et al, 'Cognitive Behavior Therapy vs. Control Conditions, Other Psychotherapies, Pharmacotherapies and Combined Treatment for Depression: A Comprehensive Meta-Analysis Including 409 Trials with 52,702 Patients' (2023) 22 *World psychiatry: official journal of the World Psychiatric Association (WPA)* 105.

[70] EM Cornett et al, 'Medication-Induced Tardive Dyskinesia: A Review and Update' (2017) 17 *The Ochsner Journal* 162.

Third, neuroexceptionalism often leads to an emphasis on the brain over the person. Consider the following examples from recent national and international soft governance:

> The brain is what makes us who we are as individual human beings.[71]
>
> The nervous system activity provides information inherent to all human beings … The nervous system activity is also instrumental in social and cultural interactions.[72]

Foregrounding the brain in this way can obfuscate the role that the social world plays in neurological and psychiatric disorders. From a governance perspective, current medical practices and regulatory structures already consider the brain's importance to our ability to lead fulfilling lives without requiring brain-specific guidelines or regulations. These frameworks address the brain's influence on autonomy and physical abilities adequately without overemphasising its special status. Yet, claims such as those above may be leveraged to make the case that the 'special status' of the brain has not been accounted for in existing governance.[73] For example, there is concern that brain-specific governance such as efforts to enshrine brain-specific human rights ('neurorights') could devalue existing human rights – especially when driven by political activism rather than by rigorous legal analysis.[74] As Bublitz astutely observes, 'strong forms of reductionism are a fine methodological position for neuroscience, which may and should try to explain as much as possible at the neural level. But one should not mistake a methodological assumption of a scientific field as a basis for ethics or public policy'.[75]

B. Critical Issue 2: Global Ethical Pluralism

There is a history of unjust treatment of marginalised communities within biomedical research.[76] Minority populations have been systemically excluded from participating in research or included without their consent (eg, Tuskegee syphilis studies).[77] Consequently, new medical treatments may not benefit these communities equally or meet their needs. Neuroscience research for the diagnosis and treatment of neurological disorders has historically neglected to consider

[71] Protecting Cognition: Background Paper on Human Rights and Neurotechnology (Australian Human Rights Commission 2024), 10.

[72] UNESCO, First Draft of the Recommendation on the Ethics of Neurotechnology (2024) 4.

[73] See also: Critical Issue, Case 3 on Neurorights.

[74] Borbón and Ramírez-Gómez (n 14).

[75] Bublitz (n 51) 17.

[76] SS Oh et al, 'Diversity in Clinical and Biomedical Research: A Promise Yet to Be Fulfilled' (2015) 12 *PLoS medicine* e1001918.

[77] J Henrich, SJ Heine and A Norenzayan, 'The Weirdest People in the World?' (2010) 33 *Behavioral and Brain Sciences* 61.

patients from culturally diverse backgrounds.[78] The harms of this neglect are compounded by the disproportionate impact that neurological diseases have on low and middle-income countries (LMICs), driven by limited healthcare access, a shortage of specialists, high prevalence of risk factors, and barriers to affordable treatment.[79]

Over the past decade, the neuroscience community has become increasingly attentive to these justice issues. Recent soft governance tools have recommended promoting equity, diversity, and inclusion within research. For example, governance tools have called on researchers to be vigilant about bias – both social and algorithmic – creeping into the design of neurotechnologies that could discriminate against minority communities:

> In addition to the risk of algorithmic bias within neurotechnologies themselves, there is also the risk that neurotechnology may deepen social and economic divides in a way that violates the right to equality and non-discrimination.[80]

> Neurotechnology systems for human use should always ensure trustworthiness across their entire life cycles. This requires, among other things, that these systems do not replicate or amplify biases …[81]

Other soft governance instruments have emphasised the importance of making accessibility and availability a core component of the design process:

> Where interventions using novel neurotechnologies have been demonstrated to be safe and effective … we would hope that the exercise of inventiveness would mean that they also become cheaper, easier to use, and more widely and equitably available.[82]

We support these soft governance tools for increasingly recognising the importance of equity, diversity, and inclusion, and believe they can and should continue to be strengthened. However, such instruments tend to originate within the Global North,[83] and largely reflect Global North values and priorities. As a result, the perspectives of neurotechnology users and developers in the Global South have been largely excluded. These international recommendations should consider how notions of 'responsible' neurotechnology governance might differ across diverse developing nations, where healthcare infrastructures and regulatory mechanisms supporting the translation of biomedical innovations may still be in their infancy.[84]

[78] OP Matshabane, 'Promoting Diversity and Inclusion in Neuroscience and Neuroethics' (2021) 67 *EBioMedicine* 103359.

[79] VL Feigin et al, 'The Global Burden of Neurological Disorders: Translating Evidence into Policy' (2020) 19 *The Lancet. Neurology* 255.

[80] Protecting Cognition: Background Paper on Human Rights and Neurotechnology (n 71) 17.

[81] UNESCO, First Draft of the Recommendation on the Ethics of Neurotechnology (2024) 13.

[82] Nuffield Council on Bioethics (ed), *Novel Neurotechnologies: Intervening in the Brain* (Nuffield Council on Bioethics, 2013) 235.

[83] LJ Robertson, NL Higgins, MJ Maier, J Gardner and A Carter, 'Ethical Governance Strategies for the Responsible Innovation of Neurotechnologies: A Scoping Review' (In press) *Journal of Bioethical Inquiry*.

[84] K Wakunuma et al, 'Reconceptualising Responsible Research and Innovation from a Global South Perspective' (2021) 8 *Journal of Responsible Innovation* 267.

Matshabane highlights several points of emphasis within neurotechnology governance documents that do not appear to be innovation priorities for the Global South, such as expensive neurosurgical neurotechnologies that require extensive clinical infrastructures and multi-disciplinary teams to support their use.[85] Likewise, neuroethics has historically focused on justice issues related to neuroenhancement,[86] such as the unfair advantage conferred to the wealthy by DTC neurostimulating devices or nootropic drugs in competitive professional or academic settings. This preoccupation has led to a relative neglect of concerning how to improve access to neurotechnologies that could be essential to basic healthcare (eg, MRIs for diagnosis):

> While we recognize that many forms of human cognitive augmentation are still in the distant future, early efforts should be made by manufacturers and insurance companies to ensure broad access to effective enhancement technologies … Given the complexity and range of possible enhancements, this recommendation serves as a reminder to keep matters of equity and access centred as development continues.[87]

Framing the largely speculative issue of potential unfair advantage in neuroenhancement as a model justice concern risks overshadowing the pressing, genuine issues of inequity and discrimination that pervade neurotechnology research and translation. Future governance tools should reconsider the relative importance of 'cognitive augmentation' and 'life-changing enhancement', against arguably more urgent and ubiquitous justice concerns such as inequitable access to neurotechnologies as diagnostic and treatment tools.

A broader, culturally informed approach to neurotechnology governance is necessary to understand how different values and healthcare priorities impact mental health policy and research. This includes considering culturally diverse understandings of mental health, and the global relevance of individualistic and Western-centric moral concepts such as autonomy and agency. The Global Neuroethics Summit Delegates make a strong case for consideration of collectivist understandings of the role of the brain in decision making.[88] They highlight for example that the irreducible relationality of the self in cultures influenced by Buddhist and Confucianist philosophies has implications for informed consent procedures in neuroscience research. Encouragingly, some governance tools have started to consider how the values and priorities of Global South countries might shape governance, with UNESCO's draft guidance warning against 'technological colonisation':

> Specific attention to underserved and historically marginalized people is vital to protect against bias, continuous disparities in healthcare, persecution, stigma, neglect, and

[85] Matshabane (n 78).
[86] C Forlini and A Erler, 'Neuroenhancement' (2020) *Routledge Encyclopedia of Philosophy*.
[87] Goering et al (n 63) 15.
[88] J Amadio et al, 'Neuroethics Questions to Guide Ethical Research in the International Brain Initiatives' (2018) 100 *Neuron* 19.

disrespect. Technological colonization through loss of culture and heritage, therefore, is a substantive threat that must be avoided.[89]

It is crucial to move beyond international frameworks dominated by Global North perspectives and priorities. Future governance tools should prioritise inclusive, culturally diverse approaches that reflect the lived realities, values, and healthcare needs of marginalised and underserved populations – globally. By doing so, the field can better align neurotechnology innovation with principles of equity, accessibility, and global justice.

C. Critical Issue 3: Balancing Regulation and Innovation

The flexibility of soft law instruments makes them especially useful in quickly evolving areas of innovation.[90] They are also highly attainable forms of international governance given political obstacles to policy reform.[91] These advantages of soft law nevertheless do not discount the need for well-designed and implemented local and national-level regulations. Technology regulation must neither stifle innovation nor allow for unchecked experimentation or commercialisation that may harm users. Overlapping or excessive regulations can lead to bureaucratic hurdles and inefficiencies, while gaps in regulation may fail to prevent unethical research practices and set research back by decades. In this section, we will use three cases to examine the scope of neurotechnology regulations, the implementation of these regulations, and finally regulations for the specific governance of neurotechnologies.

i. Case 1. Scope: 'Health' vs. 'Wellness' Consumer Neurotechnologies

A major challenge for regulators is applying appropriate controls to devices that act on the body. Issues arise when devices which interface with the body in comparable ways are marketed differently; some intended for medical use by patients, others marketed to healthy consumers. In the US, products that make medical claims are classified as medical devices and fall under the regulation of the FDA, however the FDA does not regulate products that do not make health claims. In 2016, and again in 2019, the FDA stated that it would not enforce regulations against devices that were low-risk and marketed for 'general wellness' rather than as improving health.[92]

[89] UNESCO, First Draft of the Recommendation on the Ethics of Neurotechnology (2024) 10.
[90] R Hagemann, J Huddleston and AD Thierer, 'Soft Law for Hard Problems: The Governance of Emerging Technologies in an Uncertain Future' (Social Science Research Network, 5 February 2018).
[91] JC Bublitz, 'What an International Declaration on Neurotechnologies and Human Rights Could Look like: Ideas, Suggestions, Desiderata' (2023) *AJOB Neuroscience* 1.
[92] Food and Drug Administration, *General Wellness: Policy for Low Risk Devices* (Guidance for Industry and FDA Staff, 27 July 2016) www.fda.gov/regulatory-information/search-fda-guidance-documents/

The EU's 2022 Medical Device Regulation (MDR) has laid down specific rules for a range of products 'without an intended medical purpose'. Annex XVI of the MDR specifically includes within its scope neurotechnologies that 'apply electrical currents or magnetic or electromagnetic fields that penetrate the cranium to modify activity in the brain' (Annex XVI, item 6). Thus, medical device review now applies to a growing market of DTC tDCS devices which had formerly been able to avoid medical device review in the EU due to their lack of an 'intended medical purpose'.

Many have welcomed the policy change as a safeguard against DTC device companies bypassing regulatory review, yet a specific element of the MDR expansion has drawn criticism from the neuroscience research community. Critics have noted that the MDR now includes neurotechnologies for modulating brain activity, but not those that solely monitor or record brain activity. EEG headsets and some EEG-assisted BCIs would therefore fall outside the scope of the MDR. Consumer EEG companies claim to provide insights into mental states (eg, concentration, vigilance, arousal) by interpreting electrical activity captured from the scalp, with the interpretation itself being purported to lead to behavioural improvements. Thus, commentators have argued against the exemption for neuromonitoring devices on the grounds that they present 'a subtle, and arguably more complex, set of ethical issues'.[93]

Second, Annex XVI of the MDR up-classifies non-implantable neurostimulating devices to the highest risk classification (Class III). According to Steindl (2024), the reasons for this up-classification are 'severe health-related side effects', such as 'atypical brain development, abnormal patterns of brain activity, increase metabolic consumption, fatigue, anxiety, irritability, headaches, muscle twitches, tics, seizures, vertigo and skin irritation' (6). This would subject devices such as tDCS and TMS to the same regulatory rigour as implantables such as DBS. Many have strongly opposed this up-classification, arguing that this amendment did not involve an extensive consultation with research or clinical professionals who work in the field.[94] They have disputed the claim that TMS/tES can lead to 'atypical brain development' or 'abnormal brain activity patterns', and contend that the up-classification to Class III could jeopardise the leading position of European researchers in the field and delay patient access to non-implantable devices in a healthcare delivery context. As of January 2025, an inquiry with the EU Ombudsman is underway to prompt the Commission to reassess its classification of non-invasive, non-medical brain stimulation devices.[95]

general-wellness-policy-low-risk-devices. See also A Wexler and P B Reiner, 'Oversight of Direct-to-Consumer Neurotechnologies' (2019) 363 *Science* (New York, N.Y.) 234.

[93] Wexler and Thibault (n 67) 1.

[94] C Baeken et al, 'European Reclassification of Non-Invasive Brain Stimulation as Class III Medical Devices: A Call to Action' (2023) 16 *Brain Stimulation* 564; Bublitz and Ligthart (n 51).

[95] Bublitz and Ligthart (n 51).

ii. Case 2. Implementation: Expedited Approval of Medical Neurotechnologies

Neurotechnology innovation has advanced in a financial and regulatory milieu that is perceived, in some cases, as antagonistic to clinical investigation. To address these issues, the health agencies may offer expedited review pathways to device manufacturers that meet certain conditions.[96]

While expedited review is designed to promote innovation and accelerate patient access to medical devices, they are also susceptible to misuse. The FDA's humanitarian device exemption (HDE) pathway offers unique marketing advantages that allows applications to bypass the rigours of a clinical trial. An HDE is exempt from effectiveness requirements and is subject to certain profit and use restrictions. In February 2009, the FDA granted Medtronic an HDE for the use of DBS devices for severe, treatment-resistant OCD. Notwithstanding some positive research outcomes related to DBS-OCD research,[97] the approval was criticised on the grounds that this disorder affects over 500,000 people and should not have been permitted to undergo expedited access under the HDE scheme. Critics were also dubious about DBS-OCD being awarded a determination of 'substantial equivalence' to an already-approved device, since 'a [DBS] electrode's intended use varies with stimulation of different parts of the brain'.[98] These critiques, now over a decade old, remain relevant to the responsible design of regulatory schemes today. Expedited approval programs should ensure that innovative neurotechnological interventions are subjected to appropriate clinical scrutiny.

iii. Case 3: Specific Regulations for Neurotechnology Innovation

As of December 2024, neurorights initiatives have influenced national regulations, including a constitutional amendment in Chile, a criminal law bill in Argentina, a bioethics law in France, and a Charter of Digital Rights in Spain.[99] In the US, California has passed a house bill incorporating Neurorights into existing consumer protection laws, classifying neurodata as 'sensitive personal information'. Colorado has recently introduced a similar bill.

As scholars, politicians and lobbying groups consider introducing new statutory frameworks for Neurorights, it is crucial to anticipate potential unintended consequences if such reforms are enacted without a complete understanding of

[96] Food and Drug Administration, *General Wellness: Policy for Low Risk Devices* (Guidance for Industry and FDA Staff, 27 July 2016) www.fda.gov/regulatory-information/search-fda-guidance-documents/general-wellness-policy-low-risk-devices.

[97] BJ Nuttin et al, 'Long-Term Electrical Capsular Stimulation in Patients with Obsessive-Compulsive Disorder' (2003) 52 *Neurosurgery* 1263.

[98] JJ Fins et al, 'Misuse Of The FDA's Humanitarian Device Exemption In Deep Brain Stimulation For Obsessive-Compulsive Disorder' (2011) 30 *Health Affairs* 302.

[99] JM Muñoz and J Ángel Marinaro, 'Neurorights as Reconceptualized Human Rights' (2023) 5 *Frontiers in Political Science*.

their implications. Critics of the Neurorights initiative have argued that creating new rights specific to neurotechnologies could devalue existing human rights.[100] There is continued disagreement regarding the conceptual understandings of proposed neurorights. While seminal work[101] introduced the idea of a negative right to cognitive liberty – defined as the right to refuse coercive uses of neurotechnology – it was notably absent from the Neurorights Foundation's 2024 report, which has driven significant policy change. The omission of the negative right to cognitive liberty surprised some legal scholars, who viewed this as the 'most promising and perhaps most urgently needed' given the fundamental importance of individuals' rights to freely use or refuse neurotechnologies.[102] Bublitz notes that there have been longstanding discussions about how this right could usefully complement the legal protection of persons.[103]

We share concerns regarding the potential devaluation of human rights raised by these commentators. Human rights based on the unclear or ambiguous conceptual foundations of Neurorights could undermine the value and subsequent enforcement of existing rights. Historically, human rights have emerged from careful, exhaustive deliberation, and over-expansion risks diluting their significance. It is also unclear whether the current Neurorights initiative adequately balances positive and negative rights or aligns with established norms in disability and human rights law – an area ripe for further exploration. Confusion created by neurorights premised on unsettled conceptual understandings or erroneous assumptions about the nature of the brain may ultimately hinder progress in regulating neurotechnologies.

V. Discussion and Conclusion

Neurotechnologies are promising, innovative tools for diagnosing, treating, and preventing nervous system disorders. Effective governance is essential, and individual developers and clinicians cannot address ethical issues alone. Just as we expect those developing or clinically delivering these technologies to do so responsibly, there is a need for responsibility in the design and implementation of these governance structures. In this final section, we briefly canvass two model responsible research and innovation (RRI) initiatives that may help developers achieve a balanced approach to governance.[104]

[100] JJ Fins, 'The Unintended Consequences of Chile's Neurorights Constitutional Reform: Moving beyond Negative Rights to Capabilities' (2022) 15 *Neuroethics* 26; Bublitz (n 61).

[101] Ienca and Andorno (n 57).

[102] Bublitz (n 61).

[103] W Sententia, 'Neuroethical Considerations: Cognitive Liberty and Converging Technologies for Improving Human Cognition' (2004) 1013 *Annals of the New York Academy of Sciences* 221.

[104] Responsible Research and Innovation (RRI), emphasised in the European Commission's 2013 Horizon 2020 program, is an approach that integrates inclusivity, ethical reflection, and responsiveness to societal needs throughout the research and innovation process.

One key advantage of soft governance instruments is their capacity to influence hard governance. They can guide courts in interpreting standards, clarify the substance of human rights, and inspire additional binding measures at both national and international levels. For example, Anderson argues that an effective way to accelerate patient access to novel health technologies is unilateral collaboration with regulatory agencies globally to harmonise regulatory requirements.[105] Toward this end, Anderson and others give as an example the International Medical Device Regulation Forum (IMDRF), which promotes the development of useful and relevant international safety and efficacy standards for innovative devices, a scaffold for a single premarket review process for innovative devices, and establishing working groups to develop clear guidance to support prospective regulatory convergence in these areas.[106]

Competitive dynamics within innovation ecosystems must be front of mind when designing governance structures, as the interests of key stakeholders may not always align. For example, the NIH BRAIN initiative's public-private partnership for neurotechnologies, conferred a host of advantages to developers. For investigators, the funding provided access to tailored research tools that acted as proof-of-concept prototypes for future products, while for commercial manufacturers, the program minimised the risks of exploratory research, speeding up the pace and extent of scientific discovery and innovation.[107] However, the sustainability of industry engagement with the research community remains uncertain. If investors withdraw from research involving implantable devices, patients may be left with obsolete devices, while manufacturers face insolvency and investigators are unable to supply replacement hardware components.[108] Complex questions regarding the enduring responsibilities for neurotechnologies that fail to traverse the translational 'valley of death' must be addressed within the framework of neurotechnology governance.

Finally, neurotechnology governance must balance innovation with responsibility. It expects that stakeholders collaborate to build governance structures that are flexible yet robust enough to handle evolving challenges. Initiatives like those from the IMDRF and the NIH BRAIN initiative illustrate paths forward, underscoring the value of both soft and hard governance measures to ensure these technologies not only advance scientific discovery but also safeguard societal interests and patient welfare in the long term.

[105] L Anderson et al, 'FDA Regulation of Neurological and Physical Medicine Devices: Access to Safe and Effective Neurotechnologies for All Americans' (2016) 92 *Neuron* 943.

[106] International Medical Device Regulators Forum, *IMDRF Strategic Plan 2021–2025* (IMDRF, 2021) www.imdrf.org/documents/imdrf-strategic-plan-2021-2025.

[107] DA Borton et al, 'Developing Collaborative Platforms to Advance Neurotechnology and Its Translation' (2020) 108 *Neuron* 286.

[108] N Higgins et al, 'Post-Trial Access to Implantable Neural Devices: An Exploratory International Survey' (2024) 6 *BMJ Surgery, Interventions, & Health Technologies* e000262.

PART III

Death

7

Life After Death? The Ethical, Legal and Social Implications of Cryonics

EMMA KOWAL AND NEERA BHATIA

I. Introduction

The desire to transcend death is a central theme in religious, philosophical, and mythological traditions of human societies across the world and through time.[1,2] In Ancient Egypt, for example, immortality was deeply tied to the belief in an afterlife where the soul could live eternally if effectively preserved through mummification and funerary rites. Greek philosophy also explored immortality, particularly in Plato's *Phaedo*, where Socrates argues for the soul's indestructibility and eternal existence. Monotheistic religions such as Christianity and Islam conceptualise immortality as an afterlife governed by divine judgement. Daoist traditions in China emphasise immortality through meditative practices, seeking to achieve enlightenment through internal transformation and harmony with the Dao. The variety of beliefs about immortality in different cultures and religions can be conceptualised along two axes: first, as either physical (eternal life in a bodily form) or spiritual (the persistence of the soul beyond death); and second, as either individualistic (the persistence of the individual soul after death) or collective (eg, the absorption of the soul into a collective consciousness after death).[3] Anthropological perspectives on death and immortality see beliefs about death, possible afterlives or resurrection as expressions of cultural beliefs about how life should be lived.

In the late twentieth and early twenty-first centuries, a few hundred people have taken the highly unusual step of having their dead bodies frozen and stored in the hope of being revived in a future time when the diseases that caused their death can be cured and when ageing has been overcome by technological means. In some ways, this practice is analogous to earlier religious and cultural practices and beliefs

[1] MH Gorisse, 'Global Perspectives on Death and Immortality' (2024) 60 *Religious Studies* S1.
[2] DM Coulter-Harris, *Chasing Immortality in World Religions* (McFarland Publishers, 2016).
[3] K Wiredu, 'Immortality' in VY Mudimbe and K Kavwahirehi (eds), *Encyclopedia of African Religions and Philosophy* (Springer Verlag, 2021).

about the afterlife.[4] Cryonics (alternatively called cryogenics) reflects a belief in life beyond biological death, but by means of advanced biomedicine rather than divine intervention. In this modern form of belief, technological optimism replaces metaphysical forces as the path to immortality. Advocates of cryonics argue that future scientific breakthroughs in fields such as nanotechnology or regenerative medicine may allow for the reanimation and restoration of cryopreserved individuals, effectively granting them a form of life extension. Cryonics is often associated with what have been called 'transhumanist' philosophies that seek to surpass biological limitations through technological enhancement.[5] In relation to the two axes of belief about death and immortality discussed in the previous paragraph, cryonics sits at the extreme 'body' end of the body-spirit scale, and at the extreme 'individualist' end of the individual-collective scale. It assumes that preserving the physical body – either the entire body or just the brain – is the path to life extension, and that it is the individual person that will return, if, and when, they are revived. As we will discuss, the likelihood of a cryopreserved body or brain being restored to life in the future is incredibly small. However, it raises many interesting questions about novel uses of technology and how they could or should be regulated.

This chapter asks how we should understand this new approach to immortality and what legal, ethical and social issues it raises. We first briefly explain the history of cryonics and then explain how it is performed. Subsequent sections examine the social and ethical issues raised, and some of the legal implications of the practice. In our exploration of the ethical, regulatory and social implications of cryonics we focus on developments and discourse in Australia and the United Kingdom (UK).

II. History

Cryonics has its technological roots in the field of cryobiology, the study of the effects of extremely low temperatures on biological systems. This science had its roots in the seventeenth century, when natural philosophers such as Robert Boyle and Antonie van Leeuwenhoek conducted experiments on the effects of cold on living organisms. Boyle, for example, investigated the effects of freezing on biological tissues, while Leeuwenhoek observed that microscopic organisms could be revived following exposure to freezing temperatures. In the nineteenth century, John Hunter experimented with freezing and reviving tissue samples, demonstrating that cells could survive cryogenic conditions.[6]

The modern discipline of cryobiology emerged in the mid-twentieth century when advances in biochemistry, physics, and cell biology enabled a better understanding of the effects of freezing on cellular structures. A major breakthrough

[4] S Dein, 'Cryonics: Science or Religion' (2021) 61(4) *Journal of Religion and Health* 3164.

[5] T Fuchs, *In Defence of the Human Being: Foundational Questions of an Embodied Anthropology* (Oxford University Press, 2021).

[6] J Radin, *Life on Ice: A History of New Uses for Cold Blood.* (University of Chicago Press, 2017).

came with the discovery of cryoprotectant substances, such as glycerol, which prevent the formation of ice crystals that would otherwise cause irreparable cell damage during freezing or thawing. In the 1940s and 1950s, scientists such as James Lovelock and Peter Mazur conducted pioneering research on the mechanisms of freezing injury and cryoprotectant efficacy, leading to significant progress in the cryopreservation of cells, tissues, and even organs. In the twenty-first century, cryobiology plays a crucial role in many fields, including reproductive medicine, organ transplantation, and conservation biology.[7]

While cryobiology is a well-established and respected scientific field, cryonics has a far more controversial history and is considered a pseudoscience by mainstream scientists. Robert Ettinger, known as the 'father of cryonics', launched the field with the publication of *The Prospect of Immortality* in 1964.[8] The book proposed that freezing the bodies of people who had just died would enable their preservation until some future time when they could be brought back to life by not-yet-existing technologies. He self-published the book in 1962, and it caught the attention of science fiction author Isaac Asimov, who helped it find a commercial publisher. This association between the science fiction community and cryonics is a persistent theme in the history and rationality of the practice.[9]

The institutional basis of cryonics began in 1965 with the Cryonics Society of New York, soon followed by other societies on the east and west coasts of the United States. The first person to be frozen was psychologist Dr James Bedford, who was cryopreserved in 1967 after dying of cancer. He remains frozen today. The Alcor Life Extension Foundation was founded in 1973, followed by the Cryonics Institute, founded in 1976 by Robert Ettinger himself. More recent additions to the cryonics industry include Oregon Cryonics based in the United States, the Russian company KrioRus,[10] and the Chinese company Yinfeng Life Science Research Institute. The latest cryonics company and the first to be based in Australia, Southern Cryonics, froze its first "patient" in May 2024.[11] In the next section, we turn to the technical aspects of freezing a body just after death.

III. Technical Aspects

The technical processes used to cryopreserve bodies have varied over time and between companies, but they all aim to freeze bodies as soon as possible after the person has been pronounced dead. At the time that a medical practitioner declares

[7] J Radin and E Kowal, *Cryopolitics: Frozen Life in a Melting World.* (MIT Press, 2017) 3–26.

[8] RCW Ettinger, *The Prospect of Immortality* (Doubleday and Co Publishers, 1964).

[9] R Doyle, 'Disciplined by the Future: The Promising Bodies of Cryonics' (1997) 6(4) *Science as Culture* 582.

[10] A Bernstein, *The Future of Immortality: Remaking Life and Death in Contemporary Russia* (Princeton University Press, 2019).

[11] E Somerville, 'Southern Hemisphere's first cryogenically frozen client at rest in regional New South Wales facility' (*ABC News Online*, 23 May 2024), www.abc.net.au/news/2024-05-23/sydney-man-first-cryogenically-frozen-holbrook-regional-nsw/103879454.

that the patient has died, they cease to have legal personhood but are considered by cryonics companies to be a 'patient'. The first technical challenge for the cryonics process is logistical and social: a team of experts from a cryonics company, often based in another country to the hospital where the dying person is located, must be there at the time that death is declared (or as soon after as possible), and have convinced hospital staff and treating doctors that they should be allowed access to the deceased person to perform what appear to be medical procedures.

Once these initial logistical and social obstacles are overcome and the cryonics team have access to the body, the goal of the cryopreservation process is to preserve as much of the body's biological function as possible through rapid cooling while avoiding tissue damage from the freezing process itself. In the first phase, the heart and lungs are connected to a machine that artificially maintains circulation and perfuses the body in cold water to reduce the body temperature to close to zero degrees Celsius. At the same time, an anticoagulant drug is administered to prevent blood clotting, while cryoprotectants are circulated, a process called vitrification. Once the body is vitrified, it is moved to the company facility and then further cooled over several days to the temperature of liquid nitrogen – minus 196 degrees Celsius. Finally, the body is stored along with the other cryopreserved 'patients' of the company.[12]

Many cryonics 'patients' choose the option of only preserving their head or just their brain: options called 'neuropreservation'. This is much cheaper than storing a whole body due to the reduced space and power required to maintain the head/brain at extreme low temperatures. While the proportion of people choosing neuropreservation over full body preservation is not available across the whole industry, Alcor states that as of 2020, 51 per cent of their customers choose neuropreservation.[13] Proportions may be similar industry-wide. Cryonics providers suggest several potential benefits to preserving only the head/brain: cryopreservation of a head/brain is technically easier and therefore likely to be better preserved; moving a whole body across state or international borders poses legal and administrative barriers that are less or non-existent for moving a head/brain, avoiding delays that can further worsen the technical outcome; and the remainder of the body can be cremated and the ashes offered to relatives to scatter or keep.

This method operates under the assumption that personal identity and consciousness reside entirely within the brain's neural structures, particularly in the synaptic connections that may store memories and produce personality traits. Consumers who choose this option are likely to believe that in the future, bodies will be easily synthesised, and the brain can be 'uploaded' to a new body. Those who choose to preserve their whole body are likely to believe that preserving the whole body increases the chances of a successful revival, as it maintains

[12] BP Best, 'Scientific Justification of Cryonics Practice' (2008) 11(2) *Rejuvenation Research* 493.
[13] Alcor Life Extension Foundation, www.alcor.org/docs/Neuro-and-Whole-Body-Options.pdf.

the complete biological context of the person, including the intricate connections between the brain and the rest of the nervous and endocrine systems.

Whether someone chooses to preserve their brain/head or their whole body, the possibility of revival relies on huge future advancements in molecular nanotechnology, regenerative medicine, and neuroscience. Currently, the techniques developed in cryobiology are most commonly applied in the field of reproductive medicine for freezing and reviving gametes (eggs and sperm), embryos, and by blood banks for freezing red blood cells in donated blood.[14] Successfully thawing multicellular structures has proven to be far more difficult due to the ice crystals that can form and disrupt the architecture of the tissue or organ. While there has been some reported success in freezing and reviving tissues and small organs in mammals – most notably a rabbit kidney that successfully worked for nine days following thawing[15] – the technological tools and processes required for cryopreservation and successful revival of human organs, much less a brain or whole body, are at least some decades away.[16] The technology required to 'upload' the neural information from a brain to a computer or synthetic body and thereby reconstitute a human are even more speculative.[17] Thus, it is highly unlikely that any body or head frozen in a cryonics facility will ever be 'alive' again. However, the chance is not zero: it *is* possible. For advocates of cryonics, this non-zero possibility is all that is required to justify cryopreservation, given that the alternative is death – a version of Pascal's Wager that is sometimes called the Cryonics Wager.[18] As one blogger writing about cryonics put it: 'If you knew your plane was to crash and you had to choose between dying instantaneously or trying out an experimental parachute with a better than zero chance of staying alive, what would you choose?'[19] We now turn to discuss some of the ethical and social implications of cryonics.

IV. Social and Ethical Implications

Cryonics raises a host of social questions. One place to start in addressing them is the intersection of cryonics with varying interpretations of life and death. The definition of death in industrialised societies has shifted over time as medical technology has progressed. Historically, death has been primarily defined by

[14] TH Jang et al, 'Cryopreservation and its Clinical Applications' (2017) 6(1) *Integrative Medicine Research* 12.

[15] GM Fahy et al, 'Physical and Biological aspects of Renal Vitrification' (2009) 5(3) *Organogenesis* 167.

[16] A Parihar et al, 'Cryopreservation: A Comprehensive Overview, Challenges, and Future Perspectives' (2023) *Advanced Biology* 2200285.

[17] P Hopkins, 'Why Uploading will not Work, or, the Ghosts Haunting Transhumanism' (2012) 4(1) *International Journal of Machine Consciousness* 229–43.

[18] D Shaw, 'Cryoethics: Seeking Life after Death' (2009) 23(9) *Bioethics* 515–21.

[19] OM Stan, 'Cryonics Suspension – Debating Life Finitude, Extending Time Capital and Cancelling Death' (2016) 7(2) *Journal of Comparative Research in Anthropology and Sociology* 71–91, 83.

the cessation of the heartbeat and breathing, known as cardiopulmonary death. With the emergence of life support technology, organ transplantation, and intensive care, all around the middle of the twentieth century, the concept of death became more complex. Patients with no chance of waking up due to irreversible brain and/or organ damage could be kept alive on life support. The concept of 'brain death' was devised in the late 1960s to solve this problem, positing that a person could be brain dead while their breathing and circulation continued to be supported by external means.[20] This definition gained widespread social and legal acceptance, allowing for the ethical removal of life support (and facilitating organ donation).

The advent of cryonics goes hand in hand with an attempt to redefine death. Cryopreservation of whole bodies with the intent to revive them requires that the person not be considered dead but in some other state that holds the possibility of becoming the same person again in the future. An alternative definition of death that serves this purposes for some cryonics companies is 'information-theoretical death'.[21] This term is used to describe a period of time beyond clinical or legal death, but before the irrecoverable loss of the bodily information that cryonics advocates believe is sufficient to reconstitute a person. Cryonicists believe that in the window between legal death and information-theoretical death, the memories and personality of the person will be salvageable with the help of future medical technologies – if the person is cryopreserved according to company protocols. Farman describes this notion of personhood that cryonics seeks to preserve as our 'informatic selves'.[22] As long as neuronal patterns are retrievable from the brain, individual personhood can theoretically be reconstituted in a future body. The finality and irreversibility of death is soundly rejected by the cryonics community: a leading cryonics company Alcor describes their service as 'pausing the dying process'. Accordingly, the industry rejects any association between cryonics and resurrection. Rather than bringing dead people back to life, they consider themselves to be preserving dying people so that future technologies can treat their diseases, analogous to an induced coma.[23]

Philosopher Melanie Swan's analysis of a 2017 survey of 316 cryonics customers and supporters (only the second academic study of the cryonics community to be conducted and the first since the 1970s) considered their views of personhood. The predominant motivation of survey participants, 70 per cent of whom were members of cryonics companies, was the potential to be revived in the future so that they could experience the future world while retaining their memories of their

[20] 'A definition of irreversible coma. Report of the Ad Hoc Committee of the Harvard Medical School to Examine the Definition of Brain Death' (1968) 205(6) *JAMA* 337–40.

[21] T Romain, 'Extreme Life Extension: Investing in Cryonics for the Long, Long Term'(2010) 29(2) *Medical Anthropology* 194–215.

[22] A Farman, *On not dying: Secular immortality in the age of technoscience* (University of Minnesota Press, 2020).

[23] Dein (n 4) 3164–76.

current life. Most believed that brain preservation was the most important aspect of cryonics, as personality and selfhood are located in the brain.[24]

It almost goes without saying that inequality is inherent to cryonics, with only a privileged few able to afford membership to a cryonics organisation. Anthropologist Tiffany Romain's study of the United States cryonics community found that there was a particular demographic that was massively overrepresented. The cryonics movement appeals to 'primarily a small fraction of white, male, atheist, Libertarian, middle- and upper-middle-income, computer engineering "geeks" who believe passionately in the free market and its ability to support technological progress'. She found that a belief in the benefits of radical life extension go hand in hand with a subculture that is 'technophilic, biological materialist, American, atheistic, Libertarian, and masculine in nature'.[25]

Cryonics can be thought of as a subset of transhumanism, a philosophical movement aimed at overcoming human biological limitations, including death.[26] Transhumanists believe that technological advances in genetics, nanotechnology, synthetic biology and artificial intelligence will lead to a form of 'post-human' intelligence far beyond anything that humans can currently reach.[27] In a typical transhumanist imagined future, the neural patterns of cryopreserved brains will be uploaded into a non-physical body. Many cryonicists take extreme measures to safeguard their health and live as long as possible, so that the best possible body and/or brain can be delivered for cryopreservation. The longer they live, the better the cryonic technology will be and the higher the chance of successful reanimation.

Approaches to cryonics are part of what Kowal and Radin have termed 'cryopolitics'. Cryopolitics is a variation of what French philosopher Michel Foucault explored through the concept of 'biopolitics'. Biopolitics refers to the state's politicisation of human life, whether that be at an individual or population level. The dictum of biopolitics is to 'make live and let die', meaning that the modern state allows people to die through neglect, but focuses primarily on maximising the potential of the population through measures such as antenatal care and education. In a time when cryopreservation of many different forms of life is possible, cryopolitics describes a mode of politicisation where people and populations are 'made to live' by the state but are not allowed to die. Cryopreservation extends life indefinitely, impacting how well lives can be lived.[28]

Others have discussed the kind of world and environments that 'patients' of cryonics might return to in the future (if it is successful). Gibson speculates about

[24] M Swan, 'Worldwide Cryonics Attitudes About the Body, Cryopreservation, and Revival: Personal Identity Malleability and a Theory of Cryonic Life Extension' (2019) 58(4) *Sophia* 699–735.

[25] Romain (n 21) 196, 205.

[26] Farman (n 22).

[27] J Bialecki, 'Strange Aeons: Transhumanism, H.P. Lovecraft, and the Affective Index of Posthuman Dread' (2022) 33(3) *The Australian Journal of Anthropology* 428–41.

[28] E Kowal and J Radin, 'Indigenous Biospecimen Collections and the Cryopolitics of Frozen Life' (2015) 51(1) *Journal of Sociology* 63. See also A Friedrich and S Höhne, 'Regimes of freshness: Biopolitics in the Age of Cryogenic Culture' (2016) 3 *Medicine Anthropology Theory* 112–54.

future material and social obligations, responsibilities and challenges that might be faced by those who undergo cryonics. He considers the post-cryopreserved 'patient' to be analogous to having 'refugee' status. In that, while present-day refugees flee 'geographical' locations, cryopreserved 'refugees' would be fleeing 'temporal' locations – while remaining in the exact geographical location.[29] A cryogenically preserved 'patient' who has been reanimated after, for example, a millennium Gibson suggests would be able to claim residency in a completely new time period/era. The 'patient' would return to a world with drastically changed 'social structures, political entities, economic systems, ecological processes and other factors'[30] – all fundamentally different to the world they left behind.

If the 'patient' is the only person in their family to opt for cryonics they would return to a world with no family or next of kin, which Shaw has referred to as a 'loneliness argument'.[31] Thau suggests that in fact, 'patients' who are reanimated will eventually 'get bored' of having such a long existence on the planet. Life may simply become tedious, where a person feels no further reason to live, or they have reached all their life goals and ambitions.[32] When we conventionally consider death, there is a certainty attached to it. Putting aside any religious or cultural beliefs about what happens to the body or mind 'after death', most people understand that once a person dies, they do not come back to life in a physical or anatomical sense. One concern that has been raised about cryonics is the lack of 'death certainty'. Thus, as Huxtable notes, devaluing death (certainty of when death occurs) and devaluing science (and its advancements).[33] Cryonics, therefore, threatens the very fact of death and the act of dying, when death occurs or will occur, and knowing that death is absolute. Cryonics might be thought of as leaving people in a state of 'death limbo'. A follow on from this is linked to a person's next of kin. When a person dies, in a conventional sense, their family or next of kin know that death is final and absolute. This, then allows them to associate grieve the loss of their loved one. There is an association of grief that can be linked with death, there is also a physical corpse/body that allows a family to mourn in the presence of a body – cryonics would not allow for this type of mourning or grief to occur.

This has been described as 'death denial'. While much of the literature focuses on the 'patient' and ethical or social arguments in favour or against cryonics in a broad sense, very little has been written about the impact on the bereaved family members of the cryogenically preserved 'patient'. The human mourning process in conventional dying is an essential part of the human experience. Hillenbrink and Wareham describe mourning the death of a loved one as a vital part of coping

[29] RB Gibson, 'The Cryonic Refugee: Appropriate Analogy or Confusing Rhetoric' (2022) 28(2) *The New Bioethics* 97, 98.

[30] ibid 102.

[31] Shaw (n 18) 515, 516.

[32] T Thau, 'Cryonics for all?' (2019) 34(7) *Bioethics* 638, 643.

[33] R Huxtable, 'Cryonics in the Courtroom: Which Interests? Whose Interests?' (2018) 26(3) *Medical Law Review* 476, 495.

with loss and ensuring emotional and psychological well-being.[34] This is coupled with certain tasks and rituals associated with death including: (i) performing funeral rites, (ii) accepting the irreversibility of a loss and impossibility of reunion, (iii) adapting to life without the deceased and (iv) emotionally repositioning the deceased so that life can continue.[35] The authors note that each of the tasks is unlikely to be actioned when a person is cryogenically persevered. Thus, not allowing family/next of kin to fully mourn the loss of their loved one. The impact of this can be severe, in not being able to move on or ever having closure about the death of their loved one. This might even go to the extreme of family not being able to connect in their current relationships due to focusing on the memories of the deceased.[36] Cryonics might be thought of as a disruptor of the grieving process for the remaining family/next of kin due to the lack of certainty that we derive from death in a conventional manner and a formal burial or creation process.[37]

Other practical considerations concern the cryonics industry itself and the consequences that could arise when facilities cease operating, malfunction or are negligent in the care of 'patients'. Of relevance too, are matters concerning natural justice and immortality. At what point do we say that a person has had their fair innings? When is it a good time to pass the world on to the next generation and consider the population size the environment and sustainable futures?[38]

V. Cryonics and the Law

In the context of the law and the legal landscape, various frameworks have been established, amended and reformed over time to protect and assist people from premature death, or at least nudge people into making better choices to extend their lives. Some frameworks or strategies are governed under law, such as an obligation to wear a seat belt when driving or other mandated safety precautions in work environments or sporting pursuits. Others are more implicit in deterring people from determinants in unhealthy food choices, overconsumption of alcohol or actively discouraging the use of tobacco.[39] While these choices and mandates are reasonable and well-understood, the practice of cryonics is starkly radical in that it proposes to stall death, holding a person in a state of suspension, with the potential promise of reanimation and life again. The technical, social and ethical

[34] R Hillenbrink and CS Wareham, 'Mourning the Frozen: Considering the Relational Implications of Cryonics' (2024) 50(6) *Journal of Medical Ethics* 388, 389.

[35] ibid 389.

[36] ibid 390.

[37] A Ahmed and S Dein, 'The Death of Cryonics: Factors Related to its Poor Uptake' (2022) 2(6) *European Journal of Theology and Philosophy* 1.

[38] Shaw (n 18) 515.

[39] B Baer Arnold, 'Thawing out Personhood: Australian Law and Cryonics' 2020 17(1) *Canberra Law Review* 43–60, 44.

issues of cryonics have been detailed and considered at length.[40] Nonetheless, many of these discussions pose more questions than answers and revolve around three possible outcomes about cryonics: (i) if it is successful; (ii) if it is unsuccessful or (iii) if it remains uncertain. Other debates about cryonics have framed arguments about cryonics being a highly speculative 'possibility' rather than a very likely 'probability'.[41]

In this section we explore some of the legal implications of cryonics that too often remain under-investigated or receive sparse attention.[42] One reason for this might be because of the little likelihood of success of reanimating a person who has been cryogenically preserved ever becoming a reality. Notwithstanding this, the extent to which aspects of the law that cryonics might impact is expansive. Arnold highlights that the implementation of cryonics raises concerns about human rights; taxation; crime; consumer protection; trusts and personhood.[43] Additionally, other areas that are relevant in a legal discussion about cryonics extend to contract law, negligence,[44] as well as other disciplines such as bioethics, philosophy, anthropology, medicine and science (amongst others).

It is a long-held principle that no property rights exist in a deceased body[45] – the 'no property' principle. Further, in common law, it is well established that an executor or the next of kin of the deceased has the right to possession of the body for the exclusive purpose of burial.[46] The origins of the 'no property principle' can be loosely traced as far back as the sixteenth century in *Haynes Case* where the Courts determined that a dead person did not have property rights.[47] Later in

[40] For example, F Minerva, *The Ethics of Cryonics: Is it Immoral to be Immortal?* (Palgrave Macmillan, 2018); C Mercer and TJ Trothen, 'Cryonics: Buried, Burned, or … Frozen' *Religion and the Technological Future: An Introduction to Biohacking, Artificial Intelligence, and Transhumanism* (Springer, 2019); J Shao, 'Cryonics Wager: An Analysis' (2024) *International Journal of Philosophical Studies* 1–14.

[41] N Bhatia and J Savulescu, 'Cryonics: Is freezing bodies all hype, hope, or is it just logistical and ethical hell?' (ABC News Online) www.abc.net.au/news/2016-11-24/cryonics-hype-hope-or-hell/8050278.

[42] However, see the recent book by P de Gioia Carabellese and C Della Giustina, *The Law of Cryonics: A Legal Philosophical and Financial Analysis* (Routledge Press, 2024).

[43] Baer Arnold (n 39) 43.

[44] We will not engage in discussion about cryonics and euthanasia in this chapter. This is however an issue that has received some academic attention. See G Andrade and M Campo Redondo, 'Cryonics, euthanasia, and the Doctrine of Double Effect' (2023) 18(7) *Philosophy, Ethics, and Humanities in Medicine* doi.org/10.1186/s13010-023-00137-5; A Buben, 'Dying to Live: Transhumanism, Cryonics, and Euthanasia' in M Cholbi and J Varelius (eds), *New Directions in the Ethics of Assisted Suicide and Euthanasia* (Springer, 2023).

[45] See M Quigley, *Self Ownership, Property Rights, and the Human Body* (Cambridge University Press, 2018); R Hardcastle, *Law and the Human Body, Property Rights, Ownership and Control* (Hart Publishing, 2007); W Bonython, and B Baer Arnold, 'Privacy, Personhood and Property in the Age of Genomics' (2015) 4(3) *Laws* 377–412.

[46] See eg *The Queen v Fox* (1841) 2 QB 246, 114 ER 95 (QB); *The Queen v Scott* (1842) 2 QB 248, 114 ER 97 (Assizes); *Williams v Williams* (1882) 20 Ch D 659 (Ch); *The Queen v Price* (1884) 12 QBD 247 (QB); *Union Bank of Australia v Harrison, Jones and Devlin Ltd* (1910) 11 CLR 492; *Rees v Hughes* [1946] KB 517 (CA); *Dobson v North Tyneside Health Authority* [1997] 1 WLR 596 (CA); *Smith v Tamworth City Council* (1997) 41 NSWLR 680 (SC).

[47] In this case Haynes was charged with petty larceny and the felonious taking of winding sheets. *Hayne's Case* (1614) 12 Co Rep 113; 77 ER 1389.

Exelby v Handyside the Court more openly acknowledged the 'no property' in an action brought against a doctor in relation to the bodies of two babies joined by a birth defect. The action was dismissed and the Willes CJ noted that 'no person had property in corpses,[48] the Court in *R v Kelly* affirmed the "no property principle"'.[49] However, over the last century, the issue of property rights in a dead body has been called into question and exceptions to the general principle exist in various jurisdictions including Australia, the United Kingdom (UK) and the United States (US).

The 'work and skill' exception was first recognised in the Australian case of *Doodeward v Spence*.[50] This seminal case considered whether the corpse of a foetus could be the subject of property. It concerned a doctor who attended a mother after the stillbirth of her two-headed foetus. The doctor had acquired it, preserved it in spirits in a bottle, and kept it in his office as a curiosity. After the death of the doctor, some 40 years later, the father of the plaintiff, Doodeward, bought the bottle and its contents at an auction. The plaintiff exhibited the bottle for financial gain. However, a sub-inspector of police, Spence then seized the exhibit under warrant and arrested Doodeward, who was subsequently prosecuted for indecent exhibition of a corpse. The plaintiff demanded the return of the exhibit. The bottle was returned to him and the spirits without the foetus that was retained at a university museum. The issue of ownership went to the Supreme Court of New South Wales where Pring J stated that there was no right of property in any separated portion of a human body.[51] However, the High Court of Australia established that property rights did exist in a dead body and held:

> … when a person has by the lawful exercise of work and skill so dealt with a human body or part of a human body in his lawful possession that it has acquired *some attribute differentiating it from a mere corpse awaiting burial*, [our emphasis] he acquires a right to retain possession of it, at least as against any person not entitled to have it delivered to him for the purpose of burial …[52]

Of relevance here is the application of the 'work and skill' principle to a cryogenically preserved person. Some scholars have suggested that the preservation techniques used in the cryopreservation process of a person might be considered 'work and skill'.[53] Mullock and Romanis suggest that the process is more complex than simply deep freezing a corpse and then thawing it to convert it back to its pre-preservation state.[54] Rather, the authors state that cryopreservation involves more advanced scientific processes that in fact *change* the corpse from its natural state.

[48] See *Exelby v Handyside* (1749) 2 East PC 652.
[49] *R v Kelly* [1999] QB 621, 630.
[50] *Doodeward v Spence* (1908) 6 CLR 406.
[51] *Doodeward v Spence* (1907) 7 SR (NSW) 727 (SC).
[52] *Doodeward v Spence* (1908) 6 CLR 406, para 414.
[53] A Grubb, 'I, Me, Mine: Bodes, Parts and Property' (1998) 3(4) *Medical Law International* 299.
[54] A Mullock and EC Romanis, 'Cryopreservation and Current Legal Problems: Seeking and Selling Immortality' (2023) 10(2) *Journal of Law and the Biosciences* 1, 25.

Insofar as exercising 'work or skill' on a human body giving it attributes differentiating it from a mere corpse awaiting burial – if the exception were to apply to cryonics and it could be established that property rights are to be conferred on the cryogenically persevered person this gives way to a range of other relevant and related questions.

It has been highlighted that the facility holding the cryogenically preserved body might hold property rights over the body, further causing conflict or doubt about disposal of the body. If it were to be found that there is a property in the body and its ownership rests with the cryonic storage facility, then any potential claims to the body by the next of kin for the purposes of disposal for the '*purposes of burial*' might be overridden.[55] Arnold describes the 'frozen body' as one with 'no personhood and no legal rights'.[56] He emphasises that the 'frozen body' cannot vote, has no standing in litigation, or cannot fundamentally hold property as it is not recognised as a living 'legal' person.

To date, only France and British Columbia (BC) in Canada have specific laws stating that cryonics is unlawful. No other jurisdictions have specific legislation that expressly states that cryonics is an unlawful practice – thus leaving it largely unregulated. It has been noted by Arnold that most jurisdictions do recognise that it is an offence to 'permanently store a dead person in a domestic freezer',[57] but no legal explicit prohibition about larger facilities. The state of BC has made it clear that 'freezer storage' is an offence and applies to larger facilities. The funeral legislation prohibits 'sales, and offers of sale, of arrangements relating to cryonics and irradiation'. Stating:

> A person must not offer for sale, or sell, an arrangement for the preservation or storage of human remains that is based on
>
> (a) cryonics,
> (b) irradiation, or
> (c) any other means of preservation or storage, by whatever name called,
>
> and that is offered, or sold, on the expectation of the resuscitation of human remains at a future time.[58]

In France, cryonics is also unlawful, and the only lawful forms of body disposal are burial or cremation. Additionally, bodies can be donated to science. Despite the prohibition on cryonics in France, the law is somewhat relaxed in that bodies can be taken to other countries for cryogenic freezing.

Cryonics has received the attention of the UK Courts, garnered media exposure, and received academic commentary from legal, bioethical, and philosophical scholars (amongst others). Since the establishment of Southern Cryonics, it has

[55] ibid 26.

[56] B Baer Arnold, 'Putting Death in the Freezer: Cryonics as Technology, Law and Ethics' in J Casas-Roma, J Conesa and S Caballé (eds), *Technology, Users and Uses: Ethics and Human Interaction Through Technology and AI* (Ethics International Press Limited, 2023) 326.

[57] ibid 321.

[58] Cremation, Interment and Funeral Services Act, s 14 [SBC 2004] CHAPTER 35 www.canlii.org/en/bc/laws/stat/sbc-2004-c-35/latest/sbc-2004-c-35.html.

also captured considerable media attention in Australia.[59] The case we discuss below has been discussed elsewhere in several bodies of work – therefore its discussion here remains brief.[60]

The case of Re JS (Disposal of Body) involved a 14-year-old teenage girl in the UK (known as JS) who was diagnosed with a rare cancer. In 2016 the High Court determined that she had the lawful right to have her body cryogenically preserved immediately after her death, in the hope that she might be reanimated in the future if a cure should become available.[61] JS had spent several months conducting internet research on cryonics, and she decided that it was something she wished to pursue. JS said, 'I want to live and live longer, and I think that in the future they might find a cure for my cancer and wake me up. I want to have this chance. This is my wish.'[62] Her parents were divorced, and JS had not seen her father for several years. Despite this, both parents were legally entitled to make decisions about the posthumous disposal of her remains. Her mother supported her wish, and her grandparents had secured the funds to cover the cost of the cryogenic preservation. The case went before the High Court because her parents were in dispute about consenting to the cryogenic preservation. Her father initially did not agree with JS's wishes but eventually agreed on the provision that he could view her body after her death, to which JS refused. This led to an application for the Court to intervene and resolve the dispute. Under the Children Act 1989, Jackson J was required to consider JS's welfare as the paramount consideration in the case. While undoubtedly uncharted territory for Jackson J, the judge found JS was of sound capacity, and a bright intelligent young person with the ability to articulate her strongly held views of her current situation in deciding to be cryogenically preserved.[63]

Jackson J noted that cryonics was not regulated under the Human Tissue Act 2004, cryonics sits outside the scope of the Act and beyond its remit.[64] Nonetheless, the request from JS to be cryogenically preserved and shipped to the US was not in itself illegal or unlawful, albeit perhaps costly (£37,000). The judge determined that JS's mother could make arrangements for her body to be preserved and shipped to the US. The hospital in the UK supported and cooperated with JS and her family along with Cryonics UK who were made aware of JS's request. However, the novelty of this case was evident in that Cryonics UK – the

[59] E Somerville, 'Southern Hemisphere's first cryogenically frozen client at rest in regional New South Wales facility' (*ABC News*, 23 May 2024) www.abc.net.au/news/2024-05-23/sydney-man-first-cryogenically-frozen-holbrook-regional-nsw/103879454.

[60] H Conway, 'Frozen Corpses and Feuding Parents' Re JS (Disposal of Body) (2018) 81(1) *Modern Law Review* 132; Mullock and Romanis (n 54) 1; F Cranmer, 'Cryonics and the law: Re JS (Disposal of Body)' (2016) *Law & Religion UK*, lawandreligionuk.com/2016/11/19/cryonics-and-the-law-re-js-disposal-of-body/; Huxtable (n 33) 476; A Benn, 'Re JS (A Child) (Disposal of Body: Prospective Orders): [2016] EWHC 2859 (Fam): High Court of Justice (Family Division): Jackson J: 10 November 2016' (2017) 6(2) *Oxford Journal of Law and Religion* 413.

[61] *Re JS (Disposal of Body)* [2016] EWHC 2859 (Fam) para 6.

[62] ibid para 10.

[63] ibid para 9.

[64] ibid para 14.

organisation assisting the hospital was found to have been: (i) under-equipped and disorganised; (ii) placing pressure on the hospital to allow for procedures that had not been agreed upon.[65] This somewhat haphazard approach to preparing for JS's body to be shipped to a cryonics facility in the US may not come as a surprise.

The Human Tissue Acts and other relevant legislation permit and regulate the freezing of sperm, eggs and embryos (gametes) to later be thawed for use. It is unlikely to have been in the contemplation of legislators or draftspersons that there would come a time or need to consider the freezing of entire bodies or brains for the potential reanimation in the future. Jackson J noted that it may be thought that the events of the case suggest that there might be a need for better regulation of cryonic preservation in the UK if cryonics were to happen again in the future or as an increasing practice.[66] It is more plausible, however, as Conway suggests regulation is not an 'urgent task'.[67] The author highlights that there is only a small proportion of people who may seek to be cryogenically preserved in any given year, and as highlighted in JS, the cost associated with cryonics is no small feat.[68] Rather, Conway discusses more demanding issues that require our attention about the disposal of the dead body (corpse). Noting that although cremation and burial continue to dominate as preferred methods of body disposal, other possibilities influenced by our consciousness of the environment, and commercially more viable (than cryonics) are being explored.

Some of these alternatives, Conway explains, include: resomation (liquefication using alkaline to dissolve the body) and promession (liquid hydrogen that cools the body, then the brittle remains are shattered by the application of ultrasonic vibration).[69] Others have discussed the 'green burial movement' – that has seen a growing demand for human composting (in part due to the COVID-19 pandemic) of the body after death. Also known as 'natural organ reduction' this process uses heat and oxygen to speed up the microbial process that converts the body to soil, with some companies promising to turn bodily remains into trees after death.[70] Each of these alternatives provide strong challenges to the viability of cryonics commercially and ethically, and perhaps with fewer legal challenges.

VI. Conclusion

As of March 2025, cryonics company Alcor had only 248 'patients' (frozen bodies) and under 1500 'members', people who pay an annual subscription to access cryonics

[65] ibid para 68.
[66] ibid para 15.
[67] Conway (n 60) 132, 135.
[68] ibid.
[69] ibid 136.
[70] K Paul, 'From Cradle to Compost: The Disruptors who want to make Death Greener' *The Guardian* (Australia, 19 February 2023). The practice is legal in several US states.

in the event of their death.[71] The other major company, the Cryonics Institute, has similar numbers. The small numbers reflect the extreme nature of the intervention and the remote possibility of reanimation. The reluctance of people to engage in cryonics is also justified by the economic realities of the industry. The business models of cryonics companies are fundamentally flawed, as 'patients' cannot continue paying for their own cryopreservation. Nearly all the first generation of cryonics companies have gone out of business, and their 'patients' have been thawed and disposed of.

While cryonics is likely to remain a fringe pursuit, the technologies used in cryonics are finding applications in mainstream medicine. Therapeutic hypothermia is used when the body is severely compromised by major blood loss or sustained cardiac arrest. The body is cooled to reduce cellular activity, reducing the need for oxygen and minimising cell death while blood transfusion takes place and/or cardiac function is restored. The highly speculative nature of the science of 'life extension' has meant that cryonics retains an aura of 'pseudoscience', science fiction, or a 'secular religion'. Despite this, it is valuable to consider the ethical and social implications of cryonic practices as such discussion lends itself to broader and deeper discussion and conversation about the moral value and weight we might place on life and death.

The law, at least in Australia and the UK has not engaged with the practice of cryonics in any meaningful manner (other than the case of *JS*). The reason for this might be due to the unlikely possibility of its success. However, with the establishment of the first cryonics centre in Australia, there is every chance that the law might be called upon to intervene in situations dealing with breaches of contract, property law, tort law or other areas of the law that relate to the operation of cryonic centres or 'patients' of such centres. Additionally, advances in nanotechnology, generative AI, quantum computing and space travel are shifting the vision of cryonics ever closer to becoming a reality.

[71] Alcor, www.alcor.org/.

8

New Funerary Methods: Technological Innovation, Sustainability, and the Role of Law

HEATHER CONWAY AND GERARD KELLY

I. Introduction

While advances in healthcare technology have increased life spans in the twenty-first century, biological death remains an inescapable reality for all of humankind. One enduring consequence is the dead body – the physical matter that must be dealt with in the interests of public health and respect for the dead. While burial and cremation have traditionally dominated the funeral landscape,[1] new technologies such as alkaline hydrolysis and natural organic reduction offer different ways of dealing with the dead in the twenty-first century.[2] Actively promoted as offering increased consumer choice[3] and – more importantly – as more environmentally sustainable options,[4] these emerging 'funerary methods'[5] are the subject of this chapter.

[1] Though the popularity of each method has fluctuated over time – see DJ Davies, *A Brief History of Death* (Blackwell Publishing, 2005) 49.

[2] Another option, around since the 1960s, is cryonic preservation where legally dead individuals are frozen in liquid nitrogen in the hope of successful future reanimation. We are not considering this option, because the body is preserved rather than transformed.

[3] GM Robinson, 'Dying to Go Green: The Introduction of Resomation in the United Kingdom' (2021) 12 *Religions* 97 and J O'Keeffe, Alternative Disposition Services: Green Burial, Alkaline Hydrolysis and Human Composting (National Collaborating Centre for Environmental Health (NCCEH) (Canada), 19 April 2023) recompose.life/faqs/what-happens-to-diseases-during-human-composting/, but Reid and Kemmis caution that approaches to legalisation could also inhibit consumer choice: CD Reid and B Kemmis, 'Killing the Funeral Industry: The Problem with States' Piecemeal Approach to Legalizing Alternative Methods of Disposition' (2024) 59 *Wake Forest Law Review* 997, 1006.

[4] As part of an ongoing, and increasingly global, debate surrounding more sustainable death styles see eg R McManus (ed), *The Sustainable Dead: Searching for the Intolerable* (Cambridge Scholars Publishing, 2022) and TD Marsh and JL Whalley, 'An Eco-Conscious Farewell' (2024) 59 *Wake Forest Law Review* 941.

[5] The term 'funerary method' as used here denotes the particular dispositive process applied to the dead body, regardless of any attendant funeral rites. The term has recently been promoted by the Law

Both alkaline hydrolysis ('AH') and natural organic reduction ('NOR') can be summarised briefly. The former involves placing the dead body in a steel container, with water and a strong alkaline compound that is warmed to a moderate temperature; over several hours, the organic material dissolves away, and the end product is a sterile liquid and bones that can be reduced to a fine powder and returned to the deceased's family (much like post-cremation ashes).[6] NOR – sometimes referred to as 'human composting' – involves placing the body into a specially designed vessel along with other organic materials (eg, woodchips, straw). With temperature and humidity levels optimised to accelerate natural decomposition, bacteria and other micro-organisms break down the body over several weeks creating a nutrient-rich soil used for compost or other regenerative purposes.[7]

The question of how individual legal systems respond to these new funerary methods raises a number of significant issues that have not been probed in any meaningful sense, and are the subject of this chapter. In Section II, we examine the legal status of these new methods, and identify how different jurisdictions are legislating for both AH and NOR to affirm their legality. More pertinently, our discussion posits a new line of inquiry by moving beyond the content of said legislative frameworks to interrogate the fundamental – if slightly more speculative – question of what purpose these laws actually serve, and the limits of legislative validation when it comes to consumer uptake. Section III locates our evaluation within the broader framework of sustainability and climate concerns, given the prominent environmental narrative that underpins both AH and NOR. It reflects on the contested nature of sustainability as it relates to funerary methods, and the scope and limits of the state's role in encouraging more environmentally friendly ways of dealing with the dead. Section III further argues that law's role in achieving the desired environmental shifts that are driving these new technologies will be necessarily more limited.

This chapter points to the existence of a hitherto unacknowledged analytical void, setting the scene for a broader research agenda that sits at the interface of law and policy. In doing so, it necessarily looks beyond law, and adopts an interdisciplinary approach to inform our argument. Two points must be borne in mind. First, we use English law as a convenient staging post for the chapter, though other jurisdictions are grappling with the same issues, and the chapter draws on legal developments and authorities from elsewhere as appropriate. Second, most of the research-base and our consequent discussion is informed by

Commission of England and Wales in its *Burial, Cremation and New Funerary Methods* project, as a means of avoiding phrases such as 'disposal of the dead' which might be considered offensive: for example, see Law Commission of England and Wales, *Burial and Cremation: Consultation Paper* (No 263, October 2024) paras 1.142–1.144.

[6] D Cirigliano, 'A Comparative Analysis of Contemporary Methods of Final Disposition' (2024) 14 *Open Journal of Applied Sciences* 1762, 1764. The body of anti-apartheid campaigner Archbishop Desmond Tutu, at his own request, underwent alkaline hydrolysis after his December 2021 funeral service in Cape Town, South Africa.

[7] ibid 1763–64.

methods and practices across western societies with socio-cultural contexts that may not apply universally.

II. The Legal Challenges Posed by New Funerary Methods

English law – like other jurisdictions – has a vast and complex doctrinal framework for dealing with the bodies of the recently deceased.[8] A reflective assessment points to what we might describe as a somewhat 'laissez faire attitude':[9] in particular, legislation only tends to materialise when circumstances necessitate a more interventionist approach. For instance, a raft of burial laws enacted up to and during the nineteenth century was driven by overcrowding in urban cemeteries and the unsanitary conditions that this produced.[10] The Cremation Act 1902 was primarily a response to the famous case of *R v Price*[11] and the lobbying efforts of the Cremation Society to ensure that cremation could be carried out legally in Britain.[12] Fast forward almost 120 years, and emergency measures authorised by the Coronavirus Act 2020 imposed sweeping restrictions on funerals to reduce the risk of virus spread during the coronavirus pandemic.[13]

In short, while there is a legislative history of the state acting in this space, it tends to be episodic and, more importantly, responsive: laws are driven by specific events or advances. Whatever legal structures are put in place for new funerary methods[14] is simply another example of this, albeit framed within a much wider narrative of how law responds to technological innovation. There is a wealth of literature on this subject,[15] and it highlights a number of recurring themes. These include legal uncertainties surrounding whether new technologies (and the issues they raise) are covered by existing laws; whether new laws are needed; and prevailing legal structures being insufficiently dynamic alongside the generally slow pace

[8] See generally H Conway, *The Law and the Dead* (Routledge, 2016).

[9] J Rugg, 'Nineteenth-Century Burial Reform in England: A Reappraisal' (2021) 16 *Histoire, médecine et santé* 79, 80. Though describing attitudes towards burial, Rugg's comments have a wider reach.

[10] See eg ME Hotz, 'Down Among the Dead: Edwin Chadwick's Burial Reform Discourse in Mid Nineteenth Century England' (2001) 29 *Victorian Literature and Culture* 21.

[11] *R v Price* (1884) 12 QBD 247. We return to the decision in *Price* below.

[12] See P Jupp, *From Dust to Ashes: Cremation and the British Way of Death* (Palgrave Macmillan, 2005).

[13] See H Conway, 'Death Rites Disrupted: Coronavirus, "Lockdown" Laws and the Altered Social Ritual of the Funeral' (2023) 74 *Northern Ireland Legal Quarterly* 211.

[14] We discuss the specifics immediately below.

[15] For a flavour, see LB Moses, 'Recurring Dilemmas: The Law's Race to Keep Up with Technological Change' (2007) *University of Illinois Journal of Law, Technology & Policy* 239; R Brownsword and K Yeung (eds), *Regulating Technologies: Legal Futures, Regulatory Frames and Technological Fixes* (Bloomsbury Publishing, 2008); and GE Marchant, *The Growing Gap Between Emerging Technologies and the Law* (Springer Netherlands, 2011).

of legislative change. The question of how law deals with new funerary methods speaks to all these themes, with the added complication that the subject-matter is human remains.

A. Legislating for New Funerary Methods

At the time of writing, law-makers in England and Wales, and in Scotland, are grappling with this question of how to regulate AH as a new funeral option that is now available to consumers (albeit not very widely).[16] The legal position is more advanced elsewhere, especially in the United States where both AH and NOR are currently available and legislated for in a growing number of states with new laws actively progressing in others.[17] The dominant approach has been to accommodate these new methods – and AH in particular – within a revised and more expansive definition of cremation.[18] Of course, new technologies often raise the question of whether they also require legal innovation, or can be dealt with under existing legal rules;[19] and new funerary methods are no different. The latter option has certain advantages here. We could point to legislative efficiency (there is, as Tekle notes, 'little need to construct additional regulatory infrastructure'[20]), and laws that are reassuringly familiar for those who apply and interpret them.[21]

[16] The current focus tends to be more on AH, given that it is well beyond the developmental stage and facilities already exist in the north of England. As part of its ongoing *Burial, Cremation and New Funerary Methods* project, the Law Commission of England and Wales is considering what appropriate regulatory frameworks might be put in place for AH and also NOR – see New Funerary Methods – Law Commission, lawcom.gov.uk/project/new-funerary-methods/. This has now been followed by a consultation paper: Law Commission of England and Wales, *New Funerary Methods: Consultation Paper* (No 272, June 2025). Meanwhile AH looks set to be regulated in Scotland, following the Scottish Government's consultation on 'Regulation of Alkaline Hydrolysis in Scotland' and subsequent consultation analysis report published in April 2024, see Alkaline Hydrolysis (Water Cremation) Regulation: Consultation Analysis Report, www.gov.scot/publications/scottish-governments-consultation-analysis-report-regulation-alkaline-hydrolysis-scotland-water-cremation/.

[17] AH is now legally available in more than half of all the US states and NOR in almost a quarter-see respectively GM Robinson, 'Alkaline Hydrolysis and Its Affordances' (2025) *Mortality*, DOI: 10.1080/13576275.2024.2445852, p 2 and Tracker: Where Is Human Composting Legal In The US? – Earth, earthfuneral.com/resources/tracker-where-human-composting-legal/.

[18] Tekle notes that this is the dominant approach with AH (see AM Tekle, 'Have a Scoop of Grandpa: Composting as a means of Final Disposition of Human Remains' (2016) 3 *Savannah Law Review* 137, 153–54, and see Fla. Stat. § 497.005 passed in 2021 for a more recent example) though isolated examples exist for NOR (see eg Assembly Bill 289 in Nevada, and effective January 2024). The alternative approach incorporates AH and NOR into existing burial and cremation laws but as separate and distinct methods of dealing with human remains. This is less common with AH (Tekle, 154–55) but more common with NOR (see eg Bill HB612 in Delaware (effective May 2024)).

[19] See eg D Friedman, 'Does Technology Require New Law' (2001) 25 *Harvard Journal of Law & Public Policy* 71.

[20] Tekle (n 18) 154.

[21] Of course, this assumes that prevailing burial and cremation laws are 'fit for purpose', and can easily subsume these new methods.

On the other hand, legislative assimilation downplays the technological variances between new and existing funerary methods,[22] and the very distinct regulatory issues posed by the former such as the effluent produced in AH.[23] There are also questions around data collection: eg the need to formally record which funerary method is chosen for death registration purposes, and to compile accurate statistics around consumer choice to inform both the funeral industry and government policy in future systems planning for death-related infrastructure. This may be more challenging where statutes simply treat new methods as variants of cremation, an approach that Reid and Kemmis decry as 'ineffective'.[24] Another potential danger is confusing consumers who have an established view of what cremation involves, and should know that what they are choosing is a technologically distinct process (not simply a supposed variant of cremation).[25]

Moving from a necessarily broad sweep of this revised legal landscape to closer inspection of the content of the actual laws, there is nothing particularly radical to note beyond legislative capture of the methods themselves. While the specifics of the relevant laws differ, they display a number of commonalities, reflecting embedded traits in burial and – more notably – cremation statutes. What we tend to see is a set of provisions that, having defined the relevant technological process(es), deals predominantly with its administrative and operational aspects, alongside any regulatory or licensing requirements. The result is value-neutral legislation that, blandly but unsurprisingly, sets out the 'rules of the road'. However, perhaps the more pertinent question – and the one that tends to be overlooked in the limited legal discourse around these new methods – is what *functions* laws governing AH and NOR actually serve.

[22] Both definitional purists and elements of the funeral sector would almost certainly rebuff the idea that AH and NOR are simply variants of cremation.

[23] 'Another reason to maintain the statutory barrier between conventional flame-based cremation and alkaline hydrolysis is that the latter produces an effluent that ends up in wastewater plants' – Tekle (n 18) 155. Legislation aside, both AH and NOR will invariably require bespoke licensing arrangements; we touch on these briefly below.

[24] Legalising AH and NOR by simply broadening the definition of cremation – while declining to specifically regulate each of the new processes encompassed by the broadened definition of cremation – is an ineffective response to these technologies: Reid and Kemmis (n 3) 1000. The authors argue that these new methods should have distinct definitions and regulatory schemes. The provisional view of the Law Commission of England and Wales, as set out in its June 2025 consultation paper, is that new funerary methods such as AH and NOR should be defined and regulated separately from existing methods: Law Commission of England and Wales (n 16).

[25] This may be more of a marketing issue (when AH is described as 'flameless' or 'water' cremation), though one assumes that law would not want to be in any way complicit in potentially misleading consumers. For a flavour of how issues might arise over the advertising of AH (even though it was not found to be misleading on the facts), see *11449 v Registrar, Funeral Burial and Cremation Services Act, 2002* 2019 CanLII 51329 (ON LAT- Ontario License Appeal Tribunal).

B. Legality, and Reflections on the Role (and Limits) of Law

An obvious response is that they legalise these new methods, hence the steady passage of laws across the United States and the positioning of this topic high up the law reform agendas of other countries- including England and Wales, and Scotland, as noted immediately above. The absence of specific legislation clearly casts doubt on whether AH and NOR are lawful ways of dealing with the recently deceased; but it does not automatically result in them being illegal as the late nineteenth century English case of *R v Price*[26] so vividly demonstrated in the context of cremation. Eighty-four year old Dr William Price was a physician and self-styled Archdruid of Wales, as well as a fervent cremationist. When his five-month-old son died, Price carried the body to one of his fields and set it alight inside a ten-gallon cask of petroleum. Locals who arrived on the scene extinguished the flames and Price was arrested. There were no cremation statutes in place in England at the time, and the question before the court was whether it was a common law misdemeanor to burn a dead body instead of burying it. Stephen J held that it was only a misdemeanor if the impugned act amounted to a public nuisance. On the matter of burning the body, the judge was emphatic:

> It may be that it would be well for Parliament to regulate or to forbid the burning of bodies, but the great leading rule of criminal law is that nothing is a crime unless it is plainly forbidden by law.[27]

Price's actions were clearly an exercise in 'test[ing] the law's silence'[28] on cremation. However, the ruling in the case is described as 'still [being] an authority about the permissibility of other – indeed of any – means of dealing with dead bodies.'[29] The working assumption would therefore be that new funerary methods such as AH or NOR may go ahead in a particular jurisdiction unless they are otherwise prohibited.[30] They would also have to be fully compliant with other generic legal requirements such as health and safety, public health, planning and environmental laws.

[26] *Price* (n 11).
[27] *Price* (n 11) 256.
[28] Tekle (n 18) 152.
[29] S White, 'A Burial Ahead of its Time? The Crookenden Burial Case and the Sanctioning of Cremation in England and Wales' (2002) 7 *Mortality* 171, 171.
[30] In other words where a particular jurisdiction lists specific ways of dealing with the dead which does not incorporate these new methods, or has passed legislation banning either AH or NOR. However, legislation that appears amenable to a wide interpretation may not be construed as incorporating AH or NOR as a funeral director in Ohio discovered. Having purchased the necessary equipment, Jeff Edwards offered AH to his customers believing it to be compatible with an Ohio statute that permitted disposition of human remains by 'burial, cremation, or other manner of final disposition'. Despite the wording of the legislation, and the fact that AH was not expressly prohibited in Ohio, a court held that only burial and cremation were approved methods in the state- see *Edwards Funeral Serv. v State*, No. 11CVH03-3772, 2011 Ohio Misc. (Ct. Com. Pl. Oct. 12, 2011) discussed in Reid and Kemmis (n 24) 998–99.

Of course, in the same way as *Price* was followed by the Cremation Act 1902 with its stated aim to 'regulate the burning of human remains',[31] legislation has either been passed or is being actively considered to incorporate AH and NOR. This is important, and not just as a means of formal validation- what we might describe as a shift from a status of non-illegality to lawfulness. Within the parameters of legality, the bigger problem is that- in the absence of legislation- new funerary methods are permissible but *unregulated*, hence the need to fill this particular legal void. From an industry perspective, companies developing these new methods have the necessary legal architecture to offer them to consumers with confidence, and to invest further in their technologies.[32] Meanwhile, burial and cremation providers are assured of regulatory parity in that AH and NOR are being held to similar operating standards.[33]

From a consumer perspective, legislation has an equally important role to play. Perhaps we are guilty of ideological bias in the absence of empirical grounding, but one suspects that there is a normative expectation – amongst the public at large – that these new methods are both lawful *and* being held to specific (suitably high) legal standards.[34] This is what is required for any technological innovation that deals with human material,[35] but for new funerary methods there is a public health element – linked to the broader welfare of society – that demands assurances that the relevant processes are sanitary and do not pose a health hazard to the living. Legislation also creates enforcement capability; legal recourse is available if the regulatory frameworks surrounding AH and NOR are not adhered to.

This benchmark of legality and all that goes with it is important. To what extent it might influence consumer perceptions of both AH and NOR – and their consequent uptake – is a much more speculative question that is beyond the scope of this chapter. For now, we simply offer a number of general observations. First and foremost, the legal rubric surrounding these new methods is permissive rather than prescriptive. The legislation (just like burial laws and cremation laws when they were first enacted) is not mandating or encouraging uptake of AH or NOR; it is, as we have noted, process-driven and value-neutral in terms of the method

[31] Title and Introductory Text to the 1902 Act. The Act applied to England, Wales and Scotland; it was later extended to Northern Ireland by what was then s 26 of the Belfast Corporation (General Powers) Act (NI) 1948.

[32] Initiating its *New Funerary Methods* project, the Law Commission of England and Wales makes the point that '[s]takeholders have told us that they want a regulatory framework so that they can operate securely and conscientiously, unlock investment, and offer greater consumer choice' – New Funerary Methods – Law Commission, lawcom.gov.uk/project/new-funerary-methods/.

[33] This is borne out by the Scottish Government's consultation analysis report on the regulation of alkaline hydrolysis (n 16) which suggests that regulatory parity with other funerary methods (and cremation in particular) is important for the funeral sector.

[34] Support for this can again be found in the Scottish Government's April 2024 consultation analysis report on the regulation of alkaline hydrolysis (n 16), which showed strong support for introducing legislation – across the funeral sector <u>and</u> from members of the public who responded to the consultation.

[35] An obvious comparator is assisted reproduction- see eg M Brazier, 'Regulating the Reproduction Business' (1999) 7 *Medical Law Review* 166.

itself. Thus AH and NOR are very much a matter of personal choice, and it is highly questionable whether the state – in passing laws of this nature – could mandate specific funerary methods, much less whether it actually has an interest in doing so.[36] Second, and following on from this, the more pertinent issue is likely to be the signaling effect of laws governing AH and NOR, and whether these might incentivise new types of consumer behaviour even if said laws are agnostic about uptake.[37] We return to this briefly in Section III when we discuss the limits of law in influencing uptake of new methods in the context of broader sustainability considerations. As an aside, the passage of legislation may have an indirect 'promotional' effect due the inevitable publicity that this attracts. That said, publicity can be a double-edged sword, depending on the framing of the media narrative and how the new method is consequently implanted in the public mindset.[38]

Third, the uptake of new funerary methods will depend on a range of factors beyond their legality. Informing and educating consumers is essential,[39] alongside the availability of AH and NOR facilities as well as funeral costs.[40] Shifting public attitudes, however, away from burial and cremation is not straightforward. There will always be a time lag; as Robinson acknowledges, 'widespread funerary change takes time to become actualised', and not just because of 'availability and accessibility.'[41] Attitudes to funerary rituals are 'often bound to tradition and resistant to change',[42] and new methods will take time to seep into the public consciousness. Canning et al also highlight 'religious and cultural norms' as being particularly significant 'given the influence of these in shaping consumer disposal practices and the likely acceptance of alternatives.'[43]

[36] For instance, during the coronavirus pandemic a draft version of the Coronavirus Bill (which preceded the Coronavirus Act 2020 in the UK) appeared to allow mandatory cremations to ensure systems were not overwhelmed in the event of a surge in deaths. The Bill was hastily amended, following a backlash from MPs and faith groups, see 'Emergency Coronavirus Legislation Altered after Muslim and Jewish Communities Raise Concern Over Forced Cremation' *The Telegraph* (23 March 2020).

[37] Though, perhaps the better view here is that – given the sensitivities around dealing with the dead and funeral choice – such laws must *appear* to be agnostic, even if the state did have some sort of vested interest in increasing uptake of new funerary methods as part of its environmental agenda. We return to this in Section III.

[38] For instance, when Co-Operative (one of the biggest players in the UK funeral market) announced plans to offer AH to customers in July 2023, one particular term was coined in several newspaper headlines: see eg '"Boil in a Bag" Funerals to Become Available in Britain' *Daily Mail* (2 July 2023); '"Boil in the Bag" Environmentally Friendly Funerals Arrive in the UK' *The Guardian* (2 July 2023).

[39] Arnold et al stress the need for a clear, coherent and attractive narrative surrounding the technology in order to appeal to the public and a global marketplace, see M Arnold, T Kohn, B Nansen and F Allison, 'Representing Alkaline Hydrolysis: A Material-Semiotic Analysis of an Alternative to Burial and Cremation' (2024) 29 *Mortality* 447.

[40] In the UK, funerals costs are at an all-time high: Funeral Costs – Cost Of Dying Report 2025 (SunLife), www.sunlife.co.uk/over-50-life-insurance/funeral-costs/.

[41] Robinson (n 17) 5.

[42] C De Spiegeleer, *Secularization and the Modern History of Funerary Culture in Europe Conflict and Market Competition Around Death, Burial and Cremation* (Amsterdam University Press, 2019) 170.

[43] L Canning, I Szmigim and C Vaessen, 'Consumer Acceptance of Radical Alternatives to Human Disposal: An Examination of the Belgian Marketplace' in S Dobscha (ed), *Death in a Consumer Culture* (Routledge, 2016) 228, 229.

Religious and cultural objections to AH and NOR have been voiced,[44] and are neither influenced nor diminished by the legality of the methods. More generally, there may be concerns around the dignity of the dead[45] and the aesthetics of what each process entails (the so-called 'ick' factor[46]) that sit outside the bounds of legality.

Legislating for these new methods is an important legitimising tool, that allows AH and NOR to take their place alongside burial and cremation. We now turn to the broader framework of sustainability and climate concerns, and how this might influence consumer choice.

III. The Sustainability of Funerary Methods and the Role of Law

Writing almost 20 years ago about the work of the modern funeral industry in western societies, Harris observed that:

> [T]he once simple and natural act of laying our dead to rest has been transmogrified into a large-scale industrial operation that, like any other manufacturing process, requires the inputs of vast amounts of energy and raw materials and leaves a trail of environmental damage in its wake.[47]

In recent years there has been a growing awareness of the environmental impact of funerals – what Rumble et al describe as a 'new ecological mentality [that] is increasingly framing the management of all the dead.'[48] We are living in a climate emergency; and the recently deceased have a role to play through more sustainable funeral practices.[49] Both AH and NOR are new technologies that are often championed as more environmentally friendly funerary methods. The discussion that follows situates them within a discourse of sustainability and the current governance landscape around funerary methods more generally.

[44] For an overview in respect of AH, see GM Robinson, 'Dying to Go Green: The Introduction of Resomation in the United Kingdom' (2021) 12 *Religions* 97. The Catholic Church has come out strongly against both AH and NOR, see eg K Lasnoski, 'Are Cremation and Alkaline Hydrolysis Morally Distinct?' (2016) *The National Catholic Bioethics Quarterly* 233. In contrast, the Church of England appears more receptive to both AH and NOR, 'Church of England May Allow Human Composting and Water Cremation' *The Independent* (7 February 2023).

[45] See eg G Scarre, 'Alkaline Hydrolysis and Respect for the Dead: An Ethical Critique' (2025) 30 *Mortality* 273.

[46] VJ Haneman, 'Alkaline Hydrolysis' (2021) 47 *ACTEC Law Journal* 55, 58.

[47] M Harris, *Grave Matters: A Journey through the Modern Funeral Industry to a Natural Way of Burial* (Scribner, 2007) 5.

[48] H Rumble, J Troyer, T Walter and K Woodthorpe, 'Disposal or Dispersal: Environmentalism and Final Treatment of the British Dead' (2014) 19 *Mortality* 243, 243.

[49] See eg C Nosi, A D'Agostino, F Ceccotti and F Sfodera, 'Green Funerals: Technological Innovations and Societal Shifts Toward Sustainable Death Care Practices' (2024) 207 *Technological Forecasting and Social Change* 123644.

A. Funerary Methods and the Contours of Sustainability

The concept of sustainability has gained significant popular and political attention, particularly in recent years as the climate emergency unfolds. Yet the concept remains innately complex, broad, and multidisciplinary.[50] At its core, sustainability captures the notion that future generations should inherit the Earth in such a way that they are no worse off than generations today.

To chart the boundaries of sustainability as it relates to funerary methods, it is helpful to first consider the counterpoint: the (extent of the) negative environmental impacts of traditional methods.[51] It is often observed that the actual and potential environmental effects of burial and cremation are well documented, but such evaluations are also jurisdiction-specific: as Keijzer has observed 'the standard procedures and environmental norms of both burial and cremation can differ amongst countries'.[52]

Traditional burial involving interment within a cemetery, burial ground, or graveyard requires considerable resources to produce coffins and headstones. In the UK 85 per cent of coffins are made from particle board.[53] Artefacts like metal fittings can contain heavy metals, whilst coffin handles may be made from single use plastic.[54] The materials used to line the coffin and clothe the deceased often include barely degradable polyester, whilst headstones are frequently made of non-biodegradable materials, such as granite. The environmental hazards arising from substance release or accumulation are often much less clear. Indeed, some scholars have observed that cemeteries are 'best interpreted as special kinds of landfill'.[55]

Unlike traditional burial, cremation does not require the preservation, potentially in perpetuity, of burial grounds.[56] Nonetheless, the environmental credentials

[50] AB Damico, JM Aulicino and J Di Pasquale, 'What Does Sustainability Mean? Perceptions of Future Professionals across Disciplines' (2022) 14 *Sustainability* 9605.

[51] AC Forstmann, GE Martin, M Valdez Orezzoli, JY Zu and M Heitmayer, 'Sustainable Death: Promoting Adoption of Green Passing' (2023) 15 *Sustainability* 4082, 2.

[52] For example, differences in air pollution standards and/or permissible mercury emissions: see E Keijzer, 'The Environmental Impact of Activities After Life: Life Cycle Assessment of Funerals' (2017) 22 *The International Journal of Life Cycle Assessment* 715, 728.

[53] Environmental Stewardship Group, 'Climate Change, Our Legacy? Reflections on the State of the Bereavement Sector and the Climate Emergency' (*Environmental Stewardship Group*, September 2021) assets.website-files.com/60377e04191a1fe9c269e15e/61b76943563af05b02adba7f_ESG%20REPORT%202021.pdf.

[54] ibid: according to the Environmental Stewardship Group, 3,000,000 single use plastic coffin handles are used annually.

[55] BB Dent, SL Forbes and BH Stuart, 'Review of Human Decomposition Processes in Soil' (2004) 45 *Environmental Geology* 576.

[56] In the UK, the reuse of graves has historically been less common, though this is changing. Section 5 of the Highgate Cemetery Act 2022 provides that the burial authority may disturb or authorise the disturbance of human remains interred in a grave in the cemetery for the purpose of increasing the space for interments in the grave or conserving the cemetery, but only inter alia if they have been interred for a period of not less than 75 years. This can be contrasted with Greece where, due to severe overcrowding in major urban centres, it is common for remains to be disinterred 'after three to five years when family members are forced to face (often un-decayed) (sic) remains of loved ones': see

of this method are the subject of increasing scrutiny. The principal environmental concerns regarding cremation focus on the release of combustion gases (such as nitrogen oxides), heavy metals, and polychlorinated dibenzo-p-dioxins and dibenzofurans (PCDD/Fs), among other persistent organic pollutants (POPs).

The release of combustion gases into the atmosphere is recognised as a particular environmental concern associated with cremation. Eastwood, for example, has observed that cremating one body emits 400kg of CO_2 which is equivalent to taking a 500-mile round trip by car.[57] The range of potential environmental concerns associated with cremation as a funerary practice has led Robinson to conclude that '[w]hile traditional burial is more damaging to the environment than cremation, considering that cremation covers nearly 80% of UK funerals, in terms of relative scale, it poses a much bigger impact on the environment'.[58] Such assessments, of course, are highly jurisdiction-specific.

Mercury is another environmental pollutant emitted during cremation and crematoria have been identified as the largest single source for mercury emissions in the UK.[59] For this reason, some jurisdictions have acted to impose tightened environmental regulation concerning the release of mercury from crematoria. For example, the UK introduced a requirement for the cremation industry to remove mercury from 50 per cent of cremations and worked collaboratively with the industry to advance this target.[60] It would be misguided to conclude that the sustainability landscape governing funerary methods is static or, as McManus aptly puts it, 'adaptation is always happening'.[61]

The research base identifying and evaluating environmental risks associated with newer funerary methods such as AH and NOR is even more limited. AH is often advanced as 'an environmentally sound method of corpse disposal'.[62] Similar to cremation, it does not involve the land-locking of burial grounds and the gamut of environmental risks associated with traditional burial. Resomation Ltd, currently the UK's only manufacturer of AH equipment, emphasises that AH 'produces no airborne emissions and the solid leftover mercury-containing amalgam is collected and safely recycled.'[63] To this extent, AH potentially addresses the principal environmental concerns associated with cremation.

G Blagojević, 'Problems of Burial in Modern Greece: Between Customs, Law and Economy' (2013) 61 *Bulletin of the Institute of Ethnography SASA* 43.

[57] S Eastwood, 'Thinking Outside the Box: Can Education About the Environmental Impacts of Traditional Body Disposal Methods, and Communication of More Sustainable Alternatives Influence People's Body Disposal Decisions' in McManus (n 4) 93.

[58] G Robinson, 'Alkaline Hydrolysis in the United Kingdom' in McManus (n 4) 76, 83.

[59] Based on data compiled by the UK's National Atmospheric Emissions Inventory, Robinson has observed that cremation is responsible for 16% of the UK's mercury emissions: see G Robinson, 'Alkaline Hydrolysis in the United Kingdom' in McManus (n 4) 76, 83.

[60] This has been implemented in England by way of ministerial direction under statutory regulation: Environmental Protection (England) (Crematoria Mercury Emissions Burden Sharing Certificate) Direction 2010 which came into force on 18 March 2010.

[61] R McManus, 'Conclusion' in McManus (n 4) 170, 171.

[62] Robinson (n 58) 76, 87.

[63] Resomation Ltd, 'Saving Our Environment' resomation.com/about/saving-our-environment/.

However, AH also raises new and different environmental considerations, particularly as the climate emergency unfolds. AH requires approximately 1,500 litres per cycle, a very significant volume of water when compared with current average daily water use statistics.[64] There is, at this point, limited data to assuage concerns that such water usage represents a scalable and sustainable model, particularly if AH were to emerge in the coming years as a popular funerary method. Research modelling the potential environmental implications of expanded use of AH during periods of water use restrictions is also particularly scarce.[65] NOR is also advanced as 'using significantly less energy and resources' than other funerary methods.[66] Similar to AH, it does not require coffins or involve the release of combustion gases, but there is a dearth of research evaluating the benefits of human composting in comparison to more established funerary methods.[67] For public health reasons, however, it is recognised that NOR may not always be suitable. Recompose, an American company specialising in NOR, acknowledges that '[t]here are three rare diseases that disqualify a body from undergoing human composting: Ebola, prion diseases such as Creutzfeldt-Jakob Disease, and active tuberculosis'.[68] At this point, comprehensive evaluations of the potential environmental effects of 'new' funerary methods remains under-explored or unexplored.

Perhaps the most detailed evaluation completed to date has been a 2011 assessment by the Netherlands Organisation for Applied Scientific Research (TNO) which concluded that:

> The general conclusion regarding the environmental impact of the funeral technique for an average deceased in the Netherlands is that the total environmental impact is highest for burial followed by cremation …. The impact of resomation is (probably) lowest of all funeral techniques.[69]

However, it is also important to recognise that the choice of funerary method is but one element of the potential environmental impacts of funerals. Independent of the chosen method, the environmental impacts of a range of associated funerary

[64] Robinson (n 58) 88. This is not insubstantial: according to Water UK, the trade association for the water industry, the average person in the UK uses 142 litres of water a day compared with 121 litres in Germany. See Water UK, 'Vast majority of Brits have no idea how much water they use each day' (*Water UK: News*, 31 August 2020) www.water.org.uk/news-views-publications/news/vast-majority-brits-have-no-idea-how-much-water-they-use-each-day.

[65] For example, after a record-breaking hot summer in 2022, much of England and Wales was recovering from drought as late as November, with temporary use bans still in place in some areas: Water UK, 'Winter Water Resources FAQs' (*Water UK: News*, 11 November 2022) www.water.org.uk/news-views-publications/news/vast-majority-brits-have-no-idea-how-much-water-they-use-each-day.

[66] K Blinne, 'Compost Me: A More-Than-Humanifesto' (2025) *Mortality*, DOI: doi.org/10.1080/13576275.2024.2411610.

[67] J O'Keeffe, 'Alternative Disposition Services: Green Burial, Alkaline Hydrolysis and Human Composting' (National Collaborating Centre for Environmental Health (NCCEH) (Canada), 19 April 2023) recompose.life/faqs/what-happens-to-diseases-during-human-composting/.

[68] Recompose Ltd, 'What Happens to Diseases During Human Composting?' recompose.life/faqs/what-happens-to-diseases-during-human-composting/.

[69] E Keijzer and HJG Kok, 'Environmental Impact of Different Funerary Technologies' (The Hague, Netherlands Organisation for Applied Scientific Research (TNO), 2011) 54.

practices (eg, including preparation of the body, sending funeral cards, and any farewell ceremony) are 'much larger than the … burial techniques themselves'.[70] Consistently, Keijzer has observed that '[t]he climate change impacts of a funeral in comparison to the other activities during a person's life are … very small'.[71] Indeed, her research suggests that the carbon footprint of funerals is 97kg CO_2 equivalents per burial or 210kg CO_2 equivalents per cremation.[72] These are both less, for example, than the 227kg indicative CO_2 equivalents emissions of a round trip flight from London to Glasgow.[73]

B. Sustainability, and Reflections on the Role (and Limits) of Law

Current evidence suggests that the environmental impacts of funerary methods – whilst perhaps not negligible – are also not a basis for profound societal concern and, by extension, energetic governmental activity.[74] However, as Young has observed, 'as we move deeper into an era of human-dominated ecosystems, it is no longer appropriate to assume that human actions are relatively minor factors in the operation of macro-scale biophysical systems'.[75] It is ethically discomforting to acknowledge that a certain quotient of environmental harm is acceptable, such that it is not visible as 'harm'; that it is instead to be contained, rather than avoided.[76] As Nosi et al also emphasise, reducing the environmental impact of a funeral is important, partly due to an emerging concept of sustainability that 'encompasses the entire human existence'[77] – to which we would add the cumulative impact of what is currently almost 60 million deaths globally per year.

However, the surrounding legal landscape influencing funerary methods and their environmental effects is not static. In some instances, such as the release of mercury during cremations, legislative changes beyond the governance of funerary methods will sharply reduce any potential environmental ill effects. This is not to say that the state has – or should have – minimal interest in the regulation

[70] ibid 5.
[71] Keijzer (n 52) 728.
[72] ibid 727–28.
[73] UK Department for Transport, 'Journey Emission Comparisons: Indicative Dashboard' (*UK Department of Transport*, October 2023) maps.dft.gov.uk/journey-emission-comparisons-interactive-dashboard/index.html.
[74] At least not when compared to the wide range of human activities requiring urgent moderation and reduction to avert the prospect of potentially catastrophic climate change.
[75] OR Young, 'Governance for Sustainable Development in a World of Rising Interdependencies' in MA Delmas and OR Young (eds), *Governance for the Environment: New Perspectives* (Cambridge University Press, 2009) 12, 19.
[76] S Humphreys, 'Climate Justice: The Claim of the Past' in A Grear and C Gearty (eds), *Choosing a Future: The Social and Legal Aspects of Climate Change* (Edward Elgar Publishing, 2014) 134, 145.
[77] Nosi et al (n 49) 2. The authors invoke the concept of the 'sustainability mindset' advanced by Rimanoczy: see I Rimanoczy, *The Sustainability Mindset Principles: A Guide to Developing a Mindset for a Better World* (Routledge, 2020).

of funerary methods, but rather that the evidence suggests that the state's interest is unlikely to be shaped by urgent concern about the contribution of funerary methods to climate change or other environmental issues. Instead, it is likely that individual jurisdictions will continue to legalise new funerary methods based on a range of societal considerations, including social, cultural and economic. It is clear too that the presence (or absence) of some funerary methods from existing legal frameworks – for reasons not only related to sustainability – influences law reform.[78]

In many respects, the incremental pace of law reform to recognise new funerary technologies should not surprise us.[79] Francis Seymour Haden, writing in 1888, bemoaned the government's legislative inactivity on matters concerning the disposal of the dead:

> It is surely in every way surprising that, whilst providing by law for a better drainage, the prevention of floods, and the over-crowding of dwelling, we should, *unlike any other people in Europe*, have as yet made no provision for the larger and more serious question of the safe and proper disposal of the bodies of the dead.[80]

Much of the contestation and debate which surrounded the construction of new urban cemeteries and latterly cremation during the Victorian period is also evident in contemporary discussions concerning new funerary methods.[81] Moreover, as Jupp has observed, '[c]remation was not the obvious, natural or necessary successor to churchyard burial'.[82] This unpredictability around the potential popularity of funerary methods and the pace of societal uptake remains, and we see little evidence of a consistent state interest to shape or influence public preferences around funerary methods. To this extent, unlike governance experimentation in many environmental policy domains, the state does not appear to be either 'rowing' or 'steering' with respect to policy around funerary methods.[83] Instead, this remains a policy sphere where there is de minimis state intervention, much less regulation. This raises the question, what then is the role of the state as it relates to funerary methods?

[78] In Greece urban burial overcrowding was a significant factor in the legalisation of cremation in 2016, the last EU Member State to do so.

[79] The pedestrian pace of reform in this field is not unique to the UK. For example, Slabbert and Labuschaigne, considering legalisation of AH in the South African context, have observed that '[a]quamation is once again an example of technology developing faster than legislation' – M Slabbert and M Labuschaigne, 'Aquamation: Legal Nail in Burial and Cremation's Coffin?' (2021) 54 *De Jure Law Journal* 359, 369.

[80] FS Haden, *The Disposal of the Dead: A Plea for Legislation and a Protest Against Cremation*, 2nd edn (Bemrose & Sons, 1888) 14 (emphasis in original).

[81] Scholz suggests London's 'Magnificent Seven' suburban cemeteries were met with a chorus of protest and were much less influenced by public health reform than private profit: M Scholz, 'Over Our Dead Bodies: The Fight Over Cemetery Construction in Nineteenth-Century London' (2017) 43 *Journal of Urban History* 445. Separately, see Scarre (n 45) engaging with contemporary debates concerning AH.

[82] Jupp (n 12) 11.

[83] N Gunningham, 'Environment Law, Regulation and Governance: Shifting Architectures' (2009) 21 *Journal of Environmental Law* 179.

There is, at a minimum, an important role for the state by providing definitional guidance and, to the extent environmental concerns are relevant, enforcement capability.[84] In some areas of environmental law, the increasing diversity of governance arrangements often defies traditional hierarchical assumptions and the state/non-state binary with the state acting in concert with private actors and civic partners to advance its policy objectives. As discussed in Section II, the state, by explicitly legalising and defining new funerary methods, is conferring legitimacy on such methods, even whilst remaining agnostic as to whether any particular method is normatively preferable or superior.[85] In other words, we think that the inclusion of new funerary methods within the legislative menu of those explicitly recognised by law confers the state's imprimatur on the validity of those new methods: the law is recognising that they are as valid as other more societally-established funerary methods, and this has a signalling effect. Though beyond the scope of this chapter, there is an expansive literature to suggest that laws have an expressive function, and that this then contributes to shaping the context within which individual citizens make decisions.[86] This is true, even for value-neutral legislation – which we consider laws governing funerary methods to be – and, in particular, the new technologies that we have been discussing here.

Beyond the potential implications of formal legalisation, other factors are at play. First, as McManus and Schafer have observed, '[f]unerals demand that considerable material, emotional and symbolic expectations are met'.[87] Unless the funeral has been pre-arranged,[88] it could represent 'a classic "distress" purchase' with those involved 'hav[ing] little experience of arranging a funeral … and show[ing] a reluctance to shop around or seek out information'.[89] Second – and to re-engage with the theme of sustainability – there is now an increasing public awareness of the environmental consequences of individual lifestyle choices. This growth of ecological consciousness, particularly for those who pre-arrange their funeral, is likely to prove more impactful than the state's minimalist legislative approach. Yet the two are not disconnected: the state's far-reaching decarbonisation agenda advancing ambitious climate action across multiple policy domains

[84] Gunningham has identified three clear roles for the state: definitional guidance, participatory incentives, and enforcement capability. Given the state's agnostic position with respect to funerary methods – a position which we do not see as likely to change – participatory incentives are less relevant at this time. N Gunningham, 'The New Collaborative Environmental Governance: The Localization of Regulation' (2009) 36 *Journal of Law and Society* 145.

[85] We are reminded, by analogy, of the law's traditional approach to religion in charity law (prior to statutory reform in 2006) that '[a]s between different religions the law stands neutral, but it assumes that any religion is at least likely to be better than none': *Neville Estates Ltd v Madden* [1962] Ch 832, 853, per Cross J.

[86] C Sunstein, 'On the Expressive Functions of Law' (1996) 144 *University of Pennsylvania Law Review* 2021.

[87] R McManus and C Schafer, 'Final Arrangements: Examining Debt and Distress' (2014) 19 *Mortality* 379, 379.

[88] ibid 385.

[89] UK Office of Fair Trading (OFT), *Funerals: A Report of the OFT Inquiry Into the Funerals Industry* (OFT, 2001) 1.

has normalised the importance of sustainability.[90] Meanwhile, increasing public interest in funerary methods advanced as being more environmentally sensitive could 'raise the interest of policy makers in pushing for more sustainable ways of passing'.[91] It is reasonable to surmise that an individual's ecologically-influenced choices in life might also have an appreciable relationship to their preferred funerary method. Whilst such a potential link is under-researched, Nosi et al 'found that individuals' concern for the environment – resulting from an altruistic orientation – can be a significant predictor of their intention to adopt a green funeral'.[92] Incremental change influenced by individual altruistic motives represents a very different uptake trajectory to the 'fully fledged intervention' and 'communication campaign' promoting 'green passing' which Forstmann et al have advanced.[93] Such incremental change, however, would not be any more remarkable than historical shifts in the relative popularity of funerary methods. As Davies has noted, 'the emergence of cremation as a dominant mode of dealing with corpses in the UK has been one of the most remarkable pieces in the jigsaw of social change over the last century'.[94]

We see little evidence that the state will actively endorse a particular funerary method and, indeed, we see good reason why the state should choose to proceed with caution. First, the environmental impact of all funerary methods is not substantial when compared with the environmental impacts generated throughout an individual's life. Second, even if the state was inclined to advance a particular funerary method, recent legislative experience during the pandemic suggests that this would prove challenging to implement.[95] Given the very significant non-environmental considerations, the threshold for state intervention to direct policy in this field is much higher. However, advancing sustainability cannot be the province of governmental actors alone. Effective progress towards the fundamental transformation(s) which the climate emergency requires necessarily involves reframing the crisis at smaller scales. As Mathjissen has observed, '[i]n popular parlance we can witness an increasing use of terms like green, eco-friendly and environmentally-sustainable'.[96] It seems plausible that individuals sensitive to these considerations and the ecological impact of their choices during

[90] This is not universal: in a number of jurisdictions climate change remains a highly contested political issue and despite the long-settled consensus within climate science, reservoirs of scepticism exist: '[w]here climate policies are contested, as in the United States and Australia, this contestation is … more a question of reinvigorated opposition to climate change action per se.' M Paterson, 'Selling Carbon: From International Climate Regime to Global Carbon Market' in JS Dryzek, RB Norgaard and D Schlosberg, *The Oxford Handbook of Climate Change and Society* (Oxford University Press, 2011) 611, 618.

[91] Forstmann et al (n 51) 15.

[92] Nosi et al (n 49) 7.

[93] Forstmann et al (n 51) 15.

[94] DJ Davies, *Mors Britannica: Lifestyle and Death-Style in Britain Today* (Oxford University Press, 2015) 131.

[95] See n 36.

[96] B Mathijssen, 'Thiswordly Afterlives: The Religious, Biosocial and Ecological Sustainability of the Deceased' in McManus (n 4) 10, 116.

life might consequently be more likely to choose a funerary method which they believe aligns with those values.[97]

IV. Conclusion

New funerary methods, reliant on innovative technological processes, have now arrived on the deathcare scene. In many ways, the issues affecting both AH and NOR are the same as those with any new technology and raises familiar questions about the pace and manner in which law responds. However, new funerary methods also raise very distinct considerations, because of the subject-matter and the socio-cultural sensitivities around treatment of the dead. In this sense, interrogating funerary methods is a necessarily complex and multivalent interdisciplinary challenge.

From a legal perspective, law acts as an important legitimising tool in this new evolutionary phase of funerary methods, and one that is instrumental in laying the groundwork for uptake of these new methods. Both AH and NOR also arrive at a time of profound concern about ecological collapse and the potential for catastrophic climate change. Since so much of the discussion around these new methods is oriented around sustainability, any coherent understanding must be located within the context of the current climate emergency, and the scope for these innovative technologies to unlock ways to tackle the resultant challenges. As we have explored here, the role of law may be limited to legalising and defining these new methods, rather than steering fundamental change amongst funeral consumers. It is trite but true that only time will tell how impactful new technologies, such as AH and NOR, will prove to be.

[97] It is beyond the scope of this chapter, but the idea that ecological altruistic motives influence decision-making is resonant of Titmuss' research arguing that the UK's approach of reliance on voluntary blood donors based on altruism was more effective than the for-profit approach pursued in the United States. RM Titmuss, *The Gift Relationship: From Human Blood to Social Policy* (George Allen & Unwin Ltd, 1970).

9

The Digital Afterlife: Grieving Digitally After Death

MATTHEW GROVES AND PRUE VINES

I. Introduction

We are experiencing what has been described as the fourth industrial revolution.[1] The transformations occurring in this digital age have affected every part of society and the law is no exception. From a strict doctrinal point of view, the digital age should be unremarkable. The methodology of the common law is one of evolutionary adaptation. The common law approach does not simply allow for change; it is sustained by it. The classic conception of this process is 'one of incremental judicial development of legal principle to meet changing societal needs.'[2] Change can also occur in rapid steps or significant shifts, particularly when facilitated by new statutes. The role of statutes reflects the generally accepted view that the law of common law jurisdictions is a mixture of legislative and judicial choices that cause and respond to social change in equal measure.

Death is no exception. It has long been regulated by a mix of statute and judge made law, with differing levels of influence in differing aspects of this area. Succession law, in which for present purposes we include the rules governing funerals, burial and estate management, provides some useful illustrations of this blend. The law has long required that will makers possess sufficient mental capacity to make a valid will.[3] The rules governing capacity evolved in response to a greater understanding of mental health that arose from modern psychiatry.[4] In

[1] K Schwab, *The Fourth Industrial Revolution* (Penguin, 2017).

[2] This is how the Chief Justice of Australia described the approach of one of his predecessors: S Gageler 'The Coming Age of Australian Law' in B McDonald, B Chen and J Gordon (eds), *Dynamic and Principled – The Influence of Sir Anthony Mason* (Federation Press, 2022) 1.1.

[3] The leading modern case remains *Banks v Goodfellow* (1870) LR 5 QB 549. One reason that case remains relevant is that legislation governing capacity tends to assume capacity rather than define it: *Baker v Hewtson* [2023] EWHC 1145 (Ch) paras 11–50.

[4] A notable change was the slow judicial acceptance that the loss of capacity was not necessarily permanent and could change with suitable treatment. See, eg, *Timbury v Coffee* (1941) 66 CLR 277 (accepting that a chronic alcoholic could have periods of lucidity sufficient to have testamentary capacity).

recent years, more radical changes were sparked by legislation allowing courts to authorise wills made on behalf of people who lacked capacity.[5] These statutory or court authorised wills reflected a growing social acceptance that a legal solution was required for the rising number of people with dementia, brain injuries and other conditions. The inability of these people to meet common law capacity requirements was resolved with legislative intervention.[6]

One Australian judge recently suggested that such changes in succession law reflected 'seismic shifts' on social conceptions of personal autonomy, the increasingly 'transactional personal relationships' within families and changes to how we live and die within our wider community.[7] This chapter examines a novel aspect of that community – the digital afterlife. While digital living is deeply embedded into the lives of most people, digital death is not. Succession law has long focused on property in a narrow sense. A person's will serves to dispose of property that comprises their estate. The legal management of what is left behind has always had a narrow focus. Death always leaves behind grief which often motivates bitter disputes in succession law, but grief typically receives little direct attention in succession law disputes. That will change in the digital age because digital life has a feature that runs counter to the very purpose of succession law – an 'afterlife'. This chapter examines the legal, psychological and ethical implications of the legal afterlife and how grief might be assuaged or complicated by new technology.

II. What Happens After Death Now?

In the common law world, funerals and burials are largely outside the reach of a will. A will cannot, as a general rule, regulate the funeral or burial of its maker. The reason can be traced to a fundamental principle of property law. We may have autonomy over our own bodies, but we do not have ownership. A body cannot be owned and this cannot constitute property.[8] Testamentary instruments provide instructions to dispose the author's property. What is not property is beyond the grasp of a will. Several discrete threads flow from these first principle. Directions in a will about the funeral or burial of the will maker

[5] See eg *Wills Act 1997* (Vic), ss 21–30; *Succession Act 2006* (NSW), ss 18–26.

[6] Medical researchers have long argued that such changes mean the principles of *Banks v Goodfellow* should be revisited. See eg KI Shulman, CA Cohen and I Hull, 'Psychiatric Issues in Retrospective Challenges of Testamentary Capacity' (2005) 20 *International Journal of Geriatric Psychiatry* 63 and K Shulman, I Hull S Himal, C Peisah, S Amodeo and C Barnes, '*Banks v Goodfellow* (1870): Time to Update the Test for Testamentary Capacity' (2017) 95 *Canadian Bar Review* 251.

[7] Justice G Lindsay, 'Coping with Incapacity in a Legal Setting' (speech to the Succession Law Conference, Orange, NSW, 29 March 2025) 4, https://supremecourt.nsw.gov.au/documents/Publications/Speeches/2025-speeches/Lindsay_20250329.pdf.

[8] Unless it has been preserved through care and skill: *Doodeward v Spence* (1908) 6 CLR 406. This principle has slowly been chipped away in relation to reproductive tissue: K Falconer, 'Dismantling *Doodeward*: Guided discretion as the Superior Basis for Property Rights in Human Biological Material' (2019) 42 *University of New South Wales Law Journal* 32.

are not legally binding.[9] At the same time, however, the courts have recognised the power of executors to manage funeral burial arrangements.[10] That recognition conceals a contradiction. Funerals and burials cannot be determined by a will, yet the person placed in charge of the will also has de-facto control over them. We draw on two aspects of this problem from our jurisdiction of Australia to explain the function and obvious limits of these ad hoc principles.

Litigation about funeral and burial arrangements often narrows to one question – where should the deceased be buried? Many cases involve divorced or separated parents, who each seek the child be buried closer to where they live.[11] Other cases contain a cultural dimension. Many have wrestled with the appropriate burial place for an indigenous Australian person, which reflects the singular connection of indigenous people to 'country'.[12] The executor is normally the final arbiter of these questions but is expected to take account of cultural issues, the wishes of the deceased and their close family.[13] These cases have caused a subtle change in the apparent rigidity of the common law. Wills still cannot determine the funeral or burial of their author, *but* the person in charge of the will must consider the wishes of the deceased.[14] The extent of that consideration is unclear, but it must occur and can be reviewed by the courts.

A recurring feature of these cases is their urgency. Cases are lodged and resolved within days, usually with strong judicial encouragement because the wider community would regard 'fights over the disposal of human remains … as unseemly'.[15] That emphasis on speed and finality overlooks both the ongoing trauma of such cases and the potential that therapeutic jurisprudence offers to such cases.[16] This reflects the often narrow focus of the common law adjudicative method that limits courts to the problem at hand, the facts in dispute and so on. The ongoing nature of grief can be left unresolved, or perhaps even amplified, by judicial management of funerals and burials. The burial cases also reflect the reactive nature of much of the common law, in which existing principles are adapted

[9] In previous times, this rule served to defeat clauses that sought to spend the entire estate on an extravagant mausoleum for the will maker, while leaving the family of the deceased in poverty Directions of this nature usually contravene the rule against perpetuities, but carefully framed clauses that include a charitable purpose may be valid.

[10] *Smith v Tamworth City Council* (1997) 41 NSWLR 680. Where there is no will, courts will seek to identify the person most likely to be granted letters of administration: *Jones v Dodds* (1999) 73 SASR 328; *Burrows v Cramley* [2002] WASC 47, para 28.

[11] These parental disputes often continue well after the child has reached adulthood. See eg *Marschall v Elson* [2023] SASCA 1.

[12] *Calma v Sesar* (1992) 106 FLR 446; *Jones v Dodd* (1999) 73 SASR 328; [2020]. An illuminating study of Christian migrants in Europe found that similar questions arise elsewhere: A Hunter, 'Staking a Claim to Land, Faith and Family: Burial Locations of Middle Eastern Christian Migrants' (2016) 37 *Journal of Intercultural Studies* 179.

[13] *Smith v Tamworth City Council* (1997) 41 NSWLR 680.

[14] This approach becomes difficult when the evidence is either conflicting or incomplete.

[15] *Calma v Sesar* (1992) 106 FLR 446, 452.

[16] H Conway and J Stannard, 'The Honours of Hades: Death, Emotion and the Law of Burial Disputes' (2011) 34 *University of New South Wales Law Journal* 860, 895–96.

to new social norms. That approach is sensible when modest doctrinal steps are required.

Questions about the disposal of bodies and remains have been drawn into the courts. The leading Australian case on the disposal of ashes conceded that the rise in the number of cremations enabled courts to consider remedies that were previously inconceivable. A court would never order a body be divided, but it could order the division of ashes.[17] That finding was influenced by evidence of the growing practice of families members dividing ashes among close relatives.[18] As judges have become more familiar with disputes about human ashes, they have issued more novel orders that sometimes appear to mimic child custody orders.[19]

What happens when the doctrinal steps must be larger? In the previous chapter Heather Conway and Gerard Kelly discussed the changes in funerary methods which have developed in recent years. Our earlier mention of cremation viewed the practice narrowly. Questions about whether ashes should be divided or ordered to be handed over invite questions about what happens next. Traditionally ashes are scattered or buried in the ground or occasionally kept on the mantelpiece in an urn. The ashes which are scattered disappear; those that are buried leave a mark in the world which can be visited, and those kept in the urn may remain part of a household for a long time. A common thread in these practices is an acceptance that the transmutation of the live person into the dead person (who does not move or communicate) merges into the material world somehow and disappears. What eventually follows is the end of personhood except as a memory. It is much easier to conceive such changes, and also to manage them legally, when a physical thing such as ashes is present. That certainty will fragment in the digital age, where the physical body and digital identity are distinct. For those who die now or have died during this digital age, it may be that young people particularly may have a sense of identity which is different from the sense of identity which could exist when only the material world existed.

In one sense, digital life and digital grieving are unremarkable. The metaphysical has been part of human identity and thinking for centuries – religious identities, feeling that we can communicate with saints or ghosts (sometimes seen as a mark of insanity) or God has always existed. A common feature of the funeral and burial practices of different cultures and religions is the connection most create between rituals and healing, as well as their role in expressing collective respect for the dead and sympathy for those left behind.[20] The digital age is not necessarily metaphysical but for many it has a spiritual element that will very likely strengthen in the future. An early stepping stone in this journey has arguably

[17] *Leeburn v Derndorfer* (2004) 14 VR 100.

[18] *Leeburn v Derndorfer* (2004) 14 VR 100, para 31.

[19] *Maros v Luca* [2024] SASC 98 (order issued to give one family member permanent possession of ashes and to permanently prohibit others from ever taking possession of the ashes).

[20] H Yun Chan, 'Death, Burials and Funerals: Grieving in the Shadow of COVID-19' (2022) 3(2) *Amicus Curiae* (Series 2) 250, 254–57.

become widely accepted in plain sight. When people are unwell, it is common for relative and friends to maintain close contact remotely via social media, to check on the sick person, arrange their care and provide support to each other.[21] If our preparation for someone's death now has a digital dimension, the same will be true of the time after death, but the potential in the digital age to create new experiences involving the deceased is radical.

In the Anglo common law world the will, which is an expression of the deceased's wishes is regarded as the major dispositive instrument. Indigenous peoples have different customs to assist with grief after death.[22] In European legal systems the will may be less important and only apply to part or none of the estate. Grief manifests in multiple ways – in the Anglo-common law systems it is not uncommon for there to be a dispute within the family after the death of a person – sometimes after the reading of a will. Very often this dispute occurs because the destabilising effect of grief makes people make decisions they would not otherwise make and stirs up old feelings of loss or sibling rivalry[23] of various kinds, as well as greed. It is not too unkind to say that the law of succession has not been successful in emotionally healing these disputes. The memory of the dead, especially when it is a parent (and, as Conway notes, it is the death of the second parent that takes the child into uncharted territory)[24] may be affected by unequal distributions of inheritance and drive a dispute into extremely emotional territory because of the longstanding relationships and possible buildup of negative feeling which comes to a head when faced with a will which appears to favour another child. The death of the last surviving parent also forces a person to face their own mortality – they are in the 'front row' now. It is when facing the death of a loved one, that humans most need their other loved ones to support them, so the sibling disputes over inheritance are particularly painful. Sibling inheritance disputes in Australia are likely to lead to the largest levels of costs, apparently because plaintiffs are willing to run up costs to defeat the sibling regardless of the cost to themselves.[25] But the point is that death creates grief and can lead to serious disputes into which people who had not been disturbed by grief might not enter. That is, grief can destabilise people and make them vulnerable.

A widely known and troubling example of the digital afterlife can be taken from South Korea. A few years after her daughter Na-yeon died when aged seven,

[21] T Walter, *What Death Means Now – Thinking Critically About Dying and Grieving* (Bristol University Press, 2017) ch 8. Our habits of remotely monitoring the health of people and preparing for their deaths changed vastly during the COVID-19 pandemic.

[22] See eg K Glaskin, M Tonkinson, Y Musharbash and V Burbank (eds), *Mortality, Mourning and Mortuary Practices in Indigenous Australia* (Ashgate, 2008).

[23] H Conway, 'Where there's a Will: Law and Emotion in Sibling Inheritance Disputes' in H Conway and J Stannard (eds), *The Emotional Dynamics of Law and Discourse* (Hart Publishing, 2016).

[24] ibid p 35.

[25] P Vines, *Report:* Bleak House *Revisited? Disproportionality in Family Provision Estate Litigation in New South Wales and Victoria* (Australasian Institute of Judicial Administration Incorporated, 2011). Conway (n 23) 42 also discusses examples of people who have destroyed or dissipated estate property so no-one else can have it.

her mother was given the chance to speak with a digital avatar of Na-yeon. As with all innovative reality programs, the show provoked fascination and outrage in equal measure.[26] The difficulties that such an avatar could present to the grief and recovery of a parent are obvious,[27] but this avatar also gives life to the widely held view of many people that they can hear or speak to deceased relatives. The example of Na-yeon is quite different from the use of digital avatars of celebrities after their death. This growing practice is generally one of copyright that can easily be managed by an estate within existing laws. The creation of Na-yeon raises questions similar to the funeral cases but adds difficult new problems. If the body cannot be owned, what of its avatar? Can the creation of an avatar be ordered or prohibited by a court? We are fast approaching the time when an avatar cannot simply be created, but can also live beyond the age of its subject. Put simply, a future version of Na-yeon may grow to an adult. The more immediate possibility is that we may see the creation of avatars that can participate in their own mourning. We discuss the process of grieving digitally further below.

III. Grieving Digitally After Death

After someone dies there is normally a period of grief felt by those left behind. Grief is a significant part of the human experience which can apply to any loss, but here we will concentrate on grief after death. Funerals, funeral ceremonies and memorialisation of the deceased appear to be almost ubiquitous in every culture. All these things appear to be designed to relieve grief. It has been said that:

> The purpose of succession rules is to ease the passage of property from one generation to the next, and in doing so to also ease the monstrous fact of death in every life – the death the individual suffers which takes away everything and everybody else; and the response those left behind have to the loss of the person who has died, which includes the reminder that death will come for them too.[28]

Attitudes to death in the Western world have varied greatly over time,[29] but grief is perennial, whether it is borne stoically without mention or loudly cried into the street. Grief has been mediated by the refusal to contemplate death in much of the twentieth century in the Western world, and in other cultures and at other times

[26] An account of the show that includes comments from its creator, it discussed in L Gy-lee, '"Meeting You" Creator on his Controversial Show: "I hope it Opens Up Dialogue"' *Korea Times* (5 April 2020) www.koreatimes.co.kr/entertainment/shows-dramas/20200405/meeting-you-creator-on-his-controversial-show-i-hope-it-opens-up-dialogue-video.

[27] The program is discussed in F Fanti Rovetta and D Valentin, 'Grief and Virtual Reality: Continuing Bonds with Virtual Avatars' (forthcoming, 2025) 24 *Phenomenology and the Cognitive Sciences.*

[28] P Vines, 'Cultural Negotiation of Inheritance Law in Australia' in K Barker, K Falconer and A Fell (eds), *Life and Death in Private Law* (Hart Publishing, 2024) 217, 217.

[29] An enormous literature on this exists. See eg P Aries, *The Hour of our Death* (Random House, 1981); to E Kubler-Ross, *On Death and Dying* (Tavistock, 1970).

by complete acceptance that death is part of life. As noted above, the processes of disposal of the body (also regulated by the law of succession as well as public health laws) are not just ways of ridding ourselves of waste, but also expressions of grief and memorialisation of the deceased. Pearson observes, 'There is little that is purely functional in people's treatment of the corpse'.[30] For centuries in the west the treatment of the corpse and the various ways of memorialising it included showing the body, well-dressed and made-up in a coffin, then burying it and creating a tombstone or other memorials such as brooches holding a lock of the deceased's hair and so on. The memorial tombstone has varied from those with exhortations to passers by: 'See you there', engraved with a finger pointing upward, to expressions of love: 'fondly missed', and statements about the deceased's personality and achievements. At the same time, over the centuries the dead have been thought of as merely sleeping, as ghosts, or as completely absent – but the latter appears to be a phenomenon which has become more frequent in the twentieth century and may have accompanied the rise in cremation.[31]

The ways in which we are comforted in grief vary widely across cultures. Grief is painful and people relieve this pain through a range of rituals, for example, closing up the house, 'sitting shiva' for seven days if they are Jewish, holding funerals which include particular rituals such as burying the person facing Mecca, or the East to meet the Risen Christ. Funerals and tombstones have been discussed above. The will itself can be a communication from the dead to the living, depending on how it has been drafted. The Victorians kept locks of hair in necklaces and brooches as *memento mori*. People who were going to die wrote letters to their children to be opened years later, advising them about life. Poetry was written. Memorial poetry was common and continues to be so.[32] In the late nineteenth century photographs could be used for memorialisation when previously only drawing or painting could do.

But in our new digital world[33] we are seeing changes in funerals and in how people are remembering the deceased. It was a sudden shock to many people during the COVID lockdowns to find that they could not attend a funeral except digitally. Streamed funerals were better than nothing, but responses to the digital

[30] MP Pearson, *The Archaeology of Death and Burial* (History Press, 2003) 49.

[31] P Vines, 'Resting in Peace?: A Comparison of the Legal Control of Bodily Remains in Cemeteries and Aboriginal Burial Grounds in Australia' (1998) 20(1) *Sydney Law Review* 78 which notes the rise of protestantism's effect on perceptions of the dead and the concomitant change in attitudes to burial and cremation.

[32] See eg Alfred Lord Tennyson, 'Crossing the Bar', or C Harmer, 'Do Not Stand at My Grave and Weep', WH Auden 'Stop the Clock' and many others.

[33] For a significant time, smart media generally gave no more than a licence to the person using it. This generally ended with death, and many examples of people attempting to get access to a loved one's Facebook page or emails failed. For example, Whatsapp's contractual terms say, 'We grant you a limited, revocable, non-exclusive, non-sublicensable and non-transferable right to use our services …' Apple iCloud 's terms provide: 'Unless otherwise required by law … any rights to your Apple ID or Content within your Account terminate upon your death. Upon receipt of a copy of a death certificate your account may be terminated and all content within your account deleted.'

version indicated that people felt unsatisfied by it.[34] Of course this was a relatively unsophisticated way of having a digital funeral. The use of virtual reality and AI may reduce some of this discomfort. In some cases the deceased has determined how they wish to be represented at their funeral or for longer – perhaps by making a video of themselves speaking or, (in a more sophisticated digital process) by having an avatar created of themselves, using Artificial Intelligence (AI) to create a more-or-less authentic persona which can actually chat with mourners at the deceased's own funeral.[35]

Digital memorialisation is developing at a rapid pace. A range of ways to digitally memorialise the dead now exist. Indeed, there could be said to be a developing market in the digital management of grief.[36] A search on Bing for 'memorial poem for deceased daughter' brought 265,000 responses, suggesting a large appetite.[37] The fact that written material can be accessed easily on the internet is not an enormous change to ways of grieving. Memorial poetry is not new, but other new digital methods of 'memorialisation' also exist. For example, if a person who is a Facebook member has nominated a 'legacy contact' Facebook will allow the legacy contact to manage the page and create memorials on it. Facebook also has a 'Memorialised Account' which allows the next of kin to memorialise the process. This puts the word 'Remembering' before the name but does not allow any new connections. The account can't be changed, the dead person's social contacts are closed, and only existing friends can post. Another kind of memorial page can be set up which is open to the public. This is often done for celebrities and the public can post on these pages, often directly addressing the deceased. These different approaches to memorialisation reflect Meta's understanding of their clients' desires over the years since they first allowed memorialisation in 2007.

We have already mentioned the deceased who can speak at his or her own funeral, either by means of a simple video recording, or by the use of AI (perhaps by an avatar with which the funeral participants can converse), and the Virtual Reality creation of the deceased child made for the parent.[38] There are also sites which assist a dying parent to make a video or an AI avatar which can speak to the children at the time of their first date, marriage, first job etc. This is not very different from the letters dying parents have often written to their children to reach out to them at significant moments in their life. It is not very radical. As always with technology, the question is whether it radically changes the concept or simply transmutes the same thing into another form.

[34] T Morse, 'Digital Necromancy: Users Perceptions of Digital Afterlife and Posthumous Communications Technologies' (2024) 27(2) *Information, Communication and Society* 240.

[35] T Hollanek and K Nowaczyk-Basinska, 'Griefbots, Deadbots, Postmortem Avatars: on responsible application of generative AI in the Digital Afterlife Industry' (2024) 37 *Philosophy and Technology* article 63.

[36] ibid. See also B Nansen, T Kohn, M Arnold, L van Ryn and M Gibbs, 'Social Media in the funeral Industry: on the digitization of grief' (2017) 61(1) *Journal of Broadcasting and Electronic Media* 73.

[37] www.bing.com/search?q=memorial+poems+for+deceased+daughter&FORM=R5FD4.

[38] See above n 27.

Virtualgrave.eu is a virtual cemetery. The website explains:

> I. **We live as long as memory of us.**
>
> Think about your ancestors, think about what you know about them. Do you know their names, do you know when they lived, what they did, what kind of people they were. Few people can answer these questions. This does not mean, however, that the memory of them is dead. History is created by people whose memory should be preserved for future generations. In this virtual cemetery, we will survive to the end of human history thanks to the Internet, which will store information about us and our loved ones.
>
> II. **Virtual grave.**
>
> Death is an inevitable phenomenon. Relatives will build graves, monuments and tablets for the deceased. Our cemetery offers the possibility of visualizing memory in the form of tombs and epitaphs, as well as the possibility of lighting a candle or laying flowers, which proves the memory of loved ones who have died. We can bury our relatives in the Virtual Cemetery, just like in the real world, in single, double, family and catacombs. We can create a Virtual Cemetery where all our relatives, family and friends will be in one place, no matter where and when they lived, and where and when they died.
>
> III. Death is the only certain thing that will happen to us, and each day brings us closer to it. A living person, assuming a grave for himself, can plan his own obituary and mailing to the indicated addresses. This will allow the deceased to contact the world of the living and provide them with various information, often information that they did not pass on during their lifetime.
>
> IV. For an additional fee, the tombstone can be specially designed according to individual wishes in a form that does not resemble a tomb. This could be graphics, sound, or some other item that can be stored on the server.'

Virtualgrave.eu has a virtual cemetery and virtual catacombs for people, and a virtual animal graveyard. Fees are charged for the burial and tombstone. It also has a store where souvenirs such as virtual candles can be purchased. The pricelist gives prices for one day, 12 months, three years and forever. Findagrave.com allows people both to find real graves and to create their own virtual cemetery. Cemetery.org has been running since 1995. For a one-off fee of US$90 it provides:

> Each **custom-made memorial** has a (fixed) memorial page and a (changing) visitors' page.
>
> You may link memorials of **relatives** (see bottom of example), even **merge** memorials of partners (example).
>
> Your memorial may have a link to a **map** of the physical resting place (example).
>
> You may submit a **site photo** and information for display on the visitors page (example).
>
> We can supply a permanent **QR-Code** for display at the physical grave (example).

The proliferation of virtual cemeteries has now been joined by municipal Councils.[39]

[39] Federation Council in NSW announced a digital cemetery on 14 March 2025: www.federation-council.nsw.gov.au/News-Media/Council-launches-new-digital-Cemetery-Platform.

This memorialisation bears interesting characteristics. The memorialisation has become extremely public. It also appears to demonstrate a shift away from institutions such as churches and cemetery boards managing memorials to a highly individualised memorialisation which 'maintains the social presence of the dead'.[40] It has been argued that death is no longer separated from life and that 'twenty-first century societies are witnessing a new integration of the dead into everyday life.'[41] Digitally enhanced coffins are available with entertainment systems (music, videos) for visitors; as is 3D imagery for funeral urns, videos on You-tube as memorials and promises of 'forever'. The phenomenon of 'lurkers' and 'emotional rubberneckers' refers to profile harvesting of the dead by the living on Facebook, testament to the number of people visiting memorial sites despite having no connection with the deceased. Perhaps this is no different than walking through a cemetery in the material world.

The memorialisation websites may offer false promises of permanence. A virtual cemetery, Cherished Lives, only lasted from 2006 to 2009 when it disappeared from the net. The desire for digital memories is partly a desire for permanence, but in fact many digital sites disappear quite quickly. Digital phenomena get lost because of lost passwords or lack of access such as to photographs on the cloud or on a social media site. This can create anxiety in people who are very focused on their memorials.[42] Digital memorial sites are also relatively inaccessible to some people – the poor, sometimes the elderly, who may find it difficult to access the digital life and data of their loved one. A further difficulty is the desire of those left behind to access material used or deposited by the deceased, such as photos in the cloud or on mobile phones, in sites which are designed only for life.[43] We will discuss this further below.

Some people have been alarmed by some of these initiatives. For example, psychologists have asked whether grief might be complicated by some of these activities, particularly those which appear to assist the mourner in denying that the death has occurred. This has become an area of psychological interest. There

[40] B Nausen, M Arnold, M Gibb and T Kohn, 'The Restless Dead In the Digital Cemetery' in C Moreman and A David Lewis (eds), *Digital Death: Mortality and Beyond in the Online Age* (Hart Publishing, 2014) 129.

[41] T Walter, 'The Pervasive Dead' (2019) 24(4) *Mortality* 389.

[42] D Bassett, 'Bereaved who take Comfort from Digital Messages from Dead Loved Ones live in fear of Losing Them' *The Conversation* (13 March 2019) theconversation.com/bereaved-who-take-comfort-in-digital-messages-from-dead-loved-ones-live-in-fear-of-losing-them-109754.

[43] For example, TVNZ reported 11 June 2018: 'Grieving Widow unable to get photos off dead husband's iPhone and Apple won't unlock it for her!' Youtube: www.youtube.com/watch?v=UAklZEoul8A. The well-known case of *In Re Ellsworth* No 2005-296, 651-DE Mich Prob Ct 2005 in which the family of a US marine killed in action wanted log-in rights to his email account illustrates the problem of access to the deceased's digital material when relatives are grieving. Yahoo refused on the basis of contract and privacy. The family argued as heirs they should be able to access emails. However, the court refused to allow access. Rather, they ordered Yahoo to send a CD with the emails on it to the family. Courts have allowed the barriers to access to remain in many cases.

are concerns that such ways of attempting to comfort the griever may cause 'complicated grief', which is regarded as an abnormal condition compared with 'normal grief'. Complicated grief or traumatic grief/prolonged grief disorder/ persistent complex bereavement disorder was classified as a psychiatric disorder by the Diagnostic Statistical Manual-5 in 2013. Characteristics of the condition are 'intense yearning, longing or emotional pain, frequent preoccupying thoughts and memories of the deceased person, a feeling of disbelief or inability to accept the loss and difficulty imagining a meaningful life without the deceased person' for longer than 6 to 12 months.[44] It resembles acute grief but lasts longer and may cause further mental disorders. There is some disagreement that complicated grief exists, since it presumes there is such a thing as normal grief,[45] but it is reasonably well accepted as a concept in the mental health profession.[46] However, it is clear that people who are grieving, especially in the acute stage are very vulnerable to marketers of digital memorials and the like and may be at risk of being tipped into complicated grief.

IV. The Digital Person can be Immortal or Dead, Remembered or Forgotten – How Does this Affect Grief?

When a modern person dies, they leave digital fragments behind them which can persist or be made into new memorials. These include their emails, photographs, videos, blogs, mobile phone or other messaging, smart media pages and so on. Digital remains can be seen as extending the 'life' of a person. For example, AI can be trained on this material about a person so that it can respond in the same way that the person would have. As we have noted, this allows the digital person to converse with others, among other things. Microsoft has patented a system where the texts, emails and social media posts can be used to make a chatbot who sounds like the original person.[47] At present it is not

[44] S Nakajima 'Complicated Grief: Recent Developments in Diagnostic Criteria and Treatment' (2018) *Philosophy transactions of the Royal Society* B 373: 20170273, p 4.

[45] M O'Connor and E Kasket, 'What Grief Isn't: Dead Grief Concepts and their Digital Age Revival' in T Machin, C Bronlow, S Abel and J Gilmour (eds), *Social Media and Technology across the Lifespan* (Palgrave McMillan, 2022) 115, 119 argue that there is no evidence that there is a 'normal' way to grieve, but suggest that in the digital age some people who have grieved for celebrities and wished to memorialise them have accused digital platforms of 'blocking [access to platforms and therefore] denying ideal grieving'.

[46] Nakajima (n 44).

[47] P van Esch and Y Cui, 'Logging off Life but Living On: How AI is redefining death, memory and immortality' *The Conversation* (9 January 2025) theconversation.com/logging-off-life-but-living-on-how-ai-is-redefining-death-memory-and-immortality-246306.

possible to download a 'brain print' and so the level of authenticity of an AI person is still limited, but television series like 'Upload' in which a deceased person's brain patterns can be uploaded to an avatar in a digital world suggest it may not be as far off as we think.

Of course, in the past the dead also left things behind such as letters, jewellery, a lock of hair, printed photographs and so on. These were keepsakes which the grieving used to comfort themselves. How is digital data different? It is different because it is not corporeal and is not accessible by touch. Also, a corporeal item was more likely to be where the deceased had been, while digital data may be anywhere on the internet and is generally not accessible by touch.

For those left behind the digital world can appear to offer permanent memorials, and indeed in virtual cemeteries, as we discussed above, permanency is offered, but it must be acknowledged that digital data does disappear. This data may create a certain form of immortality, but it also may be allowed to decay or even be deliberately destroyed. And this may create other issues. From the point of view of those left behind these technologies might be comforting but they also might exacerbate grief. Those who are excluded may be very hurt:[48]

> When my son died I received no condolence cards … at his funeral his best friend told me there was a Facebook page … but I can't … I don't have a Facebook account … I feel left out and I don't know what to do about it.

Digital data in the form of avatars, Virtual Reality scenarios, cemeteries, memrial sites and so on may be damaging in supporting unrealistic connections with the dead. Avatars, digital messages and so on which are sent to people grieving at various times may startle and disrupt them, especially if they are unexpected. Safe Beyond sends messages from the deceased which are timed to arrive at significant moments in the receiver's life. Typically, this involves a person with a terminal illness paying to have these messages sent to their children on significant birthdays or significant life events. This can be alarming for the receiver.[49]

Digital data does disappear – this may happen because it is corrupted or has a bug which has not been corrected, but there are other ways in which things disappear. For example, music streaming on sites like Spotify allows the user to listen when they call it up. However, Spotify can change the version of a song, edit it or delete it to maximise their profit because few people wish to hear it. A grieving relative who listens to the song in a particular version because that is the one that is meaningful to them in relation to the deceased has no control over it, except through piracy or attempting to buy a CD which they can own. This also applies to videos, books and other things which are on streaming platforms. This is a product of the fact that these streaming services only offer a licence to the material. Digital data may also become inaccessible because the device to read it no longer

[48] D Bassett, 'The Changing Landscape of the Uncanny Valley and the Fear of Second Loss' (2021) 40 *Current Psychology* 813, 815.

[49] Nausen, Arnold, Gibb and Kohn (n 40).

exists – material on old software or, for example, on a floppy disc, may no longer be able to be viewed on a computer when it has been updated. Again, the griever may lose control of an item in a way that is less likely if it is corporeal. The constant changing of technology such as mobile phones means the permanence of data is reduced unless one can keep the old technology. As Bassett notes:

> Those who feel in control of the data: that is, those who have passwords or access to videos, messages, platforms and pages find comfort in the memories; while those who do not have [control] described feelings of disruption to their grief.[50]

There is evidence that where the griever has no control this can increase the likelihood of complicated grief. This sort of loss has been characterised as a 'second death' for the deceased.[51] Although Stokes is referring to the loss of digital remains as a second death for the deceased, and suggesting that there might be a duty not to delete that data, we suggest that this 'second death' would also be experienced by the griever, the person left behind, so that the duty not to delete might also, if it exists, be owed to the mourner as well. The possibility of this 'second death' appears to create great anxiety for some mourners, which may exacerbate their grief; and if this 'second death' actually eventuates it may also exacerbate the grief of the mourner, possibly tipping them into complicated grief.

V. Regulating Digital Grief Products?

From the point of view of the deceased there are questions about whether the deceased has rights in relation to their 'digital remains' which might end up being the subject matter of products designed to alleviate grief. Can the person while alive consent or set up their own immortality in digital form? For example, James Earl Jones gave permission to Disney to use AI to allow his voice to be used indefinitely for Darth Vader.[52] At least he consented. Many dead people have had their estate consent for them, and others have had their digital person continued without any consent at all.[53] Peter Cushing was digitally resurrected for a recent Star Wars movie.[54] Whitney Houston gave a concert as a hologram nine years after she died.[55]

[50] Bassett (n 48) 815.

[51] P Stokes, 'Deletion as Second Death: the moral status of digital remains' (2015) 17 (4) *Ethics and Information Technology* 237; D Bassett 'Ctrl+Alt+Delete: the Changing Landscape of the Uncanny Valley and the Fear of Second Loss' (2021) 40 *Current Psychology* 813.

[52] www.berkshireeagle.com/opinion/columnists/before-he-died-james-earl-jones-gave-disney-permission-to-replicate-his-voice-using-ai-instead-the-company-should-let-his-voice-rest/article_b054149c-73bd-11ef-9b69-af90b6f2bf9c.html.

[53] www.hollywoodreporter.com/movies/movie-features/alien-romulus-ian-holm-rook-ash-ai-1235982350/.

[54] www.theguardian.com/commentisfree/2016/dec/21/peter-cushing-rogue-one-resurrection-cg.

[55] S Zeitchik, 'Nine Years after she died, Whitney Houston is back to entertain you' *Washington Post* (29 October 2021).

The counter right for the deceased is the right to be forgotten, which was originally a privacy right to have one's name delisted from search engines,[56] now expanded and recognised in the European Union's General Data Protection Regulation (GDPR) 2017. This might have been a source of ways to prevent digital immortality without consent, but the GDPR does not apply to the dead.[57] In Europe each state must now create its own law on the right to be forgotten and data protection in general after death. In Australia and in other countries outside Europe, the right to be forgotten continues to be a debated subject.

It must be noted that in the traditional way of dealing with it, the material body decomposes and disappears into the earth or elsewhere in the traditional ways of dealing with it. The fact that the testator's view of what should be done with their own remains is not binding, raises interesting questions when we consider the possibility of a virtual person being developed after death. Where the 'remains' are digital – including the remnants of conversations, transactions, photographs, videos etc, making up what we might term an 'informational body' – what rules should govern the dealing with those remains? Should this be governed by the law of succession in the same way as physical remains are? Should prior consent by the deceased be the guiding principle? Unlike with a physical person there is the possibility that the digital informational body might be immortal. Should this therefore lead to a different form of regulation?

Should the continuing digital body be governed by the continuing control of the executor? Where does that leave the intestate, since without the appointment of an executor in a will, the court must appoint an administrator? Or should the analogy be more with the donation of organs, in which the deceased person's consent is, in Australia, determinative.[58] What of the grieving person left behind who might seek comfort through a digital process? At present this is a regulatory hole to deal with which consumer law may need to be developed.

It seems likely that the law of succession will remain restricted in common law to the rule that the executor has the right to decide what is done with the body of the deceased. Products which go beyond dealing with the physical body and funeral of the deceased appear to be beyond the reach of succession law. Can or should the succession law Executor's power over the deceased's remains include the power to manage the digital remains of the person? If so, that might lead to executors licensing or selling or simply allowing the digital remains to be used. There seems little appetite for this at present.

The mourner is the consumer of the digital grief products. Should regulation be through tortious liability if the product causes harm to the consumer? In particular it seems that mourners may be vulnerable to mental distress or psychiatric harm

[56] Case C-131/12 *Google Spain SL v Agencia Espanola de Protection de Datos* ECLI:EU:C:2014:317, [2014] 3 WLR 659.

[57] The European Union's General Data Protection Regulation Article 17 creates a right to be forgotten, but the GDPR does not cover death. The GDPR only covers living people.

[58] For example, Human Tissue Act 1983 (NSW); Human Tissue Act 1982 (Vic).

created for them by problems with these digital products, whether they perform as designed or fail in some way. If people are harmed negligence law may be a possible cause of action, especially in the United States and Canada where mental distress can be regarded as a harm which is compensable.[59] In other parts of the common law world, mere mental distress is rarely sufficient to establish a duty of care in negligence. Usually, a psychiatric condition is required to found such a duty.[60] In this chapter we have clearly established that mental distress or psychiatric injury is a reasonably foreseeable consequence of a lack of care in the design of digital grief products. The fact that complicated grief is defined as a psychiatric condition in the DSM-V is likely to assist in those jurisdictions where mere mental distress is not sufficient. There are other barriers to product liability including the US Restatement's insistence that 'products' be tangible,[61] and the usual difficulties with establishing breach and causation, but these are issues to be addressed elsewhere. Consumer law in statutory form protecting against defective products and misleading and deceptive conduct may also be a basis for tortious or contractual actions against platform owners and makers of digital items directed at a grieving relative.

The present regulation of the vast majority of these platforms and products is under the law of the country where the platform is situated, most often the United States and almost always it is a matter of contract law rather than property. The failure of governments to address the importance of property in the digital space, so that the vast majority of users have no property in the items they use, has created a space which necessarily takes away control from users. It is evident from the material considered in this chapter that for mourners, the sense of lack of control which arises from this legal arrangement is an even greater problem than it is for users in general.[62]

VI. Conclusion

In this chapter we have canvassed a massive range of digital products/items or systems which are designed, or just happen to be used for, relieving grief for the dead. The ability for the dead to have a form of immortality connects to the emotions of the mourner and seems to make it possible to talk with the dead, to hear them, to see them and remember them vividly. This is a new phenomenon which is changing and developing rapidly. It appears to have shifted treatment of

[59] *Saadati v Moorhead* [2017] 1 SCR 543.

[60] *Page v Smith* [1996] AC 155; *White v Chief Constable* [1999] 2 AC 455; Civil Liability Acts in Australia.

[61] See eg K Sanchez, 'Are Apps Products? Consumer Software and Products Liability' (8 April 2025) ssrn.com/abstract=5210539.

[62] Bassett (n 48) 815.

the dead in Western society from hidden to public, and to create a new individualisation of grief.

Any new technology has to be handled by the law and in doing so we need to distinguish between things which are categorically new and things which are merely old things 'in new clothes'. The things people have always done in memory of their deceased loved ones include dealing with the body and having funerals and rituals to deal with it, talking about them to others, talking to them as if they are present, making memorials, making keepsakes and so on. Many of the digital products we have discussed are versions of this and not very different from their corporeal version. How different is walking through a corporeal cemetery compared with walking through a virtual cemetery? But some really do seem different – having the physical sensation of talking with the deceased, hearing their voice while the deceased talks to mourners at their own funeral, or having an AI experience with the digitally remaining persona of the deceased do seem qualitatively different from traditional practices. As always with new technology the law can deal with some of it with existing law; and for other parts of it, needs to create new law or adapt the old law. We have shown evidence that grieving people are vulnerable to predatory marketing of these products, such as where they are misled into thinking they are speaking to their deceased loved one (for a fee) or where the digital grief app prevents them from grieving in a healthy way and creates mental health issues such as complicated grief. The law of torts is probably available for some of these harms.

We have also seen that harms can be created by the sudden loss of a digital item which has been used for support, such as a song on Spotify which the owners of Spotify have suddenly changed a version of. Access to all these digital products is not necessarily available to all, either. Many of the products we have discussed will be useful to relieve the pain of grief for those left behind, and in many ways this technology is to be celebrated. However, there are downsides to much of this technology which means it needs to be carefully calibrated to the needs of its planned users, who are demonstrably a vulnerable group. It is to be hoped that the speed of development which is happening does not sacrifice the quality and beneficial nature of the products being developed.

INDEX

Aach, John, 58
abortion
ectogestation as alternative to, 12–13, 19–20
FemTech data privacy, 28–9, 33, 38–9
forced abortion, 18
US prosecutions, 28, 38–9
access to healthcare
cryonics, 137
diabetes treatments, 95–7, 102–4
infertility treatments, 14–16, 24
neurotechnologies, 106, 113–15, 120–3
access to information
artificial pancreas technology, 101–2
afterlife
beliefs, 131–2
digital afterlife (*see* digital afterlife)
AI
avatars, 172, 176
speaking with, 169–70, 175–6
cryonics, and, 137, 145
digital funerals, 172
post-human intelligence, and, 137
alkaline hydrolysis
overview, 144, 148
regulatory development, 150–4
social perceptions, 153–4
sustainability/ environmental concerns, and, 157–63
Anderson, Leigh, 127
artificial pancreas technology
access, equitability, 94–7, 102–4
benefits of, 97–8
children, treatment of, 90–4, 102–3
choice, ethical/ moral issues, 94–5
closed-loop devices, 83–4, 88, 93–4
costs, 94, 96
cybersecurity, 93–4, 98–100
development, 83–4, 86–7
information, availability of, 101–2
open-source technology, role of, 84–5, 87–92, 103–4
parental role in treatment, 90–2, 102–3
patient choice, 91–3, 96–7, 100–2
patient privacy, 94–5
user competence and safety concerns, 89–92, 96–7
vulnerability to withdrawal of, 98, 104
artificial wombs, 10–12
see also ectogestation
Australia
cryonics, legality of, 145
embryo research regulation, 46, 52–3
rights of the deceased, 141, 166, 178
avatars
digital remembrance, implications for grief, 175–6
speaking with, 169–70, 175–6

Baer Arnold, Bruce, 142
Bassett, Debra, 177
Bedford, James, 133
Bio Bag, 10–11
biopolitics, 137
Borges, Jorge Luis, 41
brain-computer interfaces (BCIs), 110–11, 124
BRAIN Initiative, 117, 127
Braune, Katarina, 95
breast implants, 65, 70, 72–4, 77–8
Bredenoord, Annelien L, 77–8
Bublitz, Christoph, 120

Canning, Louise, 154
Chadwick, Rachelle, 18
Charo, R Alta, 55
children
artificial pancreas technology, 90–4, 102–3
China's one-child policy, 18
cryonic preservation, legality of, 143–4
infant mortality, 20
Chrisler, Joan, 16
Clark, Amander T, 56
climate change
crematoria emissions, and, 156–7
closed-loop devices
artificial pancreas technology, 83–4, 88, 93–4
neurotechnology, 109

contraception
coercive practices, 15
contraceptive autonomy, 23
Conway, Heather, 145, 169
Corbin, Bethany, 34
coronavirus, 149, 171–2
corpse disposal
alternative forms
(*see* alkaline hydrolysis; natural organic reduction)
cremation (*see* cremation)
cryonics (*see* cryonics/ cryogenics)
donation to science, 142
laws and procedures
(*see* funerary laws and practices)
development of, 149
lawful forms, 142–3
sustainability, and, 156–60, 162–3
cremation
division of ashes, 168
environmental impacts, 156–7, 159
regulation, 149, 152–3, 162
Crenshaw, Kimberlé W, 14
cryobiology, 132–3
cryonics/ cryogenics
access inequalities, 137
AI, and, 137, 145
death rituals, lack of, 138–9
definitions of death, and, 136–7
ethical implications, 137–9
global trends, 144–5
history of, 132–3
industry failure, implications of, 139, 145
legal implications
generally, 139–40
legal status, 142–4
no property principle, 140–2
work and skill exception, 141–2
neuropreservation, 134–5
regulatory developments, 142, 145
reproductive technologies, role in, 135, 144
rights of frozen bodies, 142
social implications, 135–8
technical aspects, 133–5, 145
theory of, 131–2
transhumanist philosophies, and, 132, 137
Cryonics Wager, 135
cryopolitics, 137
cultural values
death and grief, 168–71
funerary rituals, 168–9
reproductive technologies, conflicts with, 21–3
Cumberlege Report (UK), 71
cybersecurity
artificial pancreas technology, 93–4, 98–100
open-source technology, of, 98–100

Dasaolu, Babajide Olugbenga, 21
data protection
access rights, 76
anonymised data, 77, 79
data portability, and, 118
FemTech sector, in, 28–9, 31–2, 35–40
medical devices information, 75–81
neural data, sensitivity of, 118–19
patient consent, 75, 77–80
permitted disclosures, 78–80
regulatory focus, generally, 31
right to be forgotten, 178
right to privacy, and, 75–7
terms and conditions, overcomplication, 36–7
third party data sharing, 37–8
Davis, Angela, 15, 19
death
brain death, 136
certainty of, 138
corpse disposal, lawful forms, 142–3
definition, 135–6
digital afterlife (*see* digital afterlife)
facing mortality, and, 169
grief, and
digital remembrance, impacts of, 174–7
role and importance, 138–9, 170–1
memorials, 171
parents, of, 169
regulation, generally, 165–6
rights of deceased
digital rights, 177–8
no property principle, 140–2
work and skill exception, 141–2
rituals (*see also* funerary laws and practices)
cryonics effects on, 138–9
healing role of, 168–9, 171
succession laws, 165–6, 169
wills, 165–7, 169
deep brain stimulation, 108–9, 125
Denker, Hans-Werner, 55
DePuy implants, 66

diabetes
artificial pancreas technology (*see* artificial pancreas technology)
diabetes distress, 86
global trends, 83, 95–6
insulin management
challenges of, 85–6, 97–8
commercial systems, limitations of, 93–4
diabetes subtype variations, and, 93
mechanisms, development of, 85–7, 92
digital afterlife
avatars, 169–70, 172, 175–6
consent of deceased, 177–8
digital data accessibility, 172, 176–7, 180
executor rights and duties, 178
intestate, and, 178
legal/ ethical implications, 177–9
rights of deceased, 177–8
social media access, 172, 176
digital remembrance
digitally enhanced coffins, 174
grieving process, implications for, 174–7
liability for harm caused by digital grief products, 178–80
memorial websites, 174
regulatory development, 177–9
social media, 172, 176
virtual cemeteries, 173
digital technology, generally
development speed compared with regulatory speed, 30–1
gender blindness, 30
see also digital remembrance; FemTech
Dove, Edward S, 76
Drucker, Donna, 11–12

ectogestation
abortion alternative, as, 12–13, 19–20
artificial wombs, 10–12
centrality of pregnant person, 13, 16, 23
cultural implications, 21–3
decolonial perspective, need for, 21
ecogestative justice, 22–4
emancipatory potential of, 13–14, 22
embryo research time limits, 12
full gestation, 11
gender-sensitive approach, 23
intersectionality, and, 14
legal and ethical challenges, 12–14, 24–5
neo-natal incubation, 10–13
partial gestation, 11–13
regulation, rights-based approach, 22–4
reproductive choice, and, 13–16, 19–20, 23
technology development, 10–11
Einstein, Albert, 58
electrocorticography (ECoG), 111
electroencephalography (EEG), 111
embryo models
benefits of, 45
codes of practice, 50–1
'complete' embryo models, 43
definitions
legal, 52–3
ontological, 54–7
exclusion from regulation, 47–8
integrated *vs.* non-integrated models, 49–50
morally-relevant features test, 57–60
non-human animal embryo models, 43–4
origins, relevance of, 54
potentiality, 54–6
purpose, relevance of, 56–7
regulation
impact on use of, 46–7
research regulation approaches, 47–51, 60–1
treatment same as human embryos, 48–9
scientific development, 41–5
stem cell-based embryo models, 42, 50, 52
subsidiarity principle, and, 48
embryos, generally
artificial/ synthetic embryos, 42–5
assisted reproductive technology (ART) embryos, 46, 48
black box of development, 44
definitions
legal, 52–3
ontological, 54–7
fertilisation requirement, 54
human-like form, 59–60
iBlastoids, 43, 49, 53
natural embryo use restrictions, 45–7
offences for use of, 46
pain perception, 58–60
potentiality, 54–6
purpose-based interpretation, 56–7
research using
benefits, 44–5
protections, appropriateness, 42, 51
regulatory approaches, 47–51
restrictions, 45–7
time limits, 12, 43–5, 55, 59–60

shark embryos, 11
Warnock Report (1987), 59–61
environmental issues
funerary practices
carbon footprint, 159
cremation, 149, 152–3, 156–7, 159, 162
state regulatory role, 161–2
water resources, 158
see also sustainability
epilepsy, 108–9
Ettinger, Robert, 133
European Union
data protection regime, 76
medical devices regulation, 67–8, 113–15, 124
neurotechnology research regulation, 113–14

Facebook, 172, 176
FemTech
abortion data, 28–9, 33, 38–9
benefits of, 27–9, 33
data use/ exploitation, 28–9, 31, 33, 37–9
efficacy/ effectiveness, 29–30
enforcement of legal protections, 33–4, 38–40
gender stereotype reinforcement, 34–5
intimate partner violence, and, 28, 39–40
marginalised groups, and, 33–4
overview, 27
privacy protection, 28–33, 35–6
regulatory limitations, 28–30, 35, 40
sensitive health information, 35–6
user agency and choice, 32–3, 35–7
user threats and vulnerabilities, 31–3, 37–40
fertility technologies
ectogestation (*see* ectogestation)
in-vitro fertilisation (IVF), 10, 17–18
profit focus, 17–18
financialisation of healthcare, 84–5
Finn, Suki, 10–11
Firestone, Shulamith, 13–14
foetuses, rights of
obstetric violence, and, 19–20
work and skill exception, 141
Forstmann, Anne Charlotte, 161–2
Foucault, Michel, 137
freedom of thought
implantable neurotechnologies, and, 106
functional magnetic resonance imaging (fMRI), 111
funerary laws and practices
alternative methods
alkaline hydrolysis, 144, 148, 150–5
green burials, 144
natural organic reduction, 144, 148, 150–4
regulatory approaches, 150–1
regulatory challenges, 151
regulatory scope and limitations, 152–5
social perceptions of, 153–4
sustainability/ environmental concerns, and, 155–63
carbon footprint, 159
coronavirus impact on, 149, 171–2
cremation, 149, 152–3, 156–7, 159, 162, 168
cryogenics, and, 139
digital funerals, 171–2
digitally enhanced coffins, 174
disputes regarding, 167–9
division of ashes, 168
grieving process, role in, 170–1
judicial involvement in, 167–8
memorials, 171–2
social media access, 172, 176
state role in, 161–3
testamentary instructions, status of, 166–7

Gaard, Greta, 17
gender
gender blindness in technology development, 30
stereotype reinforcement, by FemTech, 34–5
Gibson, Richard B, 138
grief
complicated grief, 174–5, 177, 179
digital remembrance, impacts of, 174–7
role and importance, 138–9, 170–1

Haden, Francis Seymour, 160
Haldane, John Burdon Sanderson, 10
Hanna, Jacob H, 43–4
Hare, Richard M, 59–61
Healy, Rachael Louise, 34
Hillenbrink, Robin, 138–9
hip implants, 65–6
Horn, Claire, 12–13, 15–16, 20
human composting *see* **natural organic reduction**
Huxtable, Richard, 138

iBlastoids, 43, 49, 53
immortality beliefs, 131–2

implantable medical devices
benefits, 65
breast implants, 65, 70, 72–4, 77–8
controversies, 65–6
Cumberlege Report (UK), 71
data protection, and, 77–81
information systems (*see* medical devices information systems)
Keogh Review (UK), 70
mesh, abdominal/ vaginal, 66, 70–1
neurotechnologies (*see* implantable neurotechnologies)
patient safety, 66–7
registries, development of, 69–75
implantable neurotechnologies
access to, 106, 113–15, 120–3
benefits of, 126
brain-computer interfaces (BCIs), 110–11, 124
clinical trials regulation, 112–13
data sensitivity, 118–19
deep brain stimulation, 108–9, 125
freedom of thought, and, 106
health *vs.* wellness neurotechnologies, 123–4
Investigational Device Exemption (IDE), 112
investment trends, 105–6
medical device risk classification, 114, 124
neuroethics, 115–16
neuromodulation, 108–10
neuromonitoring, 111
neurophysiological effects, 119–20
neurorights, 116, 125
regulation
approaches, 106–7
clinical trials, 112–13
EU, 113–15, 124
expedited review pathways, 125
global ethical pluralism, 117, 120–3
humanitarian device exception (HDE), 125
innovation, balancing with, 123–7
justice concerns, 121–2
market access, 113–15
neuroexceptionalism, 116–20
soft governance, 106–7, 117–21, 127
specific regulation, 125–6
US, 112–14
in-vitro fertilisation (IVF), 10, 17–18
infant mortality, 20
infertility
artificial wombs, 10–12
costs of fertility treatment, 17–18
healthcare access inequalities, 14–16, 24
in-vitro fertilisation (IVF), 10, 17–18
surrogacy, 17
see also reproductive technologies
insulin pumps *see* **artificial pancreas technology**
International Medical Device Regulation Forum (IMDRF), 127
intersectionality
ectogestation, and, 14
reproductive justice, and, 14–15, 24
intimate partner violence (IPV), 28, 39–40
Investigational Device Exemption (IDE), 112

Keogh Review (UK), 70
Kingma, Elselijn, 10–11

Landecker, Hannah L, 56
Leeuwenhoek, Antonie van, 132
LGBTQ+
reproductive justice, and, 14–15, 24
Lynch, Michael P, 102

McManus, Ruth, 161
Malki, Lisa, 38
maternal mortality, 20, 33–4
Mathjissen, Brenda, 162
Matshabane, Olivia P, 122
Matthews, Kirstin Rw, 52–3
medical devices *see* **implantable medical devices; implantable neurotechnologies; wearable devices**
medical devices information systems
benefits, 80–1
competent bodies, 68
data publication, 79–80
device unique identifiers, 68–9, 81
EU regulatory regime, 67–8
legal and ethical issues
consent, 75, 77–81
data protection, 75–81
genetic databases, 75
independent registries, 80
misuse of private information, 75–6, 79–80
patient confidentiality, 75–9, 81
transparency, 79–80

monitoring systems, 69
UK regulatory developments
Breast and Cosmetic Implant Registry, 70
generally, 67–9
Medicines and Medical Devices Act 2021, 72–3
NHS Medical Devices Outcome Registry, 69–82
R v Paterson, 73–4
mental capacity, 165–6
minority groups
biomedical research, participation in, 120–1
FemTech use by, 33–4
reproductive choice, 14–16, 18–19
reproductive justice, and, 14–16
wills and succession practices, 169
Mir, Mina, 32, 37
Mishra, Paro, 33
misuse of private information, 75–6, 79–80
Morali, Daniel, 52–3
Mullock, Alexandra, 141–2

Nandagiri, Rishita, 21
nanotechnology, 132, 135, 137, 145
natural organic reduction
exclusions, 158
overview, 144, 148
regulatory development, 150–4
social perceptions, 153–4
sustainability/ environmental concerns, and, 158–63
Nelson, Anna, 43
neo-natal incubation, 10–12
Neuralink, 110
neuroethics, 115–16
neuroexceptionalism, 116–20
neurological disorders
global trends, 105
implantable treatment approaches (*see* implantable neurotechnologies)
neuromonitoring, 111
neuropreservation, 134–5
neurorights, 116, 125
neurotechnology, generally
access to healthcare, 106, 113–15, 120–3
brain-computer interfaces (BCIs), 110–11, 124
closed-loop stimulation, 109
deep brain stimulation, 108–9
definitions, 107–8
governance
clinical trials regulation, 112–13
EU, 113–15
frameworks, 106–7
Investigational Device Exemption (IDE), 112
special status of brain, 120
US, 112–13
innovation (*see* implantable neurotechnologies)
market access, 113–15
neuroethics, 115–16
neuromodulation, 108–10
neuromonitoring, 111
neurorights, 116
overview, 107–8
Spinal Cord Stimulation (SCS), 109
Transcranial Magnetic Stimulation (TMS) therapy, 109–10, 124
ultrasound, hi-frequency/ low-intensity, 110
Vagus Nerve Stimulation (VNS), 109
NHS Medical Devices Outcome Registry
development, 69–75
legal and ethical issues, 75–80
no property principle, 140–2
cryonics, work and skill exception, 141–2
Nosi, Costanza, 159, 162

Obama, Barack, 117
obstetric violence, 19–20, 24
Omolola, Fabiyi Oluwafunmilayo, 21–2
open-source technology
artificial pancreas technology, 84–5, 88–92, 99–100, 103–4
benefits of, generally, 87
cybersecurity risks, 98–100
healthcare implications of, 84–5
licensing, 87–8
limitations of, 90–1, 96–7, 104
tragedy of the commons, 98–9
user safety and competence concerns, 89–91, 96–7
Overall, Catherine, 12

Parker Pearson, Michael, 171
Parkinson's disease, 108
Piotrowska, Monika, 56, 58
Prakesh, Gyan, 15
privacy, protection of *see* **right to privacy**
promession, 144
Pybus, Jennifer, 32, 37

Quintal, Ariane, 97–8

***R v Paterson*,** 73–4
***R v Price*,** 149, 152
regenerative medicine, 132, 135
religion
afterlife/ immortality beliefs, 131
alternative funerary methods, and, 154–5
funerary rituals, role in grieving process, 168–9
reproductive technologies, implications of, 22
reproductive choice
coercive practices, and, 15, 21
contraceptive autonomy, 23
ectogestation, and, 19–20, 23
exploitative practices, 17
fertility technology, costs of, 17–18
influences on, 16–19, 32
marginalised groups, of, 14–16, 18–19
obstetric violence, 19–20, 24
presumptions on, 16–17
racism in healthcare, impacts of, 18–19
surrogacy, 17
reproductive health
female symptoms, devaluation of, 34
FemTech sector (*see* FemTech)
global inequalities, 14, 24, 33–4
limitations and restrictions in, 29, 32
sensitive health information, privacy protection, 35–6
reproductive justice
coercive practices, and, 15, 21
ectogestation, and, 15–16, 22–4
intersectionality, and, 14–15, 24
marginalised groups, and, 14–16
right to health, and, 23–4
reproductive technologies
artificial wombs, 10–12
costs of fertility treatment, 17–18
cryonic preservation, 135, 144
cultural implications, 21–3
ectogestation (*see* ectogestation)
FemTech (*see* FemTech)
healthcare access inequalities, 14–16, 24
in-vitro fertilisation (IVF), 10, 17–18
profit focus, 17–18
religious implications, 22
resomation *see* **alkaline hydrolysis**
right to be forgotten, 178
right to cognitive liberty, 126
right to health, 23–4
right to privacy
data protection, and, 76–9
FemTech, and, 28–33, 35–40
medical device information, 75–9
misuse of private information, 75–6, 79–80
patient confidentiality, 75–9
right to be forgotten, 178
terms and conditions, overcomplication, 36–7
right to property
deceased, rights of, 140–2
Rivron, Nicolas C, 54–5
Robinson, Georgina M, 154
***Roe v Wade*,** 33, 38–9
Romanis, Elizabeth Chloe, 15, 141–2

Sander-Staudt, Maureen, 19
Sanger, Margaret, 15
Schafer, Cyril, 161
Schofield, Behnaz, 77
Senderowicz, Leigh, 23
Sergers, Seppe, 12
social media, 172, 176
Spinal Cord Stimulation (SCS), 109
stem cell-based embryo models, 42, 50, 52
Stokes, Patrick, 177
succession, laws of, 165–6, 169
Suresh, Yogita, 33
surrogacy, 17
sustainability
funerary practices, and
alternative approaches, 157–60, 162–3
carbon footprint, 159
state regulatory role, 161–2
traditional methods, 156–7
infant and maternal mortality, 20
reproductive technologies, and, 21
water resources, 158
Swan, Melanie, 136–7

Taylor, Mark J, 76
Tekle, Asmara M, 150–1
test tube babies, 10
Transcranial Magnetic Stimulation (TMS) therapy, 109–10, 124
transhumanist philosophies
cryonics, and, 132, 137
Tsamasaase, Tloto, 9

ultrasound, 110
United Kingdom
artificial pancreas technology, availability, 84, 90–4, 102–3
cryonics, legality of, 143–5
embryo research regulation, 43, 47, 50–1
FemTech
data privacy, 28, 31–2, 34, 36–40
regulation, 29, 35
funerary practices
alternative methods, 157
cremation, law development, 152, 162
environmental impacts, 156–7
implantable medical devices
NHS information systems (*see* medical devices information systems)
regulation, 67–9, 81
rights of the deceased, 141
United States of America
abortion, data privacy, 28, 38–9
alternative funerary methods, 150
digital remembrance, liabilities of, 179
neurotechnology research regulation, 112, 114–15
rights of the deceased, 141

vaginal mesh, 66
Vagus Nerve Stimulation (VNS), 109
Vertommen, Sigrid, 21
Vig, Stella, 80
virtual cemeteries, 173

Wareham, Christopher Simon, 138–9
Warnock Report (1987), 59–61
wearable devices
equitability of, 94–7
investment trends, 105–6
privacy protection, 28–33, 35–6, 94–5
see also artificial pancreas technology; FemTech
wills, 165–7, 169, 171
***Womb City* (novel),** 9
work and skill exception, 141–2
Wright, Ronald, 97

Żernicka-Goetz, Magdalena, 43–4

www.ingramcontent.com/pod-product-compliance
Ingram Content Group UK Ltd.
Pitfield, Milton Keynes, MK11 3LW, UK
UKHW020818290926
15470UKWH00003B/1229